CLARENDON LAW SERIES

Edit

INTRODUCTION TO THE LAW OF PROPERTY

BY

F. H. LAWSON
Professor of Comparative Law in the University of Oxford

CLARENDON PRESS · OXFORD

Oxford University Press, Walton Street, Oxford OX2 6DP

OXFORD LONDON GLASGOW NEW YORK TORONTO MELBOURNE
WELLINGTON CAPE TOWN IBADAN NAIROBI DAR ES SALAAM LUSAKA
ADDIS ABABA DELHI BOMBAY CALCUTTA MADRAS KARACHI LAHORE
KUALA LUMPUR SINGAPORE JAKARTA HONG KONG TOKYO

ISBN 0 19 876064 7

First published 1958
Reprinted 1975, 1977

Printed and bound in Great Britain by
Redwood Burn Limited
Trowbridge & Esher

TO C. H. S. F.

PREFACE

THIS book is intended for two classes of readers, law students who are approaching the study of the law of property for the first time and non-lawyers who wish to obtain a rapid and summary view of what is usually regarded as a highly technical and obscure part of English law. Hence it is an explanatory, not a learned book. Indeed a comparative lawyer, who never professed, as a college tutor, to do more when teaching Real Property than get his pupils over the first, most menacing hurdles, dare not claim any proficiency other than that of an experienced teacher. But although there are many learned books on property law, the only short introductory works are historical in character. I have written this book because I think there is room for an account which for the most part neglects history and employs a mixed analytical and functional method. If it were more pretentious, I might even say that it attempts to present something of a philosophy of the subject.

The Law of Property has the reputation of being one of the most difficult branches of English law, and its reputation is not undeserved. But its difficulty will be found on closer inspection to be of a different order from that of most other branches. For whereas the law of contract or of torts, which in detail seems straightforward enough, only gradually unfolds its real difficulties to the student, the law of property presents its most difficult features to the beginner, but becomes relatively easier as he gradually comes to see what is its general philosophy and purpose. However, the experience of teachers seems to show that it takes the student quite an appreciable time to reach that stage.

Yet it should be possible, by a concerted and deliberate attack, to carry the beginner through this initial difficulty more quickly than has hitherto been the case. That is the main purpose of this book. It proceeds from the belief that there are clear patterns in the English law of property, which are not evident to the student until he has his attention forcibly directed to them. On the other hand, those patterns are to some extent disturbed by exceptions and minor inconsistencies, which are apt to assume undue prominence in elementary books. Some of them are historical survivals whose importance tends to be exaggerated because the bias of teaching in this subject, perhaps more than in any other part of English law, has been historical. Doubtless even now a study of legal history is essential to the complete culture of a property lawyer, but it should come rather later in his education, when he has acquired some notion of the general patterns of the law. He will then be able to recognize and understand the exceptions to them; for the time being it is best to neglect most of the exceptions altogether, apart from a warning that they exist and often trouble the practising lawyer.

The book will be found to contain much repetition, for which I do not apologize. The law of property is so unfamiliar to the beginner and hence so difficult in many of its parts that it is advisable and even necessary to reintroduce constantly the same notions and explanations in different contexts. But I would warn the beginner that the *Introduction*, which forms the first chapter, may be found to be in many places more difficult than the succeeding chapters; and I would advise him to read it again when he has finished reading the book.

I have tried to portray the law of property as a whole, eschewing the familiar divisions into real and personal property, land, and chattels. There are, of course, irreducible differences between movable and immovable property, which are noted where they occur, but there is a great deal of doctrine which is common to land and movables, now, indeed, often interchangeable as component parts of funds, as for instance when trustees dispose of the one and invest in the other. It is also my firm belief that even where land and movables are treated not as parts of funds but as individual objects, there is much more in common between them than is usually acknowledged. Combined treatments of the law of property have already appeared, not merely in such a compendium as *Stephen's Commentaries*, but also in the late Sir Thomas Raleigh's *Law of Property* and the late Mr. J. A. Strahan's *A General View of the Law of Property*. For one reason or another the time was not ripe for them. It is now time for a complete reconsideration of property law as a teaching subject, and I hope this little book may lead the way.

I should not have dared to present such a book to the public had I not had the advice of friends far more expert than myself. The name of Professor A. D. Hargreaves will assure readers that if I have made mistakes, I have not done so without warning. But besides criticism he has also given me encouragement on the ground that it was high time for an outsider to show the conveyancers what they are really doing. I am also deeply grateful to my colleague Mr. R. H. Maudsley, of Brasenose College, who read and criticized the typescript in its penultimate form, and in that way, and in frequent conversations, helped me to avoid many traps and to introduce the unsophisticated student as simply as possible to a very unfamiliar body of doctrine.

My debts to the authors of the standard textbooks, which have provided me with most of my material, are too obvious to be missed. Like all who had at the time to adjust their preconceived notions to the 1925 legislation, I learnt all that I know from the *Modern Real Property* of my old friend and colleague Professor G. C. Cheshire; and no one who has the good fortune and good sense to possess his second volume of the 1928 edition of *Stephen's Commentaries* will have any hesitation in tracing back to it my desire to see Property Law treated as a coherent whole. If that volume had to be superseded as too revolutionary to suit old-fashioned notions of law teaching, Professor Hargreaves replaced it in a way that, by contributing his own characteristic way of looking at the subject, almost reconciled one to the need for reactionary change. My debt to the *Manual of the Law of Real Property* by Mr. R. E. Megarry, Q.C., especially his treatment of the 'Social Control of Land', will be no less obvious. The larger work, *The Law of Real Property*, by Mr. Megarry and Mr. H. W. R. Wade, appeared too late for me to do more than refer to it on a few occasions.

Finally, I wish to record with gratitude my obligation to Professor H. L. A. Hart, the General Editor of the series. In a part of the law where analytical problems are frequent and difficult, his aid and control have been invaluable.

F. H. L.

June 1958

NOTE: The reader should note, when he comes to p. 126, that a bill, which is now before Parliament and will probably be an Act by the time this book is published, provides additional protection, for a limited period, to tenants of premises decontrolled by the 1957 Act.

TABLE OF CONTENTS

I

INTRODUCTION

THE law of property attempts to answer a number of questions about the relations of persons to things. Many of those questions are bound to arise in any settled community where men come into close proximity to each other and compete for the control and use of valuable objects. Only in very special circumstances can the principle 'first come first served' be applied; and it may be doubted whether any society has ever existed in which men have not had things which are in some sense or other their own and which they are prepared to defend against all comers who have not some special claim to set up against them. What are these questions which the law of property attempts to answer?

Legal relations

In one's private life one encounters the law on many different occasions and in many different ways. Indeed there is nothing that one does or does not do that has not a legal aspect. The lawyer says that, whether we like it or not, we are caught up in a complex of legal relations, some of which are relatively static while others exist for the purpose of changing them. Those relations can be roughly divided into relations between persons and persons and relations between persons and things. If I am in a relation with another person, I can call upon him to do or not to do something or to submit to some conduct on my part; or, conversely, he may have similar claims on me. In all these cases each person in the relation must be identified, though there may be more than one on each side. We must know that it is John Smith that owes £100 to Tom Jones; a statement that John Smith owes £100 or that Tom Jones is owed £100 is incomplete. A creditor without an ascertained debtor or a debtor without an ascertained creditor is a contradiction in terms. But if I say that I own a specific motor-car, my statement is complete; no other *ascertained* person need come into the relation. Such a relation is a relation between a person and a thing, and lawyers call it a *real* relation to distinguish it from a *personal* relation, or a relation *in rem* as distinguished from a relation *in personam*.

In one sense, indeed, even real relations are relations between persons. Real relations would be very imperfect if they were not protected and guaranteed by law. The statement that I own Blackacre—to use a name given by lawyers to a typical, but fictitious piece of land—implies that other persons must not do anything inconsistent with my ownership, and also that I may bring an action against anyone who is guilty of such an act. Since English lawyers always tend to think of law in terms of legal proceedings before courts, they always think of legal relations as directly or indirectly giving a specific plaintiff an action against a specific defendant.

From that point of view real relations are distinguished from personal relations by the number of persons adversely affected by them. Whereas a personal relation arising, for example, out of a promise by A to pay £100 to B binds only A to B, so that if the debt be not paid, B can sue only A, a real relation is good against all comers. To take a simple example, whoever is in a position to act inconsistently with another person's ownership of property must not so act, and will be liable to an action if he does so. The identity of the person under the duty not to act is in such a case irrelevant; any person whatsoever who acts inconsistently with the owner's ownership will be liable.

Considered in this sense the classification of relations as real and personal is not exhaustive. It may well be that one person's relation to a thing is protected not against *all* comers, but only against those who know of the relation, or, to use the technical legal term, have *notice* of it. Thus if A has promised to serve B as his secretary, C is not under any duty to B not to employ A in a manner inconsistent with A's promise to B, provided he does not know of A's promise, but he will be liable if, knowing of A's promise, he induces A to break it. In other words, he must respect B's contractual relation to A, if, but only if, he knows of it. These relations which are protected only against persons who have notice of them play a very great part in the law of property. Most so-called *equitable* relations are of this kind.[1] Sometimes they are protected not only against persons who have *actual* notice but also against those who have *constructive* notice, that is to say, persons who would have had actual notice if they had acted like reasonable men. As will be explained later,[2] there are good reasons for treating relations protected against those who have notice of them as varieties of real relations. If they are so treated, it may be said categorically that the law of property deals with real relations.

Wealth

The object of the law of property is to provide a secure foundation, so far as the law can do it, for the acquisition, enjoyment, and disposal of wealth. For this reason it is, in contrast to the law of persons, and

[1] See pp. 41–50.

[2] p. 45.

especially of family law, the part of the law most closely allied to economics.

It might therefore be expected to cover the whole field of economics, and in particular not only real relations, including relations protected against persons having notice of them, but at least some personal relations. For a man may have many claims on other persons, arising from contract or otherwise, which add materially to his wealth. He may be entitled to be retained in an office or employment. If so, he is clearly the richer for it; if he can alienate that right and turn it into money by substituting some other person in his office or employment, the office or employment is still more clearly part of his wealth.

Property and contract

Moreover, the most usual, and the safest, way of acquiring wealth is by agreement with another person. The agreement may be implied in the acquisition itself, as where one person transfers a thing voluntarily, or, as real-property lawyers say in relation to land, *grants* it, to another who is willing to receive it. But very commonly the grant is preceded by a contract which binds the one person to transfer and the other to accept the property. The Romans included both transactions in the Law of Things; and indeed there is no inevitable reason why English law should not include them in the law of property. Why then should the law of property not include, besides real relations, at any rate such personal relations as arise from contract?

Some parts of contract law are indeed regularly treated both in books on property and in books on contract. If the rights created by a contract can be transferred from one person to another, English law regards them as belonging to a species of property known as *choses in action*.[3] The assignment of *choses in action*—such is the name given to such transfers—is obviously an appropriate object of study for the property lawyer. But most of the law of contract, including the principles governing the formation, performance, and breach of contracts, and the consequences of breach, deals with problems which are remote from the law of property; and some contracts, such as a contract to perform at a concert, are very remote indeed. In other words, in so far as the law of contract operates only between the contracting parties, it is not a part of the law of property.

A minor, though not unpractical, objection would be that the English law of property would then be given a size out of all proportion to other parts of private law. It already, in contrast to many other legal systems, is made to include the whole of the law of succession on death and marriage settlements. If it were also made to include

[3] See pp. 19, 22–23 below.

the law of contract, nothing of private law would be left outside except the law of persons, including family law, and the law of torts.

Real relations

To describe a real relation one must describe not only the relation itself, the link between the person and the thing, but also the person and the thing. If I am to explain what is meant by the statement that Mr. Andrews owns Gainsborough's portrait of his eighteenth-century ancestor and ancestress I must not only explain what ownership is but I must identify and describe Mr. Andrews and the portrait. Now for various reasons, partly traditional and partly practical, the classification of persons is taken out of the law of property and made the subject of a special branch of the law, the law of persons. It would be possible to separate the classification of things also from the classification of relations themselves, and this was indeed done in the German Civil Code, the most consciously systematic of all codes; but in our law other reasons, again both traditional and practical, have produced the opposite result. Both the classification of things and the classification of the relations between persons and things are subjects of the English law of property.

Persons

Although the detailed study of various kinds of persons does not belong to the law of property, it is convenient to allude to them here in a general way. Persons are classified primarily as natural persons, or legal or artificial persons. Natural persons are human beings, whereas legal or artificial persons are corporations. Among natural persons few distinctions are now made, the only important ones being between adults and infants, that is to say, persons under the age of twenty-one, and between persons of sound mind and lunatics. In time of war enemy aliens suffer serious disabilities, but for property purposes aliens hardly differ otherwise from British subjects.

Artificial persons

In England corporations are always groups of human beings, such as municipal corporations or other local authorities or companies engaged in trade or industry, or else they are successive holders of offices, such as the Crown, or a living in the Church of England; but in each case it is important to distinguish the corporation, as an artificial person created by the law, from the human beings which are its members or which represent it for the time being. Thus the corporation which is constituted by a limited company preserves its identity although all its members change, by death or by sale of their shares, and the corporation sole constituted by the parson of a parish is always the same although the parson for the time being may be replaced by a successor. Corporations are brought into existence by the law, or by human beings in accordance with the law, in order to simplify the solution of certain problems connected with the holding of property and the doing of business which might be extremely complicated if they had to be solved in terms of individual human beings.

Thus, if 5,000 persons wished to invest their money in an industrial concern, it would be extremely inconvenient to make them own the factory as individuals, to bring or defend actions personally in relation to the business, to appoint managers and engage workmen, and to take important decisions which ought not to be left to the managers. The inconvenience would be greatly enhanced if, as would almost inevitably be the case, the 5,000 investors were constantly changing, whenever, for instance, any one of them sold his shares or died and was succeeded by someone else. Such difficulties are removed if the concern is made the property of a corporation called a company and the investors are given shares in the company and not immediately in the concern itself. To a very great extent corporations are treated as though they were human beings, though, as will be seen later,[4] they are also made subject to special rules. There are, for example, certain real or apparent dangers in allowing persons to acquire and hold property who are not subject to death or the other perils of human life.

Abstract things

This distinction between natural and artificial persons has a counterpart in the classification of things,[5] for over against physical objects such as cattle, motor-cars, ships, houses, and plots of land the law sets abstract things which cannot be perceived by the senses but only conceived by the mind. Some of those which are most readily apprehended are debts, shares in companies, and industrial property such as patents or copyright. All that can profitably be said of such abstract things for the time being is that, like physical objects, they are objects of value, for which men will give money. Just as corporations can ultimately be reduced to human beings at the cost of enormous complications in the practical working out of problems, so these and other abstract things can with a similar sacrifice be reduced to physical objects. Some such abstract things, though not necessarily those admitted by English law, have, it would seem, to be employed if the relations between human beings and physical objects are not to become intolerably complicated.

Still more abstract, perhaps, are what are called funds, that is to

[4] See pp. 143, 166 below

[5] See Chapter II.

say, collections of things which are for certain purposes regarded as collective units independent of their component parts, and in which the latter can be changed from time to time without changing the identity of the fund. The component parts of such a fund may themselves be abstract, though some may be physical objects. Typical instances of such funds are a trust fund and the capital of a company, which may include not only its buildings and plant but also its constantly changing stock-in-trade and even the patents it exploits.

Ownership

Having sketched in outline the sorts of persons that can have relations with things and the sorts of things they can have relations with, it is time to consider those relations themselves. This can best be done by discussing the nature of ownership.

Ownership would seem to the layman to be a simple notion. It is a simple question of *meum* and *tuum*. If the thing is mine, I own it; if it is not, I do not. Sometimes the law conforms to this simple way of looking at ownership. Thus, for example, a person may live in a house which he has bought and completely paid for, no one else has any rights over it, and he is registered in the Land Registry in London as owner; or he may have in his show-room a car which he has bought direct from the manufacturer. In both cases he can correctly say, without qualification, that the thing is his. Or he may quite reasonably say that he is an absolute owner.

But even in such simple cases it is evident that the word 'absolute' is being applied to ownership in two different senses. It means both 'indisputable' and 'unshared'. The owner is at the same moment asserting that he is without doubt entitled to the house or car and that his interest in it is undivided and complete; or, in negative terms, that no other person can say that he is entitled to regard the thing as his and that no other person can lawfully do anything to the thing which cuts down the use or reduces the value of the thing whilst he has it. The one assertion relates to what lawyers call 'title', the other to the content of ownership.

Now, some systems of law start from the position that everything has in principle an owner who is absolute in both senses. Some recognition may have to be given to persons whose titles are disputable and therefore imperfect, and an owner may have to be allowed to part with some of his powers over a thing in favour of other persons; but these are regarded as abnormalities and the starting-point is always an owner with an absolute title and an unlimited power of use and enjoyment. Now, English law, although it does on some occasions speak of ownership, does not draw any conclusions from it. Moreover, in the land law, no use whatever is made of the notion.

Title

First, then, of title. The word 'title' belongs to the vocabulary of a purchaser's solicitor who is trying to ensure that his client will be safe in buying land and cannot be lawfully turned out by anyone else. He is concerned to see that his client gets what is called a good title to the land. This might ultimately have to be tested by bringing or defending an action in which, although the plaintiff's object would be to obtain possession of the thing, he must try to prove that he has a right to the immediate possession of it. The actions by which a person protects his right to possess are usually studied as part of the law of tort, for the encroachments which give rise to them are wrongs which, in the technical language of the law, are called torts. But it is only by discussing these actions that we can get a proper view of title.[6]

Possession and limitation

We shall find that titles, except where they are, for instance, registered, are regarded not as absolute but as relative. Thus, whereas a registered holder has the *only* title, where a thing cannot be registered a holder can at best have a title which is relatively better than that of anyone else. Such as it is, it will be derived from the possession which some one or more persons have had in the past. Thus, the usual way of investigating a title to unregistered land is to trace the history of its possession; and we must therefore examine the nature of possession. But in order that purchasers may not need to go back to an infinite period in the past, Parliament has passed Statutes of Limitation to cut off rights which have not been asserted for varying periods of time.

Equitable remedies

The actions which have so far been referred to were developed by the old Courts of Common Law and are still said to be available at common law. However, side by side with the Common Law Courts the Chancellor exercised an equitable jurisdiction and developed equitable interests and remedies which have remained distinct even though now both common law and equity are administered in the same courts. They play such an important and even predominant part in the law of property that some attention must be paid to them at an early stage.[7]

Acquisition of title

How is the title to property acquired? First by transfer. One person may alienate to another by way of gift, but more usually in return for

[6] Chapter III.

[7] Chapter IV.

a price by selling it. Now the contractual element in sale, which creates rights and duties between seller and buyer, is not a matter for discussion in a book on property law; but the ways in which the property is transferred from one person to another assuredly are a necessary topic in such a book. Moreover, the preliminaries to such a transfer, especially of land, may be just as important, since they have for one of their main objects to ascertain whether the transferor's title is good.

But although things are usually acquired by transfer from another person, some modes of acquisition are original in the sense that a person becomes the first owner of things which had immediately before no owner.

Content of ownership

So much then for title. Let us turn to the content of ownership.

If a person acquires a thing he does so not merely for the pleasure of calling it his own, but because he wants to enjoy it, perhaps at the cost and trouble of managing it. Or, to put it in another way, a person wishes to possess a thing and to protect or recover his possession because it has for him value; and his title to it is like the impression on a coin, a legal guarantee of genuineness. Now the value of a thing is inferred from what can be done with it, and it is this sum of all the things that can be done with a thing which constitutes the content of ownership.

There are certain advantages to be obtained by keeping in the same hands the right or power to do all these things. A buyer normally wants them all and it is inconvenient if the seller cannot give him them. On the other hand, there has always been a need to detach some elements of ownership from others and to vest them in different persons, a need felt peculiarly in relation to land. One of the main tasks of a law of property is to reconcile these two needs.

The Romans distinguished three rights as component parts of ownership, the right to make physical use of a thing, the right to take the fruits of it, and the right to dispose of it, by alienating or destroying it.[8] For purposes of modern life we may translate them as the right to make physical use of a thing, the right to the income from it, in money, in kind, or in services, and the power of management, including that of alienation. But although the Romans distinguished them as products of analysis, they did not favour their separation in practice. They allowed the right of use, generally in conjunction with the right to income, to be detached, under the names of *use* or *usufruct*,

[8] The distinction was formulated by the medieval teachers of Roman law as one between the *ius utendi*, the *ius fruendi*, and the *ius abutendi*. The first two terms were known to the Romans; the last, which would at first sight seem to mean the right to destroy the thing, was extended to cover alienation as well.

from the right of disposal, but only temporarily, and never for longer than the lifetime of the person in whom it was vested. Moreover, the use or usufruct was regarded as inseparable from the person in whose interest it was created, and was thus not in principle marketable, though it could be sub-let; and the remaining component of ownership, the right of disposal, was seldom handled as a separate thing. This is all very rudimentary in comparison with the English way of dealing with interests in land and funds, though a mistaken application of Roman doctrine went far in the nineteenth century to put interests in physical movables into a strait jacket.

Fragmentation of ownership

The first point to make about the English way of looking at ownership is that there is no objection whatever in principle to breaking it up into fragments. Indeed a continental lawyer has been heard to remark that whereas the laws which have been greatly influenced by Roman law think of ownership as a single whole which can to some extent be split up, English law starts with the component parts and brings some or all of them together from time to time for special purposes. It is this fragmentation of ownership, or rather the constant occurrence of the fragments in varying connexions with each other, that is not only the most characteristic feature of the English law of property, but the most difficult for the student to assimilate.

Fragmentation takes place in several different ways which will be described in turn,[9] through the operation of tenure between landlord and tenant, by co-ownership, by a peculiar way of looking at rights to successive enjoyment, by the creation of rentcharges, by the detachment of powers of alienation or appointment from enjoyment, and by the use of the trust as a means of divorcing the management from the enjoyment of property. Although the resulting fragments of the composite relation which we have called ownership are themselves only simple relations between persons and corporeal or incorporeal things, yet English lawyers often think of those simpler relations as themselves constituting abstract things and so as being capable of being owned; and they attach ownership to them rather than to the corporeal or incorporeal things the enjoyment or management of which they exist to serve. This puzzling English habit adds appreciably to the difficulty which the student experiences in studying property law.

Fragmentation and the market

One way of fragmenting ownership has gradually become more important than any of the others and has been used by the property

[9] Chapter V.

legislation of 1925, a series of statutes which recast property law wholesale, to reconcile the divergent needs to concentrate and disperse the various elements contained in the concept of ownership.[10]

If property is given to trustees to hold in trust for beneficiaries the trustees are said, now mainly for historical reasons, to have the legal estate, and the beneficiaries the equitable interest. The former is merely a way of explaining that the trustees are the managers of the property and can act commercially as owners of it, enjoying wide powers of alienating it in the market; while the latter means that the beneficiaries have the beneficial ownership, which implies that they can enjoy the use and possession of it and draw an income from it. Thus by means of the trust the legal estate can be separated from the equitable interest in property and the former vested in trustees as managers of the property, while the latter is vested in beneficiaries who enjoy it. Having gone so far, Parliament could insist on a high degree of concentration as far as the legal estate is concerned, so as to confer on the managers an almost complete control over the trust property, while allowing dispersal of the equitable interest within very wide limits among several beneficiaries who take either concurrently or in succession to each other.

Back to ownership

Here at last it is proper to pause a moment and consider what meaning, if any, can be given to the words *ownership*, *owner*, and *own* in English law.[11] The result will be found to be not entirely satisfactory.

Impact of public law

The student will now have been given a bird's-eye view of what may be called the grammar of property law. Thereafter he will have the pleasanter, and on the whole easier, task of seeing how it is applied to typical problems of everyday life. That depends largely on what may be called the policy of the law. To a great extent that policy works almost imperceptibly as one judge follows another in deciding cases in accordance with what seems to him to be justice or common sense; and it is only after a lapse of time, if at all, that a policy can be detected. But sometimes, and more especially in the last fifty to a hundred years, successive governments have deliberately moved the legislature to effectuate their notions of public policy. The impact of public law on the law of property will call for notice from time to time, as it is manifested in the concern of government for good cultivation of land, the maintenance of buildings, the protection of business against unnecessary disturbance and, above all, in an immense

10 Chapter VI.

11 Chapter VII.

weight of taxation, both *inter vivos* and upon death. However, a short general chapter will serve not only to introduce the student to the topic but also to impress on him its transcendent importance in the modern world.[12]

Physical use of things

It will then be time to turn to the actual exploitation of things; and, referring back to the distinction which has already been made between the physical use of things and the income derived from them, we must consider these two in turn. We shall find the discussion will run more easily if we start by assuming that a person using a thing has the full interest in it, by reason of the fact that he has what is called the fee simple of land or what is, perhaps improperly, called the ownership of a physical chattel.[13]

The law makes a general assumption, which has now worn rather thin as regards land, that a person may use a thing belonging to him as he likes, and therefore the interesting points for discussion are the limits which the law places on such use and when and to what extent a person may use something belonging to another. One person can bind himself to another person not to use his property or may acquire from another person a right to use that other person's property, and there is little restriction that can be placed on the duties and rights so created. But they will usually operate only between these parties and are therefore a matter for the law of contract. However, certain rights and burdens can be attached to things in such a way that they continue to exist irrespective of the persons to whom those things belong; and such rights and burdens fall within the scope of property law. They attach almost exclusively to land, and are best described by the Roman term *servitudes*; only in the past year has it become possible to attach price maintenance conditions openly to goods.

Servitudes have been supplemented and to some extent replaced by the modern practice of town and country planning. Moreover, since the last war the State has even intervened to enforce standards of good husbandry and estate management on farmers and landowners. Although all of this properly belongs to public law, some account of its main outlines must be given even in a book on the law of property.

Division of enjoyment

So far it has been assumed that a person wants to take for himself directly the whole benefit from a thing. But he may in fact be willing, or even desire, to divide the benefit in some way between himself and another or between two or more different persons. The student will have become familiar with the fundamental grammar governing such

[12] Chapter VIII. [13] Chapter IX.

situations in reading about the fragmentation of ownership. He will now follow it into some of its typical applications.

The law on this subject was developed most elaborately for land, but it extends, with some variations, to other forms of property also. Here too the discussion will be most easily understood if the physical use of a thing is distinguished from the enjoyment of an income produced by it; though the physical use of a thing by one person may produce an income for another.

If agricultural land is leased to a farmer or a house let to a tenant, the landlord reserves to himself an income in the form of rent, but gives up the physical use to the farmer or tenant. The law of landlord and tenant constitutes a great part of the law of property. But a close analogy may be found in the law of movable property, for a person may, by a transaction known by the technical name of *bailment*, hire the use of a car or other machinery or of an animal or other physical chattel from another person, and something more remotely analogous may be found in the licence given by a patentee to a manufacturer to manufacture a patented article, or by the owner of copyright to a publisher to publish a book.

On the other hand, a person may want to divide up the income among several persons. If they are to take shares of the income from time to time as it falls due, there will be concurrent ownership, already discussed. He may, however, want them to take the whole of the income in succession to each other so that, for example, one person has it for his life, and then another person for the remaining portion of *his* life, and then another person absolutely. There will then be a settlement.

Since a lease is for a limited period, the whole interest in the property will come to the landlord at the end of the lease, and accordingly the time element which appears in the grant of income successively to several persons occurs there also; for the landlord has a right to the physical use of the thing after the lease comes to an end. We shall in an earlier chapter have explained summarily the technique by which these various interests, limited in respect of time, can coexist in a certain piece of property.[14] But there is one implication of such a coexistence which must be considered before examining in greater detail the various limited interests which can so coexist. Where several persons have successive interests in property, questions of capital and income arise, for a present holder may be tempted to secure a high income for himself and thereby reduce the capital to which his successors look for income in their turn. After discussing these it will be time to examine in greater detail first leases[15] and afterwards freehold limited interests, especially life interests and

[14] See pp. 65–73 below.

[15] Chapter XI.

entailed interests, contained in settlements.[16] It is mainly in relation to the latter that future interests must be considered, with special reference to the so-called Modern Rule against Perpetuities, which prevents capital funds from being tied up for too long a period, the Rule against Accumulations, and other problems which can be considered under the general rubric of the 'Dead Hand'.

Security

When granting a lease to a farmer a landlord reserves for himself a fixed income, so that the person who has the physical use of the land has the undefined residue, if any, of the income it produces. The converse occurs in the kinds of security which come within the law of property.[17] If a person is asked to lend money to a landowner he commonly insists on having the land mortgaged to him. In that case he acquires a right to a fixed income in the shape of interest on his loan together, of course, with a right to the ultimate repayment of the loan. Here again it is the person who has the physical use of the land who keeps the undefined residue, if any, of income, but he is the person who has given away a portion of his rights in the land. In other words, to use the technical language of the law, the landlord, while reserving to himself the residuary estate in the land, also reserves to himself a fixed portion of the income, whereas the mortgagor, while again reserving for himself the residuary estate, also reserves to himself the undefined residue of income.

Mortgages are only one form of real security, that is to say, security creating property rights. Other forms are pledge or pawn, and liens and charges of various kinds.

Succession

The transfer of property may take place *inter vivos*, that is to say, from one living person to another; it must take place on the death of the person to whom it belongs. Transfer on death, which is called Succession, has so many special features that it requires special treatment.[18] It comes very conveniently near the end of a book on property because it needs for its understanding an acquaintance with all that has gone before.

Registration

Even later must come an explanation of the extent to which registration is used in property law and of the various forms it takes;[19] for

[16] Chapter XII.
[17] Chapter XIII.
[18] Chapter XIV.
[19] Chapter XV.

every kind of interest in property is or may in due course be made capable of registration.

Conclusion

Finally, an attempt will be made to sum up and consider how far English property law satisfies present-day needs.[20]

[20] Chapter XVI.

II

THE CLASSIFICATION OF THINGS

THE best way to see what property means for practical purposes is to ask what a man of substance might leave at his death for his executors to pay death-duties on. He would almost certainly have shares in one or more limited liability companies, and some government stock, some life-insurance policies, and perhaps some money placed out on mortgages of land. If he was in business on his own account, he might own one office and lease another office in a large building, unsecured debts might be owing to him, he might have a stock of goods, and he might hold bills of lading for goods consigned to him but not yet delivered; he might have some petty cash (partly coin and partly notes) in a safe and a balance at the bank; and he might hold patents, trade marks, and designs, and the copyright of a book on office management; and the goodwill of his business would also be an asset. But his house and park might well be the object of a marriage settlement, by virtue of which he had only a life interest in it. On the other hand, he might have expected to succeed to another house on the death of its present tenant for life. A large portion of his personal belongings, such as his car or his books or the contents of his wine cellar, might be his own, but some of the furniture might be part of the settlement, and some of his income might be paid to him by trustees out of a trust fund. He might hold some investments as a trustee for others.

Abstract things and legal concepts

Now the first thing to notice about these various articles of property is that only a few of them are things in the sense of being physical objects. That would be true of the stock of goods in his possession, or his personal belongings, such as his car, his books, or the contents of his wine cellar. Of his petty cash the notes would be only promises of the Bank of England to pay money, and the coins would be no more than symbols of purchasing power. In his house and park and in one of his offices he would have only a limited interest, and although he had an unlimited interest in the other office the law would not use the term 'ownership' to describe his relation to it: he had only an estate in it, the nature of which must be explained later.[1] All his other belongings were clearly abstract in the sense that,

[1] pp. 66–67 below.

although they had value, the value attached directly, not to any physical object, but to creations of the human mind such as the right to receive payment of a debt or the exclusive right to make use of an invention. Moreover, all the most valuable parts of his property would be of this abstract, unsubstantial kind; and indeed the law is often tempted to treat even physical objects of property as though they were abstract entities.

One of the main difficulties the student of property law encounters at the very threshold is this presence of abstractions where he expects to find physical objects. He very soon discovers that the property lawyer takes surprisingly little interest in land or ships or motor-cars or machinery or animals or food or drink as such, and not much even in the ownership of such things, but a great deal in abstract things such as the fee simple of land, trust funds, stocks and shares, and documents of title such as bills of lading. Conversely he will discover that what he takes to be mere rights, such as the right to be paid a sum of money or the right to use a thing and receive the income from its exploitation for his lifetime, are treated as things.

The reason why the property lawyer turns all these rights and interests into things, however abstract they may be, is that since they have value, people are willing to buy them; and any valuable asset which is the object of commerce is properly treated as a thing, just as much if it is an abstraction such as a share in a company as if it is a physical object such as a ship or a motor-car. The main reason why far more attention is devoted to abstractions than to physical objects is that, since they are creations of the human mind, they can be made to conform to patterns consciously chosen for their practical utility and capacity for combination with each other. These patterns and combinations can be made the objects of a calculus which is a fit subject of study by lawyers. In comparison with them natural objects such as land or animals are too individual to serve as mathematical units of this kind.

The work of the conveyancer

A large part of the work of property lawyers consists of creating complicated arrangements known as settlements.[2] For this purpose they have to work with elements the nature and potentialities of which are exactly known. Their position is therefore very like that of a mechanical engineer designing a complicated machine; and just as the engineer cannot use as component parts natural objects which he can pick up but must have them made to a preconceived pattern, so the lawyer making a settlement must work with abstract concepts which have been made to serve typical purposes. The property lawyer

[2] See pp. 127–52 below.

differs from the engineer in that he is not free to make and use whatever component parts he likes, but has at his disposal a limited number of them which the law provides ready-made. Yet it is surprising what he can do with them in the way of new combinations.

A great deal of the law of property is concerned with describing these simple component parts, what can be done with them, and what has been done with them in the way of creating standard complex constructions. Here the student moves in a rarefied atmosphere remote from the physical world, though by no means remote from social, political, and economic policy. For these constructions are all made in order to achieve some purpose, even if only, as is frequently the case at the present day, to avoid the payment of taxes. This part of the law of property, which was worked out first for land and afterwards extended to cover such permanent sources of income as stocks and shares, is the most intellectually rewarding for the student, partly because, in its abstractness, it has strong affinities with mathematics, but partly also because it shows how an abstract calculus can be made to serve social, political, or economic policy.

No doubt in all of this the conveyancers, as the most expert property lawyers are called, have acted and still act as servants of the propertied classes, and originally very much under their instructions. Later the law became so technical that only the conveyancers knew it well enough to know where it was defective and how to reform it. Even now, when it has been greatly simplified, it is still something of a mystery and largely under their control.

Commercial instruments

Some of the same abstractness that characterizes the conveyancer's side of property law is found also in the property side of commercial law, the essential core of which is concerned with the sale of goods. Here, however, all the more interesting abstractions have been invented by the bankers and merchants themselves, leaving the lawyers to take over, refine, and systematize their creations, without ever completely catching up with the process of invention; while the theoretical elaboration of value in the abstract form of money has been the work of the economists, and the lawyers have had little to do with it.

They have, however, taken into property law several instruments, such as bills of exchange and cheques, which were invented in order to make money payments without the use of coin, and have to some extent come to treat them not as mere collections of promises but as things which can be bought and sold. They have likewise recognized and accepted the habit which merchants have acquired of treating certain documents which are really receipts for goods to be held on deposit or carried to another place as symbolizing the goods themselves, to such an extent that a sale and transfer of a document operates as a sale and transfer of the goods it symbolizes. Here there is first an abstraction by which promises to hold or deliver are treated as equivalent to the goods, and then a materialization of the abstraction, which makes the paper on which the receipt is written or printed equivalent to the receipt. It is in this way that the delivery of a warehouse receipt or a bill of lading is made equivalent to a delivery of the goods.

Public policy

The student enters yet another atmosphere when he enters the part of the law, mainly of land, where the State or other public authorities have intervened directly, to protect agricultural, business, or house tenants, or to ensure the proper use of agricultural land.[3] Even here he will find the property lawyer at his old trick of detecting or creating abstract entities, such as the statutory tenancy under the Rent Acts,[4] but on the whole policy is evident in its naked form. Here, therefore, the student hardly needs to adjust his style of thinking. His main difficulties are to recognize the precise reasons of policy behind the changes in the detail of the law, and, above all, to assimilate a mass of intricate and often repulsive detail. The land agent can often enlighten him much more effectively than the lawyer, for the land agent is better acquainted with the reasons underlying the law and the lawyer has not yet done much to translate the policy into the abstractions with which he works more securely than with raw fact or policy.

Real and personal property

English law makes a primary distinction between *real* and *personal* property, the former being interests in land other than leasehold interests and the latter movable property together with leasehold interests in land. Real property is often called *realty*, personal property *personalty* or *chattels*, leaseholds being, somewhat surprisingly, called *chattels real*, while all other chattels are called *chattels personal*. The distinction is based on historical factors which have no longer any appreciable force; and indeed leaseholds are now always included in books on real property. It is mentioned here only because the student is sure to encounter it later.

Books are still published which profess to deal with real and personal property respectively; and if the one type of book is reserved for land and the other for all other kinds of property, there is something to be said for a division of labour between specialist authors on that principle. For many purposes it is still useful to keep land apart

[3] See pp. 107, 123–6 below.

[4] See p. 125 below.

from other kinds of property. It is permanent, almost indestructible, and capable of almost infinite division and subdivision. Accordingly from the earliest periods in the history of English law it has been common to make the same piece of land serve the needs of several persons with conflicting interests. Only in fairly recent times has anything like the same elaborate apparatus been applied to personalty, and even now some kinds of chattels have to be dealt with in a very simple way. Nevertheless, the time has come to emphasize the parts of the law which apply with more or less uniformity to land and chattels, and to relegate as far as possible to the background those which are peculiar to each.

Chattels

Chattels personal are classified as *choses in possession* and *choses in action*, according as they can be enjoyed by taking possession of them or only by bringing an action. The term *chose in action* was first applied to debts, to which alone it is completely appropriate. It expresses the fact that if A owes B £100, the only way in which B can get the money against A's will is by bringing an action against him, whereas if B actually has a book in his possession he can use it at once. However, the term has been extended to all other intangible forms of property, such as patents and copyright. It would in fact be better if the distinction were expressed as one between tangible and intangible things. But, however the distinction may be expressed, it is not always easy to draw. Thus documents which give a right to call for the delivery of tangible things which are known by the name of goods are themselves tangible, but their value depends not on the intrinsic value of the pieces of paper themselves but on the value of the intangible right they symbolize to call for the delivery of the goods; whereas, although bank-notes are merely promises to pay issued by a bank and they are worth much more than the intrinsic value of the paper they are printed on, their tangible character has almost entirely banished from human consciousness the intangible promises they represent. However, as money, they must, along with coins, receive special treatment. Finally, there are collective entities, such as the capital of a company or groups of investments managed by trustees, which are best called *funds*.

Thus we have to consider (1) land; (2) goods, i.e. tangible movables other than money; (3) *choses in action*, i.e. intangible movables such as debts, patents, and copyright; (4) money; and (5) funds. The purpose of this chapter is to explain the main characteristics of these various classes of property, leaving for later discussion the uses to which they can be put and the ways in which they can be protected and transferred.

1. LAND

We are accustomed to think of land in terms of area, so that a landowner's park is said to be so many acres in extent. That is a good starting-point, but does not include all that the law means by land. Two extensions have to be made, one natural and the other artificial, by the hand of man.

In the first place, if land were only two-dimensional, it would be useless. Agriculture requires a depth of soil, and even human movement requires an air-space above the surface. Thus for practical purposes land must be thought of as having volume, and the only question the law has to answer is how far it should extend in the third dimension, that of height and depth. The solution adopted by English law is expressed in the maxim *cuius est solum eius est usque ad coelum et usque ad inferos*, that is to say, the land extends upwards to infinity and downwards to the centre of the earth. That implies that, except where restrained by other rules of law, a person may build as high as he likes and dig as deep as he likes in search of minerals, which will then belong to him. However, such restraining rules may be very important. For instance, one person may be entitled to prevent another person from building so as to obstruct the light from coming in through his windows; and, most significant of all, a landowner may no longer search for or get any of the coal under his land: that is the monopoly of the National Coal Board. Yet in principle the maxim applies. It is perhaps worthy of mention that land includes lakes and rivers within its boundaries. They are called in the technical language of the law land covered by water.

Further, in principle, whatever is attached to the soil becomes part of it. That means in the first place that things such as seeds or seedlings, which have hitherto existed as individual movable objects, lose their identity when sown or planted in the ground and become part of the land. Similarly, objects such as crops or fruit or trees, which are ordinarily thought of as things in themselves, and which will become individual movable things once they are detached from the soil, are at present part of it. Again, houses and other buildings are inevitably part of the land on which they they stand, for they had no identity of their own until they were built on it, and their materials have become merged in them. However, although a building is part of the land on which it is built, it is possible to divide it, not only vertically, as for instance into two semi-detached houses, but also horizontally into flats, each of which is a separate piece of landed property, capable of being held not merely by a tenant under a lease but in fee simple, that is to say, in a way which is equivalent to full ownership.

Movables which are merely placed on land remain movable, and doubts sometimes arise as to the status of movables buried in the soil, for instance in order to hide them.

The most difficult questions arise in connexion with what are called fixtures. The primary question is, what is a fixture? It is important where one person buys land and takes a conveyance of it from another, or where one person lends money on a mortgage of land belonging to another. The answer to the question is, generally speaking, that anything is a fixture that is not merely placed on the land, but attached to it with the purpose of making it part of the land. Anything that satisfies this definition will pass with the land on a conveyance or will be subject to a mortgage.

The second question is, granted that a thing is a fixture, may it be removed, for instance by a tenant who has affixed it to the land? Thus if a farmer builds a barn on the land let to him or if a tenant nails tapestry to the wall of a room or if a manufacturer fixes machinery to the floors of a factory which he has leased, disputes have arisen in the past out of demands by the tenant of the land, house, or factory, that he be allowed to remove the fixture. Most of such questions have now been decided in favour of the tenant; but in any case they do not concern the character of the fixtures whilst they are still fixed. The fixtures are certainly part of the land, though they may cease to be so at the wish of the tenant.

2. GOODS

Goods are defined by the Sale of Goods Act as chattels personal other than money or *choses in action*. For the purposes of the law of sale they also include what are called *emblements*, that is to say, the growing crops annually produced by the labour of the cultivator. That only means that emblements may be sold in advance as though they were already goods and that a sale of them does not fall under the rules governing the sale of land. They are actually part of the land, and therefore not goods, until they are severed from it.

A distinction is often made between goods which are fungible and those which are not. Fungible goods are mutually interchangeable; they can be replaced by equal quantities and qualities, and are estimated by weight, number, or measure. Typical fungibles are coins and raw materials. In the ordinary way it does not matter what coins are given to a person as change provided they add up to the right amount. It does not matter which particular bottles of milk the milkman delivers provided they are of the right quantity and quality. But a little reflection will show that there is no class of goods which are always fungible. Not all goods are capable of being fungible; some are always individualized. But even goods which are normally fungible can be treated as individuals. Thus coins, if valued for their rareness or their aesthetic or archaeological interest, are not fungible, because they cannot be replaced by others. In other words, goods are fungible if they are treated as such.

Similarly if the subject-matter of a sale is expressed as so many articles of a class or kind or so many units of weight of a raw material, the goods sold are at that moment unascertained. When so many articles or so much weight of raw material are set aside for delivery to the buyer, the goods become ascertained. Here, too, there are evidently not two classes of goods; the same goods were at one moment unascertained and at another ascertained by a process of human selection. Of course for a person to be willing to buy unascertained goods, that is to say, goods to be ascertained later, he must regard them as fungible, that is to say, as not depending for their value on their qualities as individuals.

Yet another distinction is made between existing and future goods. A thing which does not yet exist cannot of course be an individual object, but it can be individualized in the mind of the person ordering it, as where a person gives an order for his portrait to be painted by a named painter. Nevertheless, in general future goods are the anticipated produce of agriculture or manufacture, such as wheat, cotton, or steel rails. As such they are unascertained and also fungible.

In strict analysis unascertained and future goods are not yet goods, but a promise to deliver them implied in a sale vests a specific *chose in action* in the buyer. Such a *chose in action* may in its turn be symbolized by a document, as will be explained later.[5]

Some articles have a value so great and so dependent on their individual characteristics that some sure and permanent means are required of identifying them and the persons entitled to them. This often leads to the formation of registers, sometimes private, such as the stud-book of racehorses, sometimes public, such as the registers of ships and aircraft. Ships are indeed governed by special rules of law and are for some purposes treated almost as though they were floating plots of land.

3. INTANGIBLE MOVABLES

(*a*) *Debts and other choses in action*

If one person makes a contract with another person by virtue of which the other person makes him a promise, that promise obviously has some value. But whether it can be regarded as creating a thing will depend on whether the value can be transferred from the promisee to some other person. If it cannot be so transferred all that exists is a relation of a strictly personal kind between the promisor

[5] pp. 23–25 below.

and the promisee, which never escapes beyond the limits of contract. To be transferable, or, to use technical language, assignable, a right created by a promise must be of such a kind that it will not change its nature or content upon transfer to another person. Thus if performance is to be to the satisfaction of the promisee, the promisor cannot be forced to execute it to the satisfaction of any other person, and accordingly the benefit of the promise cannot be transferred. Similarly, if the amount that has to be paid or delivered under the promise is apt to change if the benefit of the promise is transferred, as for instance if a company bargains for the delivery of all the goods it will require of a certain kind and is then merged in a larger concern, no such transfer can be allowed to take place. Thus in practice choses in action are almost confined to promises to pay fixed sums of money or to deliver fixed quantities of goods. Even services of a fixed kind can rarely be transferred from one person to another because the transfer carries with it some taint of slavery.

A debt is an abstract thing, quite distinct from the money which will be the creditor's if it is paid. For if X promises to pay Y 2*s*. 6*d*., what belongs to Y is not the half-crown which may possibly be at that moment in X's pocket, but a totally distinct thing, namely the contractual right to be paid the 2*s*. 6*d*. Each of the two things, the half-crown and the right to be paid 2*s*. 6*d*., can be the object of distinct transfers, for X can effectually and quite properly make A the owner of the half-crown and Y can just as effectually and properly make B the owner of the right to be paid the 2*s*. 6*d*.

Choses in action in the nature of debts do not necessarily arise out of contracts, for a legatee may have a claim to be paid his legacy by the personal representatives of the deceased. But mere rights of action, such as the right to bring an action for damages for libel or even for breach of contract, cannot be assigned by one person to another, and so are not considered choses in action. The reason usually given for this is that an assignment would be champertous, that is to say, it would amount to trading in litigation and the fruits of litigation; and since the later Middle Ages interfering in the disputes of others, especially for purposes of gain, has been considered dangerous to social peace and therefore against public policy. But perhaps another reason that lay in the way of recognizing such claims as choses in action has been their indefiniteness, for the exact amount of the damages to be obtained cannot be predicted.

(*b*) *Commercial paper*

Certain types of written promises to pay money or deliver goods have become standardized and so fully acknowledged by the commercial world as to represent almost, and sometimes quite completely, the money or the goods. They are then bought and sold as if they were the money or the goods of which they are the symbols. Such documents containing promises to pay money are called negotiable instruments, while those containing promises to deliver goods are called documents of title.

(i) *Negotiable instruments.* The best-known negotiable instruments are the bill of exchange, the cheque, and the promissory note. A typical bill of exchange would run as follows:

> London, 1st January 1958
>
> £100.
>
> Three months after date pay to Mr. John Styles or order the sum of one hundred pounds for value received.
>
> To Richard Roe, Esq. John Doe

It will be observed that the document is an unconditional order by a drawer, Doe, to a drawee, Roe, to pay a fixed sum of money to a payee, Styles. The practice of using such bills of exchange arose when merchants contracted debts to other merchants at a distance. They would not wish to undergo the trouble and risk of transporting large quantities of coin or bullion and so would look for some more convenient method. Now to apply the document shown above to the simplest possible state of facts, Roe might himself owe Doe £100 and might also happen to reside in the same place as Styles. In that case the easiest way for Doe to pay Styles will be for him to order Roe to pay Styles the £100 which he owes him, Doe. But for Roe to owe Styles the £100 so as to give Styles an action against him on the bill, Roe would have to accept the bill by writing across it some such words as 'Accepted payable at the Old Bank, Oxford, Richard Roe'. Of course, bills of exchange came to be used in much more complicated transactions than the one described above, and a regular market in them arose.

Now Styles can on receipt of the bill endorse it by writing his name on the back and can transfer it by delivery to anyone he chooses. It can then be passed from hand to hand, the holder being entitled to be paid the £100 by Roe. If Roe is solvent, the bill is regarded as worth £100 and can itself be regarded as property. If the bill had been made out to *bearer*, it could have passed from hand to hand at once without endorsement. In either case a holder in due course, that is to say, anyone who has physical control of the bill which he has bought in good faith, is entitled to be paid the £100 even if it had been stolen in the meantime, or even if Roe had had a good defence on the bill against Styles. In other words, any transfer of the bill to a purchaser in good faith is a transfer of a right to receive £100 from Roe.

The same rules apply to cheques, which are only bills of exchange drawn on a banker, payable on demand, and promissory notes. An example of a promissory note is:

> Oxford, 1st January 1958
>
> £100.
>
> I promise to pay Richard Roe or order at the Old Bank, Oxford, six months after date the sum of one hundred pounds, for value received.
>
> John Doe

Most persons have in their pockets at some time or other examples in the shape of Bank of England notes for ten shillings or a pound.

(ii) *Documents of title.* The commonest documents of title are bills of lading, delivery warrants, and warehouse receipts. A bill of lading is a receipt given by the master of a ship to the consignor of goods placed on his ship for carriage to the consignee—or, as is generally the case, to the consignee or his order. It is executed in triplicate, and the master gives two copies to the consignor, keeping one for himself. The consignor then sends one of his copies to the consignee. Thereafter the consignee may, if he chooses, endorse and sell the bill of lading to another person and it may pass, like a negotiable instrument, from hand to hand. Here again the ultimate holder may call for delivery of the goods on surrendering the bill of lading, and to that extent the bill of lading represents the goods; but the representation is not so complete as with a bill of exchange—and accordingly the bill of lading is not strictly speaking a negotiable instrument—for although the master must deliver the goods to the person who presents the bill, if the bill has been stolen from, or lost by, anyone properly entitled to it, that person can recover the goods from the person who has obtained delivery, or indeed anyone who has acquired them from him. The same rules apply to other documents of title unless in some way, by custom or otherwise, they have been made fully negotiable. In the United States most of such documents of title are fully negotiable.

(*c*) *Goodwill*

Goodwill is property of a highly peculiar kind. It is the right to enjoy all the advantages of an established trade connexion. Customers who have been in the habit of dealing with a business will probably continue to do so, even if the business changes hands, and this probability is regarded as so valuable that large sums of money are commonly paid for it. So well established a head of property is it that its value must be taken into account for purposes of taxation. Yet it is an odd kind of property since only the person who has transferred the goodwill can be placed under a duty to respect it. He indeed can be restrained from soliciting his former customers and he may also agree not to carry on a competing business. But no third party can be restrained from trading in such a way as to reduce the value of the goodwill. Yet as a marketable object goodwill must be considered property.

(*d*) *Industrial property*

Also intangible, and therefore often included in choses in action, are certain rights which have recently acquired the name *industrial property*. Such are patents, registered designs, trade marks and trade names, and copyright. They are really monopolies protected permanently, or for a limited period, by law. The law governing all of them is highly specialized and is handled by experts. All that will be attempted here is a very summary account of their nature and purpose.

These monopolies fall naturally into two classes, the one perpetual, the other temporary. The former really amount to nothing more than the right to identify one's business or its products and prevent others from usurping the advantages which go with them, or, as the phrase goes, 'passing off' their goods as one's own. There is therefore no reason of public policy why they should not last for ever, for they do nothing to prevent or even discourage competitors from producing or trading without using improper means. These perpetual monopolies are trade names and trade marks.

The exclusive right to one's trade name is protected at common law and equity by 'passing-off' actions, in which the plaintiff must prove that confusion has been or is likely to be caused between his name and that assumed by the defendant or between the name attached to his goods and that placed by the defendant on his goods, and that such confusion has caused or is likely to cause injury to his goodwill. The protection of trade names is in fact only an indirect way of protecting goodwill.

A trade mark is a mark used to indicate a connexion in the course of trade between goods and the person entitled to use the mark. If registered it gives a protection free from the difficulties which sometimes encounter the plaintiff in a passing-off action. Registration is in the first instance for seven years, but it may be renewed indefinitely for successive periods of fourteen years. A trade mark could formerly be alienated only with the goodwill of a business, but it can now be alienated separately. Thus trade marks have attained an independent status and no longer exist merely to protect goodwill.

The temporary monopolies are the exclusive rights to exploit patents, industrial designs, and copyright. These are all genuine monopolies which operate to exclude competition in manufacture, trade, or the dissemination of literary or artistic work. Now it is the general policy of the law to stimulate competition, in the hope that thereby things will be produced and disseminated in the best and cheapest way. Accordingly, to grant perpetual monopolies to inventors, artists, authors, and composers would be unthinkable. On the other hand, such persons must be given some inducement to produce. Processes of manufacture can indeed be kept secret, but, while present or future employees may be restrained from divulging such secrets, once they are divulged they become public property. Thus, so long as a process remains secret, the public suffers from the existence of a monopoly but the manufacturer also suffers from the ever-present fear that it may at any time cease to be one.

The solution which has been adopted, with variations among the various classes of monopolies, goes back to the famous Statute of Monopolies of James I. It is that in return for immediate disclosure to the public, the inventor shall have a temporary monopoly, which he can dispose of for money if he wishes. After the monopoly comes to an end everybody is free to act as though it had never existed.

A patent is the exclusive right granted by the Crown, ordinarily for a period of sixteen years—which may in certain cases be further extended—of using, exercising, and vending an invention. On applying for a patent the applicant must lodge with the Patent Office a specification showing the nature of his invention and the method of carrying it into effect. In exceptional cases the specification is kept secret, but in principle the invention must be disclosed to the public, for such disclosure is the consideration for the temporary monopoly granted the patentee. The patent may yet be held to be invalid if the invention be found to contain nothing new, and it may well be imagined that some of the world's most costly and protracted litigation arises out of disputes about patents. Industrial designs can be registered and then receive protection analogous to that of patents.

Copyright is of two kinds. There is first the common law right to restrain the publication of unpublished writings. It is perpetual and survives in the hands of the representatives of the original writer. But its money value is limited since once the writing is published anybody may copy it, so that the person who has paid for the privilege of publishing it may find others making use of what he has paid for. The more valuable copyright is statutory and gives the sole and exclusive right to print or otherwise multiply copies, and, in the case of dramatic or musical works, to perform them. In most cases the right vests in the author automatically without registration, and lasts normally for the life of the author and a period of fifty years after his death, after which anyone may publish or perform.

Patents and copyright would have a very limited efficacy if they operated only within the United Kingdom. Hence every attempt is made to extend them to foreign countries. The only way to do this with patents is to take out a new patent in every country where manufacture might be undertaken by a competitor; and of course the requirements of the patent law of each country must be observed. But for many years a movement has been on foot to make copyright genuinely international, so that if an author acquires it in one country, he automatically has it in other countries also. Until the recent adoption of the international convention which has been given effect to by the United Kingdom in the new Copyright Act of 1956, most of the world adhered to what was called the Berne Convention, the only important countries which remained outside being the U.S.A. and the U.S.S.R. The U.S.A. has adhered to the new convention.

(*e*) *Stocks and shares*

The stock issued by governments and other public authorities is really only the acknowledgement of loans made to them and a promise to pay interest at a fixed rate. Some such loans are redeemable, others irredeemable.

A detailed description of stocks and shares in limited companies belongs to Company Law. But an analysis of the nature of a share in a limited company is very much in place.

It is easy to say quite shortly that a shareholder has a share in the capital of a company proportionate to the value he has contributed to it, but such a statement means nothing until it is explained. For a person may have shares, for the time being undivided, in many other things, such as land, or a collection of pictures, or a heap of coal, and in all such cases he may insist on having the property divided and so convert his share of the whole into sole ownership of a specific part; and it might therefore be thought that a shareholder of a company could force a division of the capital and take away, for instance, one particular machine, the value of which was equivalent to his share. But that is not the case. One shareholder cannot force a partition of the assets of a company; the most he can do in that direction is to get other shareholders with a majority holding to join with him in winding up the company. Nor can he sue the company for the value of his share. And yet, as is well known, the various stock exchanges provide an extraordinarily active market in shares. What advantages then does a buyer hope to gain when he buys shares?

It might be said that he hopes to be able to resell them at a profit. That is true—the real value of a share to its holder is now perhaps usually its present or future sales value—but it rather begs the question, for we should still have to ask why he in his turn can find a buyer.

It is not enough to say that he will be entitled to a share in the capital of the company if it is wound up, for as a rule he will hope that it will never be wound up. Is he then entitled to an income in the shape of dividends? Again the answer is no. Neither he nor any combination of his fellow shareholders can force the directors to declare a dividend, though if they have a majority holding of shares they may be able to dislodge directors who do not declare a dividend. However, if a sum of money is set aside for distribution to the shareholders, it must be fairly distributed so that the same dividend is paid on every share belonging to a class. Thus if there are only three shareholders, and each has a single share, any profits that are distributed must be distributed equally among them, and if their shares are unequal the profits must be distributed among them in accordance with the size of their shares. Shareholders have also voting rights at the annual general meeting of a company and may use them in order to elect the directors who are to control the management of the company, but these voting rights are perhaps not strictly speaking property.

Accordingly, from the point of view of property law, a share may best be defined as a hope, often rising to an expectation, of receiving dividends from a company, though not of any definite amount, together with a right not to be differentiated against in respect of any dividend which may be declared by the directors and an ultimate right to a share in the capital of the company if it is wound up. And, as so defined, shares have an undoubted value for which persons will pay good money, though the value may be more or less speculative.

4. MONEY

It has already been explained that money consists now of both coins and promissory notes issued by the Bank of England, and therefore in theory sometimes consists of *choses in possession* and sometimes of *choses in action*. But coins, if used as money, are only symbols of purchasing power and bank-notes are no less. Thus the distinction between coins and bank-notes is quite unreal. Both are alike treated as tangible symbols.

Money must be distinguished from other movables, for it is that with which other things are bought and it is not in itself an object of sale. It has been defined for legal purposes as comprising 'all chattels which, issued by the authority of the law and denominated with reference to a unit of account, are meant to serve as universal means of exchange'.[6] Thus money, to be current in England, must be issued as such by the Mint or the Bank of England, and must be expressed in pounds, shillings, and pence. Since it is meant to serve as a universal means of exchange, the law must allow it to pass from hand to hand freely and with the utmost security without persons taking it in payment in good faith being concerned to investigate the title of the person paying it. Thus the rule has always been that the title to current coin passes by delivery to anyone who takes it for value in good faith; and the same rule applies, as we have already seen,[7] to bank-notes. It is often said that money has no earmark, that is to say, that one coin cannot be sufficiently distinguished from another to be easily identified, and that that is the reason why a person who acquires current coin for value in good faith becomes owner. But it is just not true. Coins can be stolen and they are frequently marked so as to make detection easier; but the thief makes the shopkeeper owner of such marked coins if he uses them to buy goods. The true reason is that any other rule would make coins less useful as a universal means of exchange.

5. FUNDS

The essential nature of a fund is that it preserves its identity although its contents change. Thus persons beneficially entitled to a fund are entitled to be paid the income derived from it, and can enforce that right and alienate their interests in it, but the investments contained in it may be varied from time to time. One example of a fund has already been discussed, namely the capital of a company. The form taken by that capital is constantly changing, as debts due to the company are paid and others contracted, as out-of-date machinery is replaced and as stock-in-trade is sold and new goods manufactured; yet the capital is regarded as a continuing entity, over which debenture holders may have a floating charge[8] and in which shareholders may have shares producing dividends.

The capital of a company is a fund of a specialized character, for it is the property of an abstract person, the company, of which the

[6] Mann, *The Legal Aspect of Money*, 2nd ed., p. 7.
[7] pp. 24–25 above.
[8] See p. 162 below.

shareholders are members and debenture holders merely secured creditors; while the power of managing the business, and therefore of varying the investments, is vested in a board of directors, who are mere agents of the company but have very wide powers. It is as members of the company that the shareholders share in the capital and the dividends produced by managing it; they are not brought into immediate contact with either the investments contained in the fund or the fund itself conceived as an abstract entity.

However, it is by no means necessary to interpose an abstract person between human beings and a fund; it can be vested in human beings for the benefit of other human beings, or indeed for themselves. In English law this is done by means of a trust.

Property may be given to trustees for the benefit of persons or for purposes, usually charitable. In either case the trustees have the management of the property, including the power of alienation, subject perhaps to certain restrictions. They may not take any benefit themselves in their character of trustees, unless they are empowered by the instrument creating the trust to charge for their services, and the trust property is not available for payment of their private debts. They must obey the terms of the trust and are under a personal duty to the beneficiaries similar to that which could have been imposed on them by contract. Thus the beneficiaries, if there are any, have personal rights against the trustees. They are also regarded as having a sort of property in the trust fund.[9]

[9] See further p. 45 below.

III

THE PROTECTION OF PROPERTY INTERESTS

1. ACTIONS AT COMMON LAW

THE rules governing the recovery of property vary with the nature of the property. Some kinds of property can be possessed, others cannot. Of the former the possession can be lost and pass into the hands of a person not the owner, and recovery means a recovery of possession. Of the others some, such as patents, copyright, or goodwill, can be infringed, and the only meaning that recovery can have is a suit to restrain infringement and perhaps to obtain damages or a return of the profits made by the infringer. Where a trust fund is concerned, the only remedy can be a suit for enforcement of the trust or, in the last resort, for removal and replacement of the trustees.

Here all that can be discussed is the recovery of possession. There is a difference between land and goods. A person who loses the former can insist on having it returned to him. He can bring an action of ejectment, and if he succeeds will obtain a judgment for return of the land. If the defendant refuses to comply with the judgment, the sheriff will be ordered to put the plaintiff in possession of the land. On the other hand, it is a matter for the discretion of the judge whether he will order the return of goods or give judgment for either the return of the goods or payment of their value at the option of the defendant. Thus a person who loses goods can never be certain that he will recover them *in specie*. However, generally he is likely to feel satisfied with payment of the value, whereas, if the article in question is unique, for example a valuable picture, the judge will usually order it to be returned to him without giving the defendant any choice in the matter.

To recover possession the plaintiff must establish his title to the thing, or, in the technical language of the law, prove that he has the right to the immediate possession of it. Although this is not the same as possession itself, it is so often the case that the plaintiff can prove it only by proving that he or some other person possessed the thing previously that possession is said to be a good root, sometimes the only possible root, of title. It must therefore be described at the outset.

2. POSSESSION

Possession is one of the most difficult concepts in English, or for that matter any other, law. Part of the difficulty of understanding it comes from the fact that the legal meaning of the term does not fully correspond with its ordinary non-legal meaning. The ordinary popular meaning is intentional physical control; if I have such control over a thing that I can, if necessary, prevent anyone else from using it, I possess it. Even if possession is so regarded as a mere fact, its outline may not always be easy to recognize, still less to define; for bystanders may often legitimately disagree if asked to give their opinion whether a person has enough power to prevent others from using a thing to be regarded as possessing it. Such is especially the case if a person is temporarily absent from land. In practice indeed possession is often said to be a social rather than a physical fact, in the sense that a person will be held to possess a thing if he has the sort and extent of control that society, considered as being represented by the ordinary reasonable man, would regard as appropriate to the kind of thing and the circumstances of the case.

But this is only the beginning of the difficulty; for the judges in developing the law have made use of possession for various purposes, and in the course of doing so have given it a meaning which sometimes departs from its ordinary non-legal meaning. On the one hand, they have attributed to possessors certain advantages which may be called possessory rights or, more compendiously, the right of possession, to be carefully distinguished from the right to possess, which may, however, sometimes be inferred from it. Thus a possessor has, as such, the right to recover damages for trespass from anyone who intrudes on his possession, but he may in certain circumstances have to prove that he has a right to the immediate possession of a thing. On the other hand, the judges have made the wrongful taking of possession one requirement for a successful prosecution for larceny, for a person who takes possession of a thing with the intent to deprive another person permanently of it is a thief and guilty of the crime of larceny.

Now in certain circumstances, although a person's possession passes the ordinary tests applied by the average layman, a judge may think it improper to accord to him possessory rights, or conversely he may think it proper to accord such rights to a person whom an average layman would not regard as a possessor; or again he may hold that a person has acquired possession of a thing at a different moment from that which the average layman would have chosen, so that, for instance, a person has been held to acquire possession of the contents of an envelope not when he received the envelope but only when he knew the nature of the contents.[1]

The proper way to express this divergence between the use of the term 'possession' by laymen and by lawyers is to say that when lawyers use the term they have in mind the legal consequences of certain states of fact which, though they tend to conform to the ordinary layman's notion of possession, often depart from it; and where possession is relevant to the law of property it really means the collection of possessory rights which are collectively known as the 'right of possession'.

In what ensues we shall have to deal with this legal concept of possession and not with possession as it is regarded by the ordinary layman.

Certain persons who have physical control of a thing are held not to possess but merely to have custody of it on behalf of someone else. Thus, although a servant possesses what he has taken on his master's behalf, whether from a third party or from nobody at all, the answer to the question whether he possesses something he has received from his master or, on the contrary, his master continues to possess it through him, depends on the circumstances; he does not possess, for instance, his master's silver when he has cleaned it, but he may possess his master's luggage if he is travelling overland to meet him when he steps down from an aircraft. Other difficulties arise with regard to lodgers and tenants; the law governing the attribution to them of possession of furnished or unfurnished rooms is both complicated and doubtful. Further, the merely temporary control that a guest has, for instance, over the cutlery he is using at a dinner party is not treated as possession. His host possesses it through him. But, generally speaking, physical control does imply possession, and so tenants of land or houses, and borrowers, pledgees, or other bailees of goods possess what they have under their control; though for certain purposes the landlord and, in certain cases, the lender or other bailor are also held to possess at the same time.

Although these principles do not amount to a very neat doctrine, they afford answers to all the obvious problems which are likely to arise except one. Difficulties have arisen particularly where one person has found something in or on land possessed by another person, and the presence of the thing was hitherto unknown to the latter. Does his possession of the land or house carry with it possession of all its contents? Or if the possessor must intend to acquire possession of the contents in addition to acquiring possession of the land or house, will a general intention to acquire the contents suffice, or must

[1] This was necessary because a person is guilty of larceny only if he forms the intention to steal at the moment he acquires possession and not after.

he have directed his mind to each specific object, or at least to such specific objects as would not ordinarily be expected to be there? Again, does it matter whether the object in question was on or embedded in the land or again whether it was in or on the land when he took possession of the latter or, on the other hand, came on to it later without his knowledge? The few decisions on this topic are not easy to reconcile with each other and do not tell a very clear story. Some at least seem to turn on the special facts of the case. Perhaps some of them are unsound.

Thus a Viking ship was held to be possessed by the possessor of the land in which it had been buried centuries before, and rings found imbedded in a reservoir were held to be possessed by the owner of the reservoir. But a shopkeeper was not held to possess a five-pound note dropped by someone on the part of the floor of the shop open to the public; and the possessor of a house which had subsequently been requisitioned by the military authorities was held not to possess a brooch which was afterwards found on a ledge at the top of a window (though the true reason for the decision may be that, whatever might have been the correct view as between the finder and the military authorities, the person who, as former possessor, brought the action against the finder, had never actually taken possession of the house before it was requisitioned).

3. TITLE

Title is a shorthand term used to denote the facts which, if proved, will enable a plaintiff to recover possession or a defendant to retain possession of a thing. Even when a purchaser's solicitor insists that a vendor shall give a good title to the land, he has at the back of his mind the possibility of his client's having to recover or defend the possession of it.

A plaintiff seeking to recover possession must prove that he has a right to the immediate possession of the thing. Before examining in greater detail the meaning of this statement it is well to dispose of a number of special considerations.

Exceptional cases

First, a person who, in the ordinary acceptation of the term, is an owner, may not have a right to the immediate possession of a thing because if it is land he has leased it, or if it is a movable chattel he has bailed it, for instance hired it out, to another person for a fixed term. During the continuance of the term he cannot recover possession from the lessee or bailee, whereas, if it comes into the possession of a third party, the lessee or bailee will recover possession on the strength of his right to immediate possession, though in order to do so he may have to prove that, but for the lease or bailment, the owner would have had a right to immediate possession. On the other hand, if the lessee or bailee retains possession after the expiry of the term, the owner can recover possession by merely proving the fact of the lease or bailment and the expiry of the term; for it is said that the lessee or bailee cannot deny his title, since his own title depended on it. Nor, thirdly, can a dispossessor put the person he has dispossessed to proof of his title. All that the latter need prove is that he was in possession of the thing and the defendant took it against his will. But another way of stating this result might be that the former possession of the plaintiff is in such a case conclusive evidence of his right to immediate possession.

Self-help

On the other hand, if the dispossessor can prove his title, he is entitled to remain in possession. Thus a person who has a title but is out of possession can assert his rights by merely evicting the present possessor. But to do so may be dangerous, not merely because a forcible entry on land is a criminal offence under medieval statutes but also because disputes may arise, *inter alia*, as to whether excessive force has been used.

Proof of title

If now we assume that the plaintiff must prove his right to immediate possession against a person who has not directly dispossessed him but has acquired possession through a third party, and also that no such obstacle as a subsisting lease or bailment stands in the way, how is he to do it? The layman's obvious answer would be: Let him prove that he is the owner and all difficulties will be at an end. And indeed that is sometimes possible. There are such things as absolute titles.

The term 'absolute' is here used as meaning that the title cannot be defeated and also that it is not relative. Thus it is not merely better than other titles; it is good and they are non-existent, or at the best bad. This sense of the word has nothing to do with the content of a person's interest in a thing. He may have an absolute title to a merely partial interest or, on the other hand, he may have only a relative title to the full interest. It will be seen later that the term 'absolute ownership' sometimes alludes to absolute title and sometimes to the unlimited interest in a thing.

Absolute titles

Absolute titles occur when the title to a thing is registered and the law guarantees it. Where that is the case, the holder of the title need not consider whether there are any outstanding titles in other persons. If the title has been wrongly registered, the person injured thereby has no claim against him, but, if at all, only against the person or authority registering it. Such registered titles exist for a portion, unfortunately still only a relatively small portion, of the land in England and Wales. The Crown guarantees the title to this so-called registered land and assumes liability to pay compensation out of a fund created by levies on registered holders to anyone who can show that he has been injured by the registration of the title. In the same way, a person who has been registered as a holder of shares in a company is a shareholder for all purposes. But sometimes registration is only prima facie evidence of title, though it is usually hard to disprove.

Acquisition in good faith

It would be possible to hold, as many legal systems hold, that anyone who buys and takes possession in good faith of a movable thing from a possessor normally obtains an absolute title to it even though the possessor from whom he obtained it was not himself the owner. In that case all that a person alleging title would have to prove would be that he bought and obtained possession of the thing in good faith, and he could not be met by any defence. Our law applies this reasoning to negotiable instruments such as bills of exchange, promissory notes, and cheques. Since they are choses in action, the effect is to give any bona fide purchaser for value, or, as he is called, a holder in due course, a right to demand payment whatever may have happened to the document between its original creation and its coming into his hands.[2] The same principle applies to coins used as currency, for money could not otherwise perform its essential function of providing a universal medium of exchange.[3]

Moreover, a person who buys goods in market overt, that is to say, open market, acquires an absolute title to them. This statement must be explained lest it become a trap for the unwary. Not all markets are market overt, but only such as enjoy the privilege by express grant or prescription; on the other hand, anything bought in the open part of a shop dealing in such articles in the City of London is held to be bought in market overt. Further, even if a purchaser obtained an absolute title, he will lose it if the goods have been stolen and the thief has been prosecuted and convicted of the theft; for he will be ordered to restore them to the true owner.

[2] See p. 25 above.

[3] See p. 30 above.

Manufacture

One other case, and we have done with absolute titles. In practice, though not perhaps in strict theory, it is easy to prove a title to a movable which is a product of recent manufacture, for its existence has a definite known beginning and it will almost always be accepted, in the absence of clear evidence to the contrary, that the manufacturer is its first owner. If that is so he has an absolute title which he can transmit to others.

Relative titles

These are all exceptional, though not uncommon cases. In general titles are not absolute but relative, but in senses which are best explained by showing what a person alleging title must prove and what defences may be set up against him. If a person cannot prove an absolute title, he must rely on a past possession in himself or in some other person or persons.

Now the law also says that actual possession implies a right to possession, and so, since the defendant is *ex hypothesi* in possession of the thing, the plaintiff must at least prove that he has a better right to possession. This is usually done by showing that he or his predecessor in title, for instance a testator under whose will he claims, possessed the thing before the present possessor—which implies that it had been wrongfully taken by someone in the meantime. Normally that concludes the case, for an earlier possession prevails over a later one that is adverse to it. But what if the defendant can prove that behind the plaintiff's earlier possession there is a still earlier one adverse to it and that the title conferred by it is still in existence? Can he defeat the plaintiff's claim by proving this right of a third party, this *jus tertii*, as it is called? Clearly if the plaintiff were allowed to recover possession from the defendant, he could not retain it against the third party who has a still better title; but can the defendant say that as he could not retain it against the third party, so he cannot recover it against *him*? The matter is by no means free from doubt, and different answers may have to be given for land and movables; the defendant can point to clearer authority in his favour where movables are concerned. If he can successfully rely on the *jus tertii*, it is clear that the title on which the plaintiff can succeed in recovering possession is in principle the *best* title that can be proved in the course of the present action; if he cannot rely on the *jus tertii*, the plaintiff's title need merely be a *better* title than the defendant's.

So far the question is indeed a very unimportant one. Cases in which the *jus tertii* has been relied on are exceedingly rare. Indeed, in the few decided cases the plaintiff's pleadings admitted the *jus tertii*. It would be very surprising if defendants frequently pleaded the *jus tertii*, for they would be inviting the *tertius* to proceed against them. But when we come to conveyancing the matter assumes a totally different aspect.

Proof of title in conveyancing

The intending buyer of a thing is rarely concerned with the possible existence of title adverse to the seller's and vested in an actual possessor. He naturally tries to buy from the possessor himself. But he is very deeply interested in the question whether there may still be in existence some earlier title adverse to the seller's; for he does not want to pay for something from which he may subsequently be evicted.

The question is in fact rarely of importance except where unregistered land is concerned. The title to most unique chattels is usually well known or easily ascertainable. There is a register of shipping which, if not conclusive as to title, is almost so; the stud-book performs the same function for racehorses; the whereabouts and ownership of valuable pictures are usually well known to the dealers. Possession of the registration book is not unfortunately a perfect test of ownership of a motor-car, but in practice few owners let it go out of their possession. But most chattels are hard to trace, and in any case it would slow trade down too much if buyers tried to make sellers prove their title to ordinary objects of commerce. Thus wise buyers usually deal with reputable sellers, and trust to the probability that they will not sell what they have no right to sell; and the law relating to the contract of sale gives buyers a remedy against sellers if they have been forced to satisfy third persons with a better title. Although there is always the possibility that a seller may be insolvent and so unable to make good his loss to the buyer, that is a risk which buyers take in the ordinary course of business. If they deal with sellers of doubtful reputation, they assume an even greater risk.

However, people do not buy land, or lend money on it, without investigating title, though they have the same remedies as they would have against a seller of goods; and it leaps to the eye that the title they require will be one which is not likely to have any flaw in it. How can the seller prove that he has such a title? He can in the nature of things only prove that he got it lawfully from someone else, and that someone else from someone else, and so on. Does that mean what the philosophers call an infinite regress, on the principle that however far he goes back there is always the possibility that someone else will pop up with a better title? The difficulty is avoided by the operation of so-called Limitation Acts. They demand separate consideration.

4. LIMITATION OF ACTIONS AND RIGHTS

A person who starts with a weak title to property or property rights may find his position strengthened by lapse of time, and other persons who are able to contest his title may find their power to do so disappear. This may happen in three different ways. In the first case a person who in fact exercises the right for the period required by law will acquire an absolute title to it, and it follows that any other person who hitherto could contest it on the ground that he had a right adverse to it will no longer be able to do so. In the second case a person who allows another person to exercise for the period required by law a property right adverse to his own will lose any right of action against him. His action will be said to be statute-barred. In the third case, not only will his right of action disappear, but his right to the thing will disappear too.

In English law the first of these solutions applies only to servitudes, that is to say, to certain rights which can be exercised over another person's land. It is so closely connected with servitudes that it will be explained later in dealing with them. The second solution finds its main field of application in personal actions arising out of contract or tort. The solution applicable to property rights as a class is the third.

The difference between the second and third solutions, which might at first sight seem unimportant, is as follows. Suppose A, when visiting B, finds his book, which he lost seven years ago, on B's table. If he tries to bring an action against B to recover it, he will certainly find his action statute-barred and he will fail, for the period for physical movables is six years and the lapse of such a period will at the very least bar the action. If, however, instead of bringing an action, he picks up the book and puts it in his pocket, thus retaking possession of it, he will be able to defend his possession against B if it is only his action that is statute-barred. If, on the other hand, his right is barred also, he will not be able to resist an action by B. Lapse of time has barred the right to land since 1833, but to movables only since 1939.

The difference is of little importance so far as movables are concerned, for, as has already been said, persons acquiring movables seldom trouble themselves with questions of title. But with land the barring of title by twelve years' adverse possession is important.

It operates as follows. Let us suppose that A has the best title to a piece of land which we shall call Blackacre—that is to say, a title which has no known title superior to it—and whilst he is away B takes possession of it. B now, by the very fact that he possesses Blackacre, has a title to it, but one that can be defeated by A. If, however,

A does not take steps to recover possession for twelve years, by ousting B or bringing an action against him, he loses his title, and B's title, which was formerly the best but one, becomes the best. But his title is not a new one; it is still the same one that he obtained by dispossessing A; and this may have important consequences which are too technical to detain us here.

It might be thought that a purchaser of land would feel safe in limiting his researches into his vendor's title to a period of twelve years in the past. This is unfortunately not the case. For there may be persons who have rights in the land which will entitle them to possession at some future date. Until that time they will have no right to recover possession from an intruder, and the Limitation Act gives them twelve years from that time and not from the original intrusion in which to recover possession. No limit can be set to the period during which the purchaser should push back his investigations in order to be absolutely safe. However, as a practical matter some period must be fixed and the law has chosen to say that, unless a special agreement has been made to the contrary, a purchaser is entitled to trace back the vendor's title only to some good root of title at least thirty years old. A good root of title is some document, such as a will, which transferred the interest which the purchaser seeks to acquire, which dealt completely with the title to it in law and equity, and contained nothing to cast doubts upon the title of the vendor.

If, however, the vendor knows of some flaw in the title farther back than that root of title, it will be best for him to disclose it before the contract is signed and to insert a term in the contract binding the purchaser not to object to the flaw. If the flaw is unimportant and not such as to make it probable that the purchaser will ever be evicted because of it, he will probably be willing to accept the title, though perhaps at a slightly lower price, whereas if it is important, he may insist on a serious reduction in price or not sign the contract. But if the flaw is not disclosed and the purchaser is evicted, he can sue the vendor for damages on the covenants for title formerly inserted but now implied in the conveyance of the land.

5. EQUITABLE RIGHTS AND REMEDIES

The rights and remedies which have been discussed hitherto are said to exist or operate at law. Certain other rights and remedies must now be discussed which exist or operate only in equity. This is a distinction which is hard to grasp and which has nothing to do with the ordinary popular meanings of law and equity. Historically it is a distinction between rights recognized and remedies afforded by courts exercising different jurisdictions, on the one hand the old

Courts of Common Law and on the other the Chancellor. The Chancellor exercised what was in effect a supplementary jurisdiction, assuming at every point the existence of the common law administered by the Common Law Courts, but making good, as far as possible, its deficiencies. Thus equity never became a coherent system, though it may fairly be said that not only is the common law taken by itself a coherent system, but common law and equity taken together make a coherent system. This is more evident now that both are administered in the same courts and both common law and equitable remedies can be obtained in the same proceedings.

Equity is in no way synonymous with natural law or natural justice, though, like all good law, it aims at justice. It is now a body of technical rules and principles based, like common law, on precedent and in places modified and even codified by statute. Most of it deals in one way or another with property, but only a few of its leading principles and characteristics need be discussed in an elementary account of property law.

Conscience

Equity will only act on the person of a defendant if his conscience is affected in some way. Whereas common law remedies are granted to plaintiffs on the ground that they are entitled to them, equitable remedies are granted because it would be unconscionable of the defendant to do or not to do something to the disadvantage or advantage of the plaintiff. In one sense this may make equitable remedies more restricted than legal remedies, for whereas a person who is entitled to the immediate possession of a thing at common law is entitled to recover it even against a person who has bought it in good faith, if his interest in the thing is merely equitable he cannot enforce it against a person who has bought the thing in good faith without notice of the existence of the equitable interest. On the other hand, equitable remedies may have a wider range than legal remedies because there are many situations where, although a person has a perfect right to possess a thing at common law and is under no duty at common law, contractual or otherwise, to hand it over to another person or to hold it for his benefit, he is bound in conscience to do the one or the other. But it is well to warn the reader that equity has on occasion stretched the claims of conscience rather far, and that in modern times lawyers direct their attention not so much to the conscience which is the ultimate foundation on which equitable remedies are based, as to the specific rules which now govern them.

For the moment it must suffice to examine by way of example one great institution, the trust, and one great remedy, the specific performance of contracts. By so doing we shall incidentally learn much about the ways in which equity works in contrast to common law.

Trusts

A settlor A may by his will give property to a trustee B, in trust for his infant son C, thus providing for the management of the property during C's minority; or he may leave property to B in trust for D for life and after D's death for E. C, D, and E are called beneficiaries—each was once technically called a *cestui que trust*. In such cases the trustee is bound to hold the property for the benefit of the beneficiary. He must allow him to use it and take the income from it, and he must take all the necessary steps to protect it—if it is a fund, by varying the investments from time to time so as to preserve the capital. If the beneficiary is an infant, the trustee may have to apply part of the trust property for his maintenance and education. So stated, the beneficiary has only a personal right, a right *in personam*, against the trustee. He has no right at all at common law, but if the trustee fails in his duties to him, the beneficiary can bring proceedings in equity to have the trust enforced. This may end with an order that the trustee hand over possession to the beneficiary, that he replace trust property or its equivalent if he has got rid of it improperly, or even that he be replaced as trustee by some more suitable person. These remedies are quite different from common-law remedies, which are only two in number, an order for possession of a thing, and a judgment for a liquidated sum of money or unliquidated damages. Moreover, whereas a common-law judgment is executed against an unwilling defendant by an order to a sheriff to put the plaintiff in possession of land or sometimes of goods, or to seize and sell a sufficient quantity of the defendant's goods to pay the judgment debt, the ordinary sanction of an order issued by a court of equity is imprisonment of the recalcitrant defendant. Equity is said to act *in personam*.

Once courts of equity had elaborated the institution of the trust and a set of remedies to enforce the duties implied by it, the way was open to say that persons who had never accepted the position of trustee, but had property which they ought in conscience to hold for the benefit of other persons, should be treated as if they were trustees. They were said to be saddled with a constructive trust, and to be constructive trustees. That meant in effect that the same remedies could be used against them as if they had been trustees.

Constructive trusts

Hence came some rather surprising developments. If a trustee gave trust property in breach of trust, the question arose, what was to be the position of the alienee? It might be said that since the beneficiary had a remedy against the trustee, the alienee did not come into the picture; but the trustee might be, and probably would be in such circumstances, insolvent. Could it be said that the alienation in breach of trust was invalid and therefore inoperative? That would have been to deny the full ownership recognized by the Common Law Courts to be vested in the trustee. Accordingly the Chancellor asked whether, in all the circumstances of the case, the conscience of the alienee could be held to be affected in the same way as that of the original trustee, and to this question different answers were given according to the circumstances. If the alienee had known when he took the property that it was being alienated in breach of trust, then he had no merits and he must be treated as a constructive trustee and would hold the property on the same terms as the original trustee. If, although he had no notice of the breach of trust, he had acquired the property by way of gift without paying for it, then, as between a person who was getting something for nothing and another person who would actually lose by his getting it, the choice was easy: the former must suffer. Thus the gratuitous alienee of trust property became a constructive trustee. More difficult perhaps was the question whether, if the trustee's property was insufficient to satisfy both his creditors and the beneficiary, the creditors who took the trust property should hold it in trust for the beneficiary. In the end they too became constructive trustees. The only person who succeeded to the legal rights of the trustee without becoming a constructive trustee for the beneficiary came to be a person who took the property for value in good faith and without notice of the breach of trust. Moreover, even if he had no actual notice he would still become a constructive trustee if he would have had notice had he taken the steps to investigate the trustee's title which a reasonable man would have taken. He would then be said to have, not actual, but constructive notice. Constructive notice has played a great part in legal history, though its importance has been diminished by recent changes in the law. For, as will be explained in greater detail later,[4] almost all interests to which a beneficiary is entitled now fall into two groups. One of them, which has seldom any relation to trusts, has been made registrable, with the effect that registration is held to be equivalent to actual notice, and failure to register is fatal to the claims of the beneficiary. On the other hand, trustees are now almost invariably empowered to sell the trust property without breach of trust and reinvest the proceeds, and it is to the income of the trust fund in its new form that the beneficiary is then entitled. Of course, when the sale is not in

[4] See pp. 53, 81–84, 86, 102 below.

breach of trust any notice that a purchaser may have is irrelevant; he will acquire the trust property free from the trust.

Nature of the beneficiary's interest

So unlikely was it that trust property alienated in breach of trust should come into the hands of a bona fide purchaser who had no notice, actual or constructive, of the breach of trust, that the beneficiary's interest became almost as secure as if it had been protected by the Common Law Courts. Accordingly, in recent times an academic controversy arose whether it was still only a right *in personam* and not really a right *in rem*. The great historian Maitland, while admitting that it was almost equivalent to a right *in rem*, thought that the possible existence of a bona fide purchaser for value, who could cut off the right of the beneficiary, prevented it from quite attaining that status. The better opinion seems to be that of Professor Austin Scott, that it is in no worse position than almost all rights *in rem*, which can be cut off under the Limitation Act by a person who succeeds in retaining possession of an object for a long enough time against the will of the person entitled to it, and so is a true right *in rem*, though slightly more likely to be defeated than the interest of the trustee himself. In other words, most rights *in rem* are defeasible in some way or other, and the beneficiary's interest is not so defeasible as to forfeit the title of right *in rem*.

The question whether a right is *in rem* or *in personam* must be distinguished from the question whether a remedy is *in rem* or *in personam*. For example, a possessor of Blackacre has a right *in rem* not to have his possession intruded on, but his remedy against a trespasser will be *in personam*, that is to say, an action for damages. On the other hand, although a purchaser of Whiteacre has only a right *in personam* against the vendor, his remedy, if the latter does not convey, is specific performance of the contract, which operates directly on Whiteacre, by giving him a title to it, and so is *in rem*.[5]

Tracing

The beneficiary can therefore follow, or trace, trust property alienated in breach of trust into the hands of any person other than a bona fide purchaser for value without notice of the breach of trust or anyone who subsequently acquires it from or through him even with notice of a previous breach of trust. The full implications of this ability to trace trust property will be considered later in relation to the fragmentation of ownership.[6]

So far *tracing*, as thus described, is used only to substitute one trustee for another in respect of the specific objects originally subject

[5] See further p. 47 below.

[6] See p. 78 below.

to the trust, and to ensure the continuance of the equitable interest in them. But *tracing* can be used not merely to follow the same identifiable objects into the hands of one person after another, but also to follow the same fund into all the various specific objects which it may from time to time comprise through successive changes of investment, whether it remains in the hands of the original trustee or comes into the hands of other persons, as constructive trustees or otherwise.

Thus X may be the trustee of a fund which is entirely composed of a block of government stock. He may sell out in accordance with the terms of the trust and reinvest in industrial shares. He may then sell these in breach of trust at an undervalue to Y and disappear with the money, Y being aware of the breach of trust. The beneficiary can trace the trust property in its new form of industrial shares, so that the fund remains the same though its contents have changed, and also into the hands of Y, who will become a constructive trustee.

But it would have been just the same if X had sold the government stock in breach of trust and reinvested the money. The beneficiary would have been able to trace the trust property into the new investments and either treat them as part of the trust fund or take their value in money.

Having gone so far equity will go farther. Trustees must keep trust money in a banking account separate from their own private account. If now X paid the purchase price of the government stock into his private banking account and mixed it with his own money, it might be thought that what had taken the place of the government stock was no longer identifiable. However, equity is prepared to say that the trust fund still comprises so much money in the trustee's private account as corresponds to the purchase price.

This is perhaps not very easy to understand. The normal relation of banker to customer is that of a debtor if the customer has money in his account, and of a creditor if the customer has an overdraft. If therefore X pays the purchase price into his own account, which is at the time in credit, the banker owes him just so much more money. It might therefore be thought that the beneficiary could at best say to the banker, Pay me instead of X any money that you still owe to X, and that all other creditors of X could say the same, with the result that the beneficiary would have to compete with them on equal terms if X became insolvent. That is not, however, the case, for the beneficiary is allowed to trace the proceeds of the sale into the banker's hands. He is given what is called a charge[7] on the money still in X's account to the extent of the purchase price. This really means that if X becomes insolvent, and there is not enough money left in the account to satisfy all his creditors in full, the banker must

[7] See further p. 161 below.

pay the beneficiary out of what is still in X's account in preference to the other creditors. It is therefore simpler to say that where tracing is allowed, the beneficiary is a creditor with a preferential claim to be paid before the other creditors.[8]

Tracing is not limited to trust funds. Thus persons other than beneficiaries may sometimes treat a mass of money or investments as a separate account on which they can draw whatever may be the claims of other creditors against the person or persons who own it. Moreover, equity often gives one person a charge for a certain amount over property belonging to another. Although the latter is not called a trustee, this is really an extension of the trust concept, and its effect is to give the person entitled to the charge a preferential right to be paid out of the value of the property charged before any other creditors. This technique will be discussed later in relation to security.[9]

Specific performance

The imputation of a trust or charge is thus a very powerful equitable remedy, though trusts and charges are themselves equitable interests and not remedies. Specific performance, on the other hand, is an equitable remedy which has the indirect effect of creating equitable rights.

The only remedy common law affords for a breach of contract is a money judgment, either for a liquidated debt or for unliquidated damages. Thus if one person promises to transfer property to another, he cannot at common law be compelled to perform his promise. However, a court of equity will usually decree specific performance, ordering the promisor to convey the property, and, if he is recalcitrant, itself executing his promise through its officers.

Moreover, once a promise to convey property has come into existence which a court of equity will enforce specifically, the promisee is regarded as already having an equitable interest in the property; speaking popularly, he is regarded by equity as already the owner, although, for purposes of common law, he may not become owner until actual conveyance.

One principle of equity must be emphasized. It is said that equity

[8] This process by which one specific object can be replaced by another object as part of a fund is known to continental lawyers as *real subrogation*. If one person guarantees the repayment of a loan and is forced to pay, he is said to be subrogated to the rights which the creditor has against the debtor; in other words, he has any remedies against the debtor which the creditor would have had. The substitution of one thing for another in a fund is obviously analogous to the substitution of one person for another in a contractual claim. Hence the term real subrogation, the word *real* being added to show that it is a thing which is substituted and not a person. It would be convenient if the term were naturalized and regularly used to express a process which is indeed much more generally applied in England than on the Continent.

[9] See pp. 160–1 below.

will not assist a volunteer. A volunteer, for this purpose, is a person who has not given consideration, that is to say, has not given money or money's worth, or a promise of money or money's worth, in return for a promise. Thus a mere promise of a gift will not be specifically enforced, even though, if it is contained in a document under seal called a deed, an action for damages would lie at common law if it is not fulfilled. Equity will not intervene to perfect an incomplete gift. So far does this refusal go that equity will not construe an incomplete gift as a trust. Nor will it in general enforce an imperfectly constituted trust, that is to say, where the settlor has neither declared himself to be a trustee nor completely divested himself of the trust property in favour of the trustee.

On the other hand, not only will equity enforce a promise for consideration to transfer some kinds of property, for instance, a promise to sell land, but it will even, in favour of a person who has given consideration, treat an imperfectly constituted trust as a promise to create a trust and enforce it as a trust, as though the trust were already in existence.

Finally, specific performance will be decreed only if a common law judgment for money would be an inadequate remedy, and never for the performance of personal services. Thus only contracts for the transfer of unique objects will be specifically enforced, since if the subject-matter of the contract is not unique, the successful plaintiff can take the money awarded him as damages and go into the market and buy its equivalent. By far the commonest object of a decree of specific performance is land, for every piece of land is unique. But a sale of a specific block of shares will be specifically enforced, and if so, the shares are regarded by equity as the property of the buyer as soon as the contract is made. We shall see later that at common law too physical chattels such as ships and racehorses are usually the property of the buyer from that same moment. These points will be taken up again in treating of the transfer of property.[10]

Effects of equitable remedies

These equitable remedies have had enormous effects on English law. For as they have been extended to protect beneficiaries against increasing classes of persons, they have conferred on them rights which, though starting as rights *in personam*, have become almost as good as rights *in rem*. Indeed, from a general point of view, their most interesting effect has been this weakening of the distinction between rights *in rem* and rights *in personam*, which is absolutely essential to Roman law and the laws strongly influenced by it. Equity is usually prepared to treat a contractual right relating to property

10 See pp. 52–53 below.

not only as a right *in personam* entitling one person to a performance from another person in respect of that property, but as a right *in rem* analogous to ownership of the property.

This transformation of contractual into real rights operates, as we have seen, within three limits. It operates, first, only in favour of a person who has given consideration,[11] that is to say, money or money's worth, for them and, secondly, never against a person who has given consideration without notice of an infringement of the personal right.[12] Thirdly, the property affected must be identifiable and unique; but a trust fund and a banking account are identifiable and unique enough.[13]

Of all the various equitable interests protected by these equitable remedies the most permanent is that enjoyed by the beneficiary of a trust fund. The others, such as the equitable interest in a thing arising from a claim to specific performance of a contract, are usually very short-lived because in the ordinary course of events the contract is soon performed or specifically enforced. But a person may have an interest in a trust fund which will last all his life or which will be so permanent that he can transmit it to successors by will or on an intestacy.

One word of warning is needed. A court of equity may be willing to enforce an equitable right against one person, for instance, the other party to a contract, without being willing to enforce it against any other person, even if he has acquired property from him with notice of the right. In other words, by no means all equitable rights attach to or, in the recognized slang of the lawyer, *run with* property. Some are personal and therefore are not equivalent to equitable interests in property.

The distinction is an important one and has recently come into prominence in connexion with what are called licences, under which one person is permitted by another person, without a lease or tenancy, to occupy property belonging to him. The protection which equity is prepared to give to a licensee against his licensor has recently been enunciated in very wide terms, the licensee being entitled, if he has given value for the licence, not only to bring an action for damages if the licensor wrongfully revokes the licence, but also to be maintained in enjoyment of the property. On the other hand, recent attempts to treat such licences as creating equitable interests in land have been much criticized, and the law remains uncertain. In other words, it is probable that the licensee has an equitable right, or an *equity*, to be maintained in his possession against the licensor or persons who have acquired the premises from him, but much more

[11] See pp. 47–48 above.
[12] See pp. 44–45 above.
[13] See pp. 46–47 above.

doubtful whether he has an equitable interest in the premises which he can transmit to others.

Beneficiary's use of legal remedies

Although the normal remedies for the infringement of equitable interests are equitable remedies, a beneficiary may be deeply interested in the title to a legal right and the legal remedies that protect it. In the first place, if the legal right is not secure, the equitable interest may topple down with it, for the ultimate basis of the latter is the ability of some person having the legal right to deal with it as a court of equity directs. But, secondly, the beneficiary may, and often does, have possession of the subject matter of the trust property. If that is the case, he may use the same legal remedies as are available to any other possessor.

IV

ACQUISITION OF PROPERTY INTERESTS

1. TRANSFER OF PROPERTY

THE modes of transferring property vary with the different kinds of property transferred. Moreover, sometimes the actual transfer is and sometimes it is not preceded by preliminaries which are almost as important as the transfer itself. Thus the actual transfer of land on a sale is almost always preceded not only by a contract but also by an investigation of title; indeed at the present day the actual signing of a contract is preceded by inquiries which would not themselves be made unless they were preceded not only by negotiations but also by something in the nature of a pre-contract. On the other hand, when goods are bought for cash in a shop, contract and conveyance are rolled into one, there are usually no negotiations, and there is certainly no investigation of title. Buying a patent or copyright lies somewhere between the two. More time and care are taken than in buying ordinary goods, but there is not the same elaborate succession of stages as in the purchase of land.

Acquisition by consent

The details of these various types of conveyance can be found in the textbooks, but it may be worth while to try to generalize as far as possible. In the first place all the transfers of property discussed here are consensual, that is to say, they require agreement between the parties. This is obvious enough where there is a sale, for the seller must agree to transfer the property and the buyer to acquire it. Where there is a gift, the agreement may seem rather more shadowy, for English law does not require any actual acceptance by the donee; however, since he is at liberty to refuse the gift, from his failure to do so it may be presumed that he is willing to acquire the property in question. There are transfers of property which take place not only without the consent but against the will of the person losing it, as for example when the property of a bankrupt vests in his trustee in bankruptcy, but such transfers are best kept apart from those which are now being discussed.

Factors at work

The next question to be asked is, agreement being admitted to be necessary, what is its effect?

The law is complicated by the interaction of three different principles, which are, moreover, subject to exceptions.

First, a distinction is made between transfers which operate merely between the parties and transfers which are good for all purposes. In principle, for the former nothing more is needed than the intention of the parties that the property shall pass; for the latter something more is needed such as delivery, a sealed document, or notice to some third party.

Secondly, any transfer which is good as between the parties also binds the transferor's creditors; though sometimes they may be able to have the transfer set aside, for instance if it is in fraud of them.

Thirdly, since the law does not readily enforce promises to make gifts, gratuitous transfers do not ordinarily operate even as between the parties unless they are also done in a way which is good for all purposes; but this is subject to an exception which is hard to explain and even harder to name.

A further complication is introduced by variations in the requirement of written evidence. It would serve no useful purpose to discuss them here. It is enough to say that, in the interests of safety and clarity, it is always advisable for a transferee who does not immediately gain possession of a physical object or a document of title to get a written statement from the transferor.

Operation between parties and operation against all the world

The distinction between transfers which operate merely between the parties (though binding the transferor's creditors) and those good for all purposes is best explained by means of examples. Thus the property in ascertained goods passes from the seller to the buyer when the parties intend it to pass, and very commonly the goods will become the property of the buyer even though they are left by him in the possession of the seller. If now the seller, in fraud of the buyer, sells and delivers the goods to a second buyer, who is in good faith, that is to say, has no knowledge of the previous sale, the second buyer becomes owner of the goods. The Sale of Goods Act explains this result by saying that the seller must be taken to have had the authority of the first buyer to sell the goods to the second buyer. It is perhaps easier to see what happens if one adopts the language of the Supreme Judicial Court of Massachusetts in a decision of 1821, that the property in the goods passes when the parties intend it, 'only as between seller and buyer'; and sections 16 to 20 of the Sale of Goods Act have the sub-heading 'Transfer of Property as between Seller and Buyer'. On the other hand, if, while goods sold to the buyer are still in the seller's possession, the seller goes bankrupt, the trustee in bankruptcy, who acts in the interests of the seller's creditors, cannot resist the buyer's demand for delivery of the goods, for he is entitled only to the property of the seller, and the goods are no longer the seller's but the buyer's.

On the other hand, once the goods have been delivered by the seller to the buyer, they are the buyer's for all purposes. Even without delivery the same result would be produced if notice of the sale could be given to all persons who could possibly buy the goods subsequently from the seller in possession; but that is in practice inconceivable.

Sales of land are ordered somewhat differently. In principle, and as a matter of common law, the title to land can be transferred only by a deed, that is to say, a sealed writing executed by the transferor. A deed is necessary to pass the legal title to legal estates and interests in land and also to patents and government stock. It is an alternative method of perfecting a gift of physical movables. To be effectual, a deed requires to be signed, sealed, and delivered by the person making it. The seal need not be his personal seal; indeed most usually nowadays it is no more than a small circular piece of red paper gummed on to the document. But a deed executed by a corporation must bear the corporate seal. Delivery would normally be physical delivery to the person in whose favour the deed is made, but need not be so. It is enough for the deed to be put in circulation, for instance by the maker saying to some bystander that he delivers it as his act and deed. Even if he then locks it up in his desk it is properly delivered.

However, as soon as a vendor agrees to sell land to a purchaser a court will in the exercise of its equitable jurisdiction normally grant specific performance of the agreement and hence the purchaser is regarded as having already an equitable interest in the land.[1] Now, that equitable interest is perfectly good against the vendor and also against any person who acquires the legal estate in the land otherwise than as a purchaser for value without notice of the previous sale. Thus, a person who has agreed to purchase land is in at least as good a position as a buyer of goods, though technically the latter already has a legal title whereas the purchaser of land only has an equitable title. But if the purchaser registers the sale as an 'estate contract' under the Land Charges Act, his equitable interest is good as against any subsequent purchaser, for registration is equivalent to notice; whereas if he does not, it will be good against no subsequent purchaser. This power of registering the sale makes the position of a purchaser of land better than that of a buyer of goods. It can be made better without inconvenience to third parties because the transfer of

[1] See p. 47 above.

land is a more leisurely process than the transfer of goods, and so purchasers have ample time to search a register.

Choses in action are subject to yet another régime. For the assignee of a legal chose in action, such as a debt, to be able to sue the debtor in his own name, without joining the assignor either as plaintiff or as defendant, the requirements of the Law of Property Act must be fulfilled, among which appear the rules that the assignment must be in writing and that notice in writing must be given to the debtor. But if either, or even both, of these requirements are not fulfilled, the assignment may take effect as an equitable assignment, so long as the assignor has done all he can to divest himself of all his interest in the debt to the assignee. If, however, the debtor pays the assignor before he has notice of the assignment, the assignee cannot enforce a second payment to him; and if the assignor, in fraud of the first assignee, makes a second assignment to a second assignee who succeeds in giving notice to the debtor before the first assignee, the second assignee will take priority over the first. Yet in spite of all this an assignee who has not yet given notice to the debtor will be preferred to the trustee in bankruptcy of the assignor. In other words, the assignment may be complete as between the assignor (or his creditors) and the assignee before it is complete as against bona fide third parties.

Gratuitous transfers

So far we have been considering transfers in a general way, without reference to the question whether they are gratuitous or not, though for the most part they have been by way of sale. We must now consider the complications introduced by the refusal of the law to enforce informal promises of gifts.

It does not affect transfers which are good for all purposes. Such transfers are always more than mere promises, that is to say, they are out-and-out grants by way of delivery of goods or documents or by deed or by written declaration coupled with notice to a third party. But it does usually affect transfers which are good only between the parties. Thus if one person promises gratuitously to give money or goods to another person, no transfer takes place even between the parties; and a promise of a gift of land raises no equitable interest in the donee. On the other hand, a promise of a gift made in a deed is binding on the donor, for promises by deed are an exception to the rule that gratuitous promises are not binding. However, a deed is also a means of transferring property not only between the parties but for all purposes, and so the only difference between a valid promise of a gift and an out-and-out gift is in the intention of the donor.

So far there is no real difficulty. But there is sometimes a difficulty when a chose in action is assigned but no notice has been given to the debtor or other person under a duty to the assignor. To give a neat result the law should say that an assignment perfected by notice and so good for all purposes should operate even if it is gratuitous, but that an assignment not perfected by notice and therefore at best good only as between the assignor and assignee (and also as against the assignor's creditors) should be treated only as a promise to assign and should therefore not even operate to that limited extent if it is gratuitous. But that is not the case. Between the gratuitous promise and the out-and-out gift, good for all purposes and against all comers, equity interposes a *tertium quid* which has no name of its own.

Equity takes the same view of gratuitous promises as common law. It will not perfect an incomplete gift. If, therefore, something remains to be done in order to make the donee owner of a thing, the donor remains owner in equity as well as at common law. Generally speaking this means that something must be done, even to satisfy equity, which will make the transfer of the property good for all purposes. However, equity does not really consider the giving of notice to a debtor a part of the transfer of a chose in action, but merely as something determining priorities among claims to be paid the debt. If, therefore, the assignment is complete but for the giving of notice, it is a good equitable assignment, even though the lack of notice makes it impossible for the assignee to sue the debtor under the Law of Property Act in his own name without joining the assignor.

Even so, equity would normally require, in order to perfect the gift of a chose in action, the delivery of a document of title or a declaration of trust by the assignor. But there are occasions where all that the assignor could possibly do would be to make a declaration, if necessary in writing, that he is assigning the chose in action to the assignee; and in that case there is a good equitable assignment which, even if gratuitous, operates to transfer the chose in action as between the parties, though for lack of notice it is not good for all purposes. This in effect covers simple money debts not enshrined in a document of title and interests in trust funds—and probably nothing else.

Rationale of the main distinction

It is not unreasonable that the parties should be able to regulate according to their own wishes the transfer of property as between themselves, and, provided he furnishes sufficient evidence of his intention, that the transferor should bind those who have already given him credit; for the creditors will be fairly well protected by the power with which a trustee in bankruptcy is invested, to resume anything which third parties have acquired from the transferor whether by way of recent gift or in fraud of his creditors.

However, it is not thought reasonable that the bare agreement of the parties, even if evidenced in an informal writing, should be conclusive against a third person who acquires the thing afterwards from the transferor for a consideration, or gives him credit on the security of it, in ignorance of the informal transfer. Almost invariably some further step must be taken to bind bona fide subsequent acquirers. Usually the books state quite shortly that these further steps are necessary for the property to pass. In fact, as we have seen, they are usually necessary not as between the parties, but only if third parties are to be bound to respect the transfer.

Notice and registration

As has already been said, notice is not so much a part of certain transfers as a supplement to a transfer designed to make it good against third parties. Registration plays the same role, and indeed the two are more alike than would appear at first sight.

The purpose of giving notice of assignment of a debt or an interest in a trust fund to the debtor or the trustees is to prevent them paying the assignor instead of the assignee, and also to secure priority to the assignee over any subsequent assignees. But the matter may be looked at from another point of view. A person who is buying or lending money on the security of a debt or an interest in a trust fund is well advised to apply first to the debtor or the trustees to see if it has already been assigned, and, if so, to what extent, at the same time warning them of the forthcoming assignment to him. Thus the debtor or trustees keep, as it were, a private register of assignments.

Where land or physical chattels are concerned, such private registers would be both unsatisfactory and hard to establish. Hence public registers have been set up for various classes of things. For the present it is enough to say that registration serves two purposes, to protect third parties and to render easier and cheaper the investigation of title. Moreover, the property in registered land is transferred by entering the purchaser's name in the register.[2]

2. ORIGINAL MODES OF ACQUISITION

By far the commonest mode of acquiring property is by transfer from one who has the title to it. But there are other modes, some of which are fairly important.

Occupation

Some things can be acquired by merely taking possession of them. Even if only possession is acquired, it carries with it advantages

[2] See further pp. 173–6 below.

which have already been explained. The possessor can maintain his possession against a mere intruder and can if necessary recover it from him. But possession may in some cases give the sort of title that is usually designated as ownership. This is so where the thing of which possession is taken has been up to that time without an owner.

This can hardly occur where land is concerned, for there will always be some person with a title to a piece of land. When a squatter takes possession of land it is almost always because the true owner is away or has mistaken the boundaries of his holding or even, as occasionally happens in some parts of the country, because he has bought it so cheaply that he cannot be bothered to look after it. The true owner then loses his title only after the period of limitation has run against him.

The two cases where title is gained immediately by taking possession are where a person finds goods without a present possessor and the owner of which cannot be traced, and where a person reduces a wild animal into possession.

In the former case the only difficult question of law that occurs in practice is whether the thing found was at the time without a present possessor. There seems to be a general tendency at the present day to hold that a thing lost on premises is in the possession of the possessor of the premises; but, as has already been explained,[3] the various decisions are not easily reconciled. There may also in any particular case be a doubt whether anyone else will claim the lost property and a further doubt whether a claimant can prove his title. These doubts make it necessary for the finder, if he is to feel safe, to advertise his finding, or, better, to report it to the police. But there is no doubt whatever that if no possessor or owner can be found the finder becomes owner.

Animals

The law relating to the ownership of wild animals is rather complicated. A distinction must first be drawn between the killing of animals and the possession of living animals. The law as to the latter is relatively simple. Any person who tames or confines a wild animal so as to possess it is owner so long as he retains possession. He is said to acquire a qualified ownership *per industriam*. As soon as it escapes and resumes its wild character he ceases to own it, though he is allowed to retake it so long as he keeps it in sight and has the power and right to pursue it. This latter requirement has been held to deprive of ownership a person whose bees swarmed into the garden of a neighbour who refused him entry to retake them. Mere temporary absences will not deprive a person of title to animals which

[3] p. 35 above.

are in the habit of leaving his land and returning, but if they lose the habit, and therefore what is whimsically called the *animus revertendi*, they cease to be his. A qualified ownership is also acquired *propter impotentiam* over animals on his land which are too young to escape, and is of course lost when they can escape.

As regards the killing of wild animals the vital question is, who has the right to kill? If such a person kills he obtains permanent ownership of the dead animal, which does not cease to be his merely if he loses possession of it. The right to kill ground game, that is to say hares and rabbits, is vested in the occupier of the land on which they are found; and he cannot be deprived of it by contract or any other means. The right to kill other game is sometimes vested in a person *propter privilegium*, by royal grant or prescription, but it is usually vested in the freeholder, by whom it can be detached and let to tenants of sporting rights.

Accession and alteration

Other modes of acquisition, which play a less prominent part in English than in Roman law, are accession and alteration.

When an accessory is added to a principal object, its identity is merged in that of the latter; and so, if they belonged to different persons, the owner of the accessory loses his title. The most important cases, where buildings or other fixtures accede to land, have already been discussed in defining land.[4] Where movables accede to movables, in most cases the owner of the principal object has already acquired ownership of the accessory before incorporating it.

Alteration of objects gives rise to problems of ownership where one person manufactures a finished object from materials belonging to another. Probably the Roman solution would be accepted, namely, that if the object can be reduced to the original materials it would be the property of the owner of the materials, but if not, the manufacturer would become owner. However, there is very little authority for the following reason. The owner of the materials could in any case obtain their value from the manufacturer in an action for converting them; while, if he went farther and claimed possession of the finished object, the judge would have a discretion whether to accede to his request or not, and, if he did, could probably make him pay for the value added to it by the manufacturer. Thus the question of title would hardly arise.

[4] pp. 20–21 above.

V

THE FRAGMENTATION OF OWNERSHIP

ONE of the greatest difficulties encountered by students of property law comes from the English habit of splitting what may in a general way be called ownership into its component parts and making of each of them an abstract entity which, if not quite the same as a thing, is not very different. A full explanation of this fragmentation of ownership must come later and indeed will not be accomplished within the two covers of this book. Here it is intended to give the student a first look at some of the more important ways in which fragmentation occurs, with as full an explanation as will be intelligible for the time being.

The law governing this topic was worked out in the first instance for land and later applied to funds comprising both land and more permanent chattel interests such as stocks and shares. It has never been applied in its entirety to physical chattels, not usually because of any objection in point of principle but from lack of opportunity.

Land and chattels

For the fragmentation of ownership to be worth while the thing in question ought to be capable of yielding an income for a considerable time and its whereabouts should always be readily ascertainable. Now land possesses both these qualities in the highest degree. It is immovable and virtually indestructible. When the law was being worked out, trust funds either did not exist in sufficient numbers or were not considered important enough to be prime objects of doctrinal development, but later they were found to possess the same characteristics as land to a sufficient degree to make it appropriate to extend to them the same technique of fragmentation; for although they were and are less immune from destruction than land, they exist solely in order to furnish an income for beneficiaries, and although they are not immovable, they can be traced with sufficient ease and security into the hands of successive trustees. But physical chattels, with comparatively few exceptions, are too destructible and can be got rid of too easily for it to be worth while to split up the ownership in them among several persons according to many different principles. Ships indeed escape this generalization to some extent, and so do valuable heirlooms such as pictures and jewels. But what are rather vaguely known as 'consumer goods' have too temporary an existence and can be spirited away too easily for the law to apply to them the full apparatus of fragmentation. They will appear only occasionally in the following pages.

However, lawyers, more especially when, in the course of writing books on law, they stand a little away from their subject, feel a strong desire to generalize. In this they do not differ from other scientific thinkers. But they have also a practical end in view. The law cannot provide in advance a detailed solution for every conceivable specific problem. It must develop principles and techniques which can be applied uniformly over fields of varying extent. Hence the need to generalize.

Now the full extent to which a general principle or technique can properly be made to apply is hardly ever apparent from the start. Accordingly, generalization tends to be progressive; partial generalizations are seen to yield to wider generalizations. The process is often easy enough, though awkward exceptions may have to be admitted. Sometimes it is difficult because, whereas the common elements in two bodies of doctrine or technique may now seem to outweigh in importance the differences between them, at an earlier period the differences seemed so serious that generalization was expressly rejected.

This has been the case with realty and chattels. Above all, extremely fruitful generalizations such as the notion of tenure and the doctrine of estates have been excluded on principle from the law of chattels, for the very good reason that what at the time would have been the most important inferences to be drawn from those generalizations were clearly not applicable to chattels. But those inferences, as will be seen later, can no longer be drawn for realty either, and so the question must now be raised whether the elements common to the law of realty and the law of chattels are not important enough to justify new attempts to generalize more thoroughly the whole law of property, and in particular to apply to the somewhat rudimentary law of chattels the highly developed doctrines and techniques hitherto commonly recognized to apply only to realty. A conviction that such attempts are justified must explain what may at first sight appear to be an excessive preoccupation with obscure problems raised by bailments, and especially with the questions whether the notion of tenure and the doctrine of estates can be applied to them.[1]

Abstraction

At this point the student enters a new world, much less familiar than the one he has just left. So far he has been concerned in the first instance with remedies, and rights have appeared only as implied in

[1] See pp. 63, 72–73, and 177 below.

those remedies. He has lost something and wants to get it back, or he wants to stop someone else from interfering with it. The atmosphere became rather more rarefied when he had to understand equitable rights and remedies, but he was still in the sort of world that the ordinary man usually regards as peculiarly legal, the forensic world of the courts, of 'going to law'. The transfer of property made him acquainted with another form of legal activity, that of conveyancing, but there also there was nothing very surprising, for all he was really interested in was making certain that he got something that would stand up to a lawsuit. He was still dealing with corporeal things or with such familiar incorporeal things as debts, stocks and shares, or copyright.

Now he will find himself brought face to face with a new activity of the conveyancer and with a type of conveyancer whom he probably never knew to exist, the expert barrister who sits in his chambers in Lincoln's Inn and hardly ever goes into court, who spends his time like a spider, weaving webs of legal gossamer in which to tie up corporeal things and the incorporeal things which are the immediate objects of commerce. The purpose of all his activity is to ensure, as far as the law can ensure it, that the property interests he is dealing with shall move from one person to another for an appreciable time in the future in a perfectly predictable way and that they shall be managed in the cheapest and most efficient way, attracting the lightest possible burden of taxation. As has already been remarked—but the point is worth making repeatedly—he works with abstract entities which it takes a prolonged effort to understand completely, for only such abstractions can be, as the Americans say, 'tailored' to fit a particular purpose. What is more important for the moment is that they are precision instruments of known form and potentialities.

In other words, the student has now left the forensic world, peopled by vague and hardly definable notions like possession and title whose only purpose is to help judges deal as best they may with things which have gone wrong, a world where purchasers either trust to luck and neglect to investigate title or are willing to accept a good holding title which will probably not be attacked. He is entering the precise, sharp, logical world of the expert conveyancer, who is constantly using the most refined abstract tools in order to create complex arrangements for the future which cannot, so far as the law is concerned, go wrong and to provide with equal certainty for the happening of untoward events. The student has had a slight foretaste of this in the law of negotiable instruments and documents of title. Indeed that highly abstract thing called money lends itself, and is intended to lend itself, to something of the same precision, and the banker, who handles money most expertly, tries to make the results of his operations as predictable as does the expert conveyancer. But the more profound study of money and banking falls within the confines of commercial law.

The topics which will be discussed at this point are (1) tenure, (2) co-ownership, (3) time, (4) words of limitation, (5) rent and rent-charges, (6) powers, and (7) the distinction between management and enjoyment.

1. TENURE

The earliest fragmentation, which made all others possible, was an essential part of feudalism. That was a system of landholding which had for its main purpose the quartering of an army on the soil. In a society short of the precious metals, and therefore unable to pay for services in money, the most convenient way of providing for an expensive force of armed horsemen was for the king to give parcels of land to men of substance (so-called tenants-in-chief) upon the terms that they should provide a certain number of knights to serve for forty days a year, and then for the tenants-in-chief, as mesne lords, to give those knights, as demesne tenants, lands to hold in subordination to them. This is only the core of what was a most complicated system of landholding, under which some cultivated the land for the benefit of others besides themselves, in return for protection and justice. But it gives sufficient information to explain what is meant by tenure.

Tenure is a relation which looks both ways, towards a parcel of land and towards a lord. The tenant-in-chief held his land of the king, and the demesne tenant held his land of his mesne lord, the tenant-in-chief. In this sense tenure was a relation between lord and man, but with regard to the land itself it expressed a fragmentation of ownership among a number of persons, each of whom was regarded not as owner but only as tenant of the land. In the older books on Real Property law one often comes across the generic term *terre-tenant*, as the exact technical equivalent of what in ordinary language is called a landowner.

Tenure is a notion which the student is bound to encounter when beginning the study of property law. He must be warned not to devote much attention to it. It still exists at two points, in the quite meaningless and indeed inaccurate statement that no subject can in the technical sense 'own' land, even though he has the exclusive benefit of it, since only the sovereign can own land and all others hold it of him, and in the law of leases, which is familiarly called the law of landlord and tenant. Of the relation between a tenant-farmer or the tenant of a house and his landlord three things must be said: first, it is the only form of tenure that still has any practical meaning, secondly, it never really fitted into the feudal system, being an alien commercial element which had to be brought into some sort of artificial relation to it, and, thirdly, the relation between landlord and tenant is now in the main contractual, though controlled by modern statutes.[2]

However, tenure, since it denied in principle the unity of ownership, created a mental atmosphere favourable to the division of ownership on other lines also. If ownership could be divided between landlord and tenant, why not between persons related to the land in other ways? In legal systems which have been greatly influenced by Roman law there is a standing inhibition against the fragmentation of ownership, which is allowed only grudgingly when practical considerations exert overwhelming force.

Bailment

Tenure has no place in the law of personalty. Nevertheless, a very close analogy to the relation of landlord and tenant is to be found in that between bailor and bailee. Whenever a physical movable is delivered by one person to another for a purpose upon the understanding that it is to be returned upon the accomplishment of the purpose, there is a bailment. Now between the bailor, who hands over the thing, and the bailee, who receives it, there is a personal relation, for the bailee is under a duty to the bailor to take reasonable care of the thing and to return it in due course. But a bailment for a term also confers possession on the bailee, to the exclusion of the bailor. Thus the bailee, and not the bailor, can bring an action of trespass against an intruder, and can alone recover possession from a dispossessor. If the bailment is at will, the bailee's position is precisely the same, though it is said on rather doubtful authority that the bailor also has possession, with the rights it confers. So far there is nothing to differentiate in principle a bailment for a term from a lease of land. Moreover, such interest as the bailee has in the chattel is derived from that of the bailor, as is shown by the rule that, just as a lessee cannot be heard to deny his lessor's title, so a bailee cannot be heard to deny that of his bailor. Thus a bailment presents the same sort of mingling of real and personal relations as a lease, and to say that there is tenure between bailor and bailee would be no great offence against terminological propriety.

2. CO-OWNERSHIP

Ownership of the same thing at the same time and in the same way by a number of persons has been general from early times. Indeed,

[2] See pp. 117–26 below.

some students of primitive law think that ownership by communities such as families, tribes, and clans everywhere preceded ownership by individuals. Roman law admitted common ownership and it has survived everywhere in one form or another.

Even in the modern world there are many occasions on which this may happen. A man may, for instance, die intestate leaving two unmarried sons who go on living together in his house; they do not choose to divide it into two self-contained flats but use most of the rooms in common. In many countries marriage usually makes some at least of what was hitherto the separate property of each of the spouses their common property; and in England it is common for husband and wife to operate a joint banking account. Or two men may run a business in partnership, which involves using the same factory or office in common.

English law has always known two kinds of co-ownership, in accordance with which several persons enjoy what are called concurrent interests. They are called respectively joint ownership and ownership in common. In speaking of land the terms joint tenancy and tenancy in common are used. The difference between them is that whereas if one owner or tenant in common dies, his share passes to his successors, whether by will or on an intestacy, one joint tenant's share accrues on his death to the other joint tenants, so that when all the joint tenants but one are dead the last survivor becomes sole owner or tenant.

Lawyers have tried to explain this right of survivorship in a thoroughly artificial way by saying that whereas tenants in common are regarded as holding undivided shares in the land, each share being capable of being alienated, joint tenants do not own shares, but each joint tenant owns the whole, subject to the concurrent ownership of the other joint tenants. When one dies the others do not in theory acquire anything that they had not already, but are merely relieved of the presence of a competing tenant.

Thus, if property is given to A, B, and C as joint tenants or without any additional words at all they take as joint tenants because there is nothing to show that they are to have shares in the property. But if land was given to A, B, and C with the addition of words which show that they were to have shares in it, for instance the word 'equally', before 1926 they became tenants in common.

The right of survivorship at first sight gives such unfair results that it is difficult to see how anybody should want to give property in joint tenancy or joint ownership. A moment's reflection will, however, show that joint tenancy or ownership is an extremely convenient form of ownership for trustees. For the ownership of trustees is for the purpose of management and not enjoyment. Now it is only where a number of persons have concurrent rights to enjoy a thing that the right of survivorship produces unfair results; on the other hand, it is very convenient that the interest of one of a number of managers should not devolve on those who succeed him on death, but should vest automatically in the survivors. If one looks upon the trustees as a committee, all that has happened is that a member of the committee has disappeared, and the others carry on as if he were still there, taking steps to add to their number if it becomes too small. Thus, joint tenancy or joint ownership is appropriate to management, tenancy or ownership in common to beneficial enjoyment of property. For this reason and others, as will be seen later, the Legislature in 1925 restricted tenancy in common to equitable interests.

3. TIME

So far we have considered cases where a person's ownership of property is limited by the competing existence, first, of a landlord or tenant, and, secondly, by that of a co-owner. In both cases their interests coexist simultaneously with his. But there is another case where, although as will be explained later, the interests are really simultaneous, they seem at first sight to be successive.

Successive enjoyment of property

Most legal systems find it necessary to allow one person to be given property for a limited time and for a second person to be assured during that time that he or his representatives will take the property after him, not as his successor but independently of any relation to him. A simple example is a grant of property to A for his life and then to B absolutely. There are many forms of legal technique by which this can be effected. The English technique is peculiar and at first sight difficult to understand.

It will help to make explanation easier if one considers what will happen if either A or B is short of money and wants to raise money on his interest in the property. Can either of them realize his interest? The first question then is to ask if either interest has an ascertainable value, and the answer is plain: both of them have. An actuary would first ask what is the price that the land—let us assume that the property in question is land—would fetch in the open market. He would next ascertain from an inspection of life tables and from information as to the age and health of A what was A's expectation of life. He would then capitalize the aggregate income that A could expect to obtain during his life. That would form the basis for an estimate of the price that an insurance company, for instance, would pay for A's life interest, or alternatively what the company would require to be paid down as a lump sum in return for an annuity of that amount, and B's interest would have a present value amounting to the difference between the present value of the land and the present value of A's life interest. There would, of course, be a speculative element, for A might die sooner or later than the actuary would predict.

Or the matter might be looked at somewhat differently. Suppose B wanted to buy out A and get the land at once. He would in effect have to buy A an annuity equivalent to the probable annual value of the land for the period that A was expected to live. Insurance companies are perfectly familiar with that kind of business. Again, they would make no difficulty in letting A have the capital value of the annuity in cash.

Now what is it that B would be buying in the last case or that any outside purchaser would be buying from A or B? In one sense what is being bought is time, the right to have now what one might have to wait a long time for. A or B buys this from the outsider, or B buys time from A. It might also be said that the outsider buys from B the land, subject to A's life interest. But it would not be so easy to say that an outsider in buying A's life interest was also buying the land. What is clear is that in buying whatever they do buy they have an eye to value and that the value of what they buy depends partly on the value of the land and partly on the probable duration of some person's interest in it. On the other hand, it is probably better to say that they buy, not the value, but something to which the value attaches, but in that case each thing to which a separate value attaches must have a present existence.

It need not therefore cause any surprise to find that English law said that the thing bought and sold was something that in some way represented the land but also contained the notion of duration, and that that duration could be cut up into slices. Now the land itself in its physical aspect could be cut into slices amounting to this or that fragment of area, or even of volume, for instance, if one floor of a house is sold apart from the other floors. But although land exists in time as well as space, it is difficult—perhaps impossible—to cut it into slices each of which amounts to a period of time. For it is of no use, if you are thinking on these lines, to say that one person has the land now and the other will have it in the future; that future holding has a present market value and therefore should be treated as a present thing.

Estates

The solution adopted by English law was to create an abstract entity called the estate in the land and to interpose it between the tenant and the land. Since the estate was an abstract entity imagined to serve certain purposes, it could be made to conform to a specification, and the essential parts of the specification were that the estate should represent the temporal aspect of the land—as it were a fourth dimension—that it should be divisible within that dimension in respect of time according to a coherent set of rules, but that the whole of that dimension, the estate, should be regarded as existing at the present moment so that slices of the estate representing rights to successive holdings of the land should be regarded as present estates coexisting at the same time. Thus, although B might have to wait for A's death to enter upon the land, his estate was not later in time than A's life estate but existed simultaneously with it. This difficult idea may perhaps be rendered more intelligible if one takes the analogy of a musical score. We shall not in the ordinary course hear the fourth movement of a Beethoven symphony until we have heard the first, second, and third movements in that order; but they are all present at the same moment in the score.

This technique, giving a legal explanation to the present market value attaching to successive rights to hold property, was first worked out for land. It has since been applied to funds, and indeed some of what has just been described in the past tense now applies to funds rather than land, as will appear in the sequel. It is generally said not to apply to corporeal movables, but the matter is uncertain. In practice it would seldom be worth while trying to apply it to them.

It is a fascinating technique, supple and allowing great liberty together with security in dealing with interests in property; but its main service has probably been, by attaching ownership not to the land itself but to an abstract entity, to familiarize property lawyers with the possibility of inventing abstractions which should conform to specifications chosen with considerable freedom to serve particular purposes. With that development the law of property ceased to be earth-bound.

Since that lesson had been learnt there was no reason why other abstract entities should not be invented to serve other purposes. Henceforth it could be no objection that by adopting a particular technical solution one made it difficult, if not impossible, to discover the owner of a thing. If one could attach ownership to one abstract entity, one could attach it to another. Of course one ought not to multiply such entities unnecessarily, and one should always have practical needs in mind; but inhibitions based on the need for keeping one's eyes fixed on the physical object were quite out of place.

Three simple classifications of estates can be easily understood even at this early stage.

Estates in possession and estates in expectancy

The first is into estates in possession and estates in expectancy. If a person's estate gave him a right to the immediate possession of the land, it was said to be an estate in possession. If, on the other hand, he would have to wait for his right to possession to take effect, he had only an estate in expectancy. Thus, a grant to A for life and thereafter to B gave an estate in possession to A but only an estate in expectancy to B. However, although B's possession would be in the future and, if his estate were for life, might never fall into possession owing to his predeceasing A, his estate, though itself often called a future estate, was really a present estate in the land.

Reversions and remainders

The second classification is of estates in expectancy, which are divided into reversions and remainders. If a person, A, who has an estate in Blackacre, for instance a fee simple, gives to another person, B, an estate of smaller duration than his own, for instance, a life estate—it is called a particular estate because it is only a fragment (*particula*) of A's estate—and says nothing about what is to happen after B's death, the land is said to revert on B's death to A or his successors in title, and the residue of A's estate after B's particular estate has been subtracted from it is called a reversion. If, on the other hand, A were to direct that Blackacre should go to C for life and thereafter to D, the land would be said to remain away from A, and D's interest would be a remainder. The technical words used in such a case would normally be 'grant to C for life remainder to D'. In the two examples just given A would be called a reversioner and D a remainderman.

Vested and contingent remainders

It is also advisable to explain at once the difference between a vested and a contingent remainder. If at any moment the remainderman would be able to take possession of Blackacre should the particular estate come to an end, which would normally be by the death of a tenant for life, then his remainder is *vested*. This would be the case if the identity of the remainderman was perfectly ascertained and no contingency still needed to be fulfilled. Both he and the *quantum* of his estate were known. Hence he had a present estate *vested* in him. It was said to be *vested in interest*; it would *vest in possession*, if at all, only when the particular estate came to an end.

But Blackacre might have been given, for instance, to A for life remainder to the eldest surviving son of X, who already has children; or to Y when he reaches the age of twenty-one; or to the eldest son of Z, who is still a bachelor. All these remainders depend for their coming into effect on contingencies. Thus, in the first example, the remainder will fail unless X has a surviving son, and, moreover, the identity of his eldest surviving son cannot be ascertained until X dies. Hence there can be no present estate in remainder for want of a known person in whom it can vest. In the second example, the identity of Y is known, but he cannot take until he reaches the age of twenty-one. Hence he has no estate at the present moment. In the third example, there are two contingencies: first, Z must marry, and secondly he must have a son. Again there is no person who can have an estate. In all three cases there is nothing but a possibility that an estate will come into existence on the happening of the contingency. Hence these remainders were called contingent remainders. They were never considered to be estates; but the probability that the contingency would happen might be very great and might be worth paying for. So it is not a matter for surprise that contingent remainders eventually became alienable, like vested remainders; and they are known as future *interests*. Reversions are of course always *vested*, for the identity of the reversioner is always known and he is always ready to take if all particular estates should come to an end.

Contingent interests form a large class, of which contingent remainders are only one example. The law relating to them was at one time extremely complicated.[3] Even after the simplifications introduced by the 1925 legislation it is still complicated and presents many traps for the unwary framers of settlements and wills.[4]

Freehold and leasehold estates

The third classification is into freehold and leasehold estates, the former having an indefinite, the latter a definite duration, or one which can be made definite at the will of one of the parties concerned. The simplest examples of freehold estates are the estate in fee simple and the life estate.[5] A fee simple lasts until a present holder dies intestate and without near relatives. It is in the ordinary course of events perpetual and is the nearest thing to full ownership of land found in English law. The indefiniteness of its duration lies in the fact that although it may come to an end, no one can say at any given moment before its termination when that will be. That a life interest will come to an end is certain, but the time of its termination is indefinite. On the other hand, not only is it certain that a lease for

[3] See pp. 134–8 below.

[4] See pp. 138–45 below.

[5] A third freehold estate was the fee tail. In principle it lasted as long as the tenant had issue in the direct line, but was usually turned into a fee simple by being 'barred'. See pp. 131–4 below. All freehold estates other than the fee simple absolute in possession were in 1925 turned into equitable *interests*. See p. 83 below. However, much of what could be said of freehold *estates* is still true of what may by analogy, but somewhat inaccurately, be called freehold *interests*.

five years will come to an end, but it is also certain that, if nothing happens to terminate it prematurely, it will come to an end precisely five years after its creation. In fact lawyers have been so impressed by the definiteness of a lease's duration that when they allude to the lease as an estate rather than as an arrangement giving possession to the lessee, they always designate it as a *term of years*, or, more shortly, a *term*; and they call the lessee a *termor*.

Not all leasehold estates arise from leases in the strict sense of the term. Some are more properly called tenancies, and are of various kinds. The most frequent and most important are so-called periodical tenancies, for example, from week to week, from month to month, or from year to year. Periodical tenancies so created continue until they are brought to an end by a notice to quit on the part of either the landlord or the tenant varying with the period of the tenancy and terminating on one of the anniversaries of the original grant. They have, as it were, a definite duration for the time being and the definiteness of its duration starts up again whenever the proper day for notice has passed without notice being given.

The other possible tenancies are tenancies at will and at sufferance. The former means what it says: the landlord may terminate it at any moment by ejecting the tenant and the tenant likewise may throw it up at any moment. However, the payment of rent by a tenant at will, on a yearly basis, makes him a tenant from year to year, subject to termination by a half-year's notice. But for its capacity for enlargement into a yearly tenancy the title of a tenancy at will to be called a leasehold estate would be doubtful enough. A still weaker title would be that of a tenancy at sufferance, which arises when a tenant holds over, that is to say, wrongfully continues in possession after the expiration of his term or his tenancy, but is not ejected by the landlord. But they were, both of them, like all other leaseholds, accounted smaller in *quantum* than even the shortest freehold estate.

The distinction between freehold and leasehold estates has a practical justification which has remained virtually the same from the thirteenth century to the present day. Leasehold estates have always been thought of on commercial lines. Persons have always been willing to invest in terms of years, whether by purchase, or by taking them as security of loans of money, or merely in order to secure possession of land for a guaranteed period as tenants of farms or house property. Long terms of as much as ninety-nine years have commonly been granted at low rents to persons who undertake to build on the land. On the other hand, although freehold interests other than the fee simple have a present actuarial value, they are not marketable to the same extent as leasehold interests; and certainly no one would at the present day give a life interest to a person with the intention that he should turn it into ready money. A life interest is meant to provide an annual income for an indefinite number of years. In other words, freehold interests, other than the fee simple, have always been used mainly in order to provide for different members of a family, whereas leasehold interests have been used as objects of commerce.

Nevertheless, in the past it was sometimes found convenient to take a lease for a number of lives, usually three in number. For those accustomed to modern terminology the name *lease* was a misnomer, since the estate created by it, being of indefinite duration, was a freehold one. On the other hand, the lease was, like most other leases, a commercial transaction, though frequently entered into for lives in order to make the lessee a freeholder and so eligible for the county franchise before the Reform Bill of 1832. The lives were those of specified persons, not including the lessee himself, and the lease lasted until the death of the last survivor of the three. An annual rent was paid and commonly also a substantial fine at the commencement and each renewal of the lease. Such leases were in 1925 turned into leases for a fixed term of ninety years, which can, however, be terminated by notice after the death of the last survivor.

Estates and chattels

It has always been an article of faith that the doctrine of estates does not apply to chattels. In the Middle Ages, when the doctrine of estates came into existence, hardly any movable property was permanent enough to produce the same sort of periodical income as land, or the stocks and shares of the modern world. Hence there was little temptation to carve estates out of them such as life estates or estates tail. Nor were chattels permanent enough to be made subject to tenure. Thus it was neither against principle nor inconvenient to say that a person could own chattels. To be sure one might want to lend or hire out or pledge a chattel, and so, by what lawyers call a bailment, to deprive oneself temporarily of the physical use of it. But this would be done in the way of business or friendship and not in order to provide successively for members of the family. It was sufficient therefore to attribute the possession of the chattels to the borrower, hirer, or pledgee as a bailee.

Since there was no marked tendency to use chattels to endow successive generations of a family, neither life estates nor estates tail were in principle allowed; and the doctrine of estates was never applied to chattels. But though before 1926 no estate tail was allowed to subsist in a chattel, for a long time testators had occasionally bequeathed chattels to one person for life and then to another person and, out of the favour which is usually accorded to a testator's wishes, effect was given to such bequests. However, they never became common enough for lawyers to make up their minds how to fit them into the general body of doctrine governing personalty; and indeed they gave rise to too great practical difficulties ever to become very popular. It was found preferable to give the chattels to trustees to hold successively in trust for the beneficiaries; and the Chancellor was willing to recognize such bequests for life and in remainder, though never an interest in chattels corresponding to an estate tail in land. However, means were found of settling chattels to go with the land and so to sidetrack this prohibition of entails of personalty; and eventually, in 1925, entailed interests were allowed to be created in personalty.

However, all these limited interests, whatever be their subject-matter, works of art or other heirlooms or, much more commonly, stocks and shares, are always created by way of trust and therefore in effect exist in funds rather than specific movable objects. From the mere fact that the doctrine of estates—or something closely analogous to it—can exist in trust funds it does not by any means follow that it can also exist in specific physical chattels such as ships or horses or motor-cars.

It is still certain that the legal ownership of such objects cannot be carved up so as to create in them life interests or entailed interests; but, as will be explained later, in that they do not now differ at all from land. The real question is whether a bailment creates what might be fairly called a limited estate in a physical chattel comparable to the periodical tenancy or the term of years created by a lease. We have already seen that there is good reason to regard the relation between bailor and bailee as something equivalent to tenure.[6] Can we find something equivalent to an estate?

Bailments and estates

Bailments do indeed raise very interesting theoretical questions which do not seem to have called for a solution. They have usually been discussed in terms of ownership and possession, but as conferring possession they differ in no way from leases of land. Do they then, like leases, confer real rights to their objects and are they in fact, though not ostensibly, subject to a doctrine of estates in the same rather imperfect way?

Some bailments, for example by way of pledge, undoubtedly confer real rights good against purchasers from the owner of the chattel. Bailments at will, under which the bailor can resume possession at any moment, cause no difficulty. Of course the purchaser can oust the bailee. There is authority for saying that if a person charters a ship

[6] See p. 63 above.

for a term, any other person, such as a purchaser, who has notice of the charter-party must take the ship subject to it. Apart from ships, which in many ways strongly resemble land, there seems to be no authority on the question whether a purchaser could oust a bailee for a term such as a hirer for a fixed period. In fact a would-be purchaser would almost always have notice of the bailment and, unwilling to risk the trouble and doubtful success of an attempt to oust the bailee, would probably either refuse to buy or pay only for the right to have the thing after the bailment came to an end.

In that case he would really be buying a reversion. That term is commonly used in such a connexion. But is it rightly so used? There are one or two cases which allow the owner of a chattel out of possession, and therefore not entitled to bring an action of trespass, to bring an action for damage to the reversion, that is to say, permanent physical damage to the thing itself. Thus there is warrant for the use of the word reversion. The only doubt—it goes mainly to classification and does not effect the substance of the law—is whether by calling the owner's interest in the chattel the reversion the law subjects it to a doctrine of estates.[7] Perhaps the best answer that can be given to that question is that the doctrine of estates was not invented to deal with terms of years, to which it has always been applied with some difficulty and with more than the usual amount of artificiality, and that bailments of chattels present no greater difficulty. Certainly the interconnected elements of time and *quantum* which went to make the doctrine of estates are present in both.

4. WORDS OF LIMITATION

In an exact art such as conveyancing it has always been important to draft documents in the most precise terms and for that purpose to develop a technical vocabulary leaving nothing in doubt. Once fragmentation of ownership according to time was admitted it became necessary to distinguish estates at their creation; and fixed forms of words had to be used to create certain kinds of estates. Although some of the formalities have been relaxed in course of time, others have been retained or even made more rigid.

A distinction has always been made between words of purchase and words of limitation, the former designating the person to whom the estate is given and the latter the nature of the estate. Thus, if land is given to A for life or in fee simple, the words 'to A' are words of purchase and the words 'for life' or 'in fee simple' are words of limitation.

The basic rule of the modern law is that if land is given to a person

[7] See p. 60 above.

without words of limitation, for instance, 'to A', he acquires all that the donor has to give. If the donor has a fee simple, A gets a fee simple; if he had only a life interest, A gets only a life interest, or rather, an interest *pur autre vie*, that is to say, one which will last for the life of the donor. If, therefore, a person who has a fee simple in Blackacre wishes to give only a life interest in it to A, he must make his meaning clear. He will usually do this by giving it 'to A for life', but this is not strictly necessary. Anything in the instrument creating the life interest which indicates his intention will suffice. Thus a grant 'to A remainder to B' shows that A's interest is to come to an end in order that B may take after him, and the most natural inference is that A shall take only a life interest.

Normally it is not now necessary to use any words of limitation if the donee is intended to get a fee simple. A grant to A will suffice. But it is customary, in order to avoid doubts, to use words of limitation, thus, 'to A in fee simple'. Occasionally even now an alternative form is used, namely, 'to A and his heirs'; it was much commoner in instruments executed before 1926 and before 1882 it was the only permissible form. The words 'and his heirs' were necessary at common law in order to show that A had an estate capable of continuing after his death and of descending to his heirs if he died intestate, but since A had acquired the full power of alienating his fee simple, the succession to it was not guaranteed to his heirs and hence the grant gave nothing directly to them. Thus the words 'and his heirs' are not words of purchase but only words of limitation.

In contrast to this relaxation in the words necessary to create a fee simple, the requirements for an entailed interest, which plays an essential part in the so-called strict settlement, have been made stricter. Since 1925 the words of limitation must include the words 'and the heirs of his body' or 'in fee tail', or 'in tail', whatever the kind of instrument in which they occur.[8]

5. RENT AND RENTCHARGES

The income derived from the exploitation of a physical object must always be produced ultimately by some physical use made of it. But it is not at all necessary that all the persons who enjoy the income should do the physical work of producing it. Commonly, some person or persons work on the thing but share the income from it with others. A similar situation may arise in relation to monopolies such as patents or copyright. Others besides the manufacturer or publisher may derive an income from them.

In theory the sharing of the profit could take any one of three

[8] Entailed interests are explained at pp. 131–4.

forms: the user could take a fixed sum, paying the whole of the residue to another person, he could pay a fixed sum (which might vary from time to time) to that other person and keep the residue for himself, or they could share the profit according to a fixed or variable proportion.

The first relation would in fact take the form of a contract binding the user to manage the property for a fixed salary or wage; he would have no right *in rem* to the property and the service would be temporary lest it should smack of slavery. The third relation is known in France as *métayage* and in the Southern States of the United States as *share-cropping*. It occurs especially where the landlord has to provide not only the fixed plant of a farm but also some or all of the working capital and prefers to go into a sort of working partnership with the cultivator instead of merely employing him; though the cultivator has a right *in rem* to the farm. This arrangement is not used in England.

In the second solution the actual user of a thing pays what may in the general way be called a *rent*, though for physical movables it is often called a *hire* and for patents and copyright a *royalty*. The relations of the party to the thing may vary greatly. Where corporeal chattels are concerned, there will almost always be a bailment and the limited interest, such as it is, will be in the bailee. A manufacturer or publisher may exploit a patent or copyright either under an out-and-out assignment or under a licence which will leave the ownership of the patent or copyright unchanged. The same variety exists in respect of land.

If a landowner wants to get his land back eventually, he leases the land to a lessee in return for a money rent, and both lessor and lessee have rights *in rem* over the land. On the other hand, he may be quite willing to sell the land and so dispose of his interest in it for good, but may be prepared to meet the needs of a relatively indigent purchaser by accepting, as is often done in Manchester and Bristol, in place of a lump sum down, a perpetual rent, or, as it is often called, a fee farm rent. Where that is the case, he retains no estate in the land and so has not the security for the annual payments that the lessor automatically has. Accordingly he requires the purchaser to execute a deed creating a rentcharge on the land, which gives him certain powers of enforcing a payment of the rent. It is in reality a form of security. Rentcharges are also often expressly created for other purposes.

Not only has the owner of a rentcharge a number of remedies at common law and by statute if the rent is not punctually paid, but it is also usual to include in the deed an express proviso for re-entry on the land in case of non-payment. Upon re-entry the land becomes forfeit to the owner of the rentcharge, who thereupon reacquires the estate which he originally had in the land. There are provisions for redemption of rentcharges at the option of the owner of the land subject to them.

6. POWERS

Another division of property rights results from the use of powers. Normally the ownership of an interest in property carries with it the power to manage and dispose of it. This power can indeed be restricted without any portion of it being vested in another person. Thus, if one person holds the fee simple of land in trust for another person in fee simple, although he has the legal estate in the land, he can be restrained by a court of equity from alienating it without the consent of the beneficiary.[9] Such restrictions, though of little importance as far as land is concerned, can be quite important for chattels such as valuable pictures or furniture. They produce a restriction rather than a fragmentation of ownership.

However, fragmentation does occur where one person has the enjoyment of an interest but another person has powers of managing or of alienating it or of otherwise determining who shall enjoy it. A clear functional distinction can be drawn between three different kinds of powers.

Some powers exist to enable persons who have no beneficial interest, or at most a limited one, to manage property and, in so far as they include the power of sale, it is for the purpose of preserving the capital by getting rid of one investment and acquiring a better one. A second kind exists for the purpose of enabling a person who has acquired a security, such as a mortgage, over a thing, to sell it for instance in order to enforce his security and so obtain the money to which he is entitled. The third kind of powers is used to make the beneficial enjoyment of property move more flexibly among a number of persons. The first kind of power forms much of the subject-matter of the next section, which deals with the distinction between management and enjoyment;[10] the second is best studied in relation to security;[11] the third falls to be discussed at once. These powers are called powers of appointment.

Powers of appointment

It is quite possible for a person, A, who is settling property on marriage or by will, to give a life interest to B followed by a gift to such person or persons as B shall appoint. In other words, the donor

[9] See further p. 79 below.

[10] See p. 77 below.

[11] See pp. 156–7, 160–2 below.

of the power, A, delegates to the donee of the power, B, the task of selecting the persons to take after B. If the power is expressed in that unrestricted form, it is said to be a general power. B can, if he chooses, appoint even himself and so a general power is equivalent to ownership in the donee. But since there is no obvious advantage to be gained by giving a person a general power to appoint to an interest instead of giving him the interest itself, general powers are not often met with in practice. A much commoner kind of power is the so-called special power of appointment, in such a form as 'to B for life remainder to such of his children as B shall appoint'. The appointment can then be made only within a class, and since the class does not include the donee, the power is not equivalent to ownership. Moreover, if the donee uses a special power to obtain an advantage for himself, by extracting, for instance, a payment to himself from the person appointed, he is guilty of a fraud on the power and the appointment is void.

A power is not itself an estate or interest but merely enables the donee to create an estate or interest in himself or some other person or persons; though for many purposes a general power is regarded as an interest.

7. THE DISTINCTION BETWEEN MANAGEMENT AND ENJOYMENT

The freedom of invention developed in handling estates has proved particularly useful in enabling the distinction between management and enjoyment of property to be expressed in terms of law. It must, of course, first be decided as a matter of policy whether management shall be allowed to be divorced from enjoyment, or whether on the contrary a person who is to enjoy the benefits of property should not also be forced to undertake, if not the actual management of the property, at least to the full extent the risk of mismanagement by others. It must be said at once that English law has taken the former view; it allows, though it does not of course compel, the management to be detached from the beneficial enjoyment.

Trusts

It is also obvious that there must be some personal relation between the manager and the beneficiary, under which the former may be made liable to the latter if he wrongfully mismanages the property. That relation is in English law called a trust. The manager is *trustee* for the beneficiary. But the question still remains, what are the relations of trustee and beneficiary to the thing held in trust? It would have been possible to say either that the trustee owns the property but is under a duty to manage it for the benefit of the beneficiary, who has nothing more than a correlative personal right against the trustee, or on the contrary that the beneficiary owns the property but gives full powers of management to the trustee, who stands in no direct relation to the property but acts merely by delegation of property rights vested in the beneficiary. English law has taken neither course, but has in effect said that both trustee and beneficiary own the property in different ways, or, more accurately, that neither owns the property in the strict Roman sense of the term ownership, but each owns a different interest in it, called respectively the legal estate and the equitable interest. It says that to ask in such a situation who owns the physical object is an improper question, just as it would be improper to ask whether a tenant for life or a person entitled to the land after his death owned the land itself.

The legal and the equitable estate

We have already seen that not only the trustee but the beneficiary has a right *in rem* over the trust property, for the beneficiary can trace it into the hands of any holder of it who has not taken it bona fide for value without notice, actual or constructive, of a breach of trust.[12] There might none the less have been some tendency to treat this right as a mere *chose in action*,[13] that is to say, as the property aspect of the personal rights which the beneficiary may have against the original trustee or later constructive trustees. But it became necessary to treat it as a separate equitable estate comparable to the legal estate; for the same desire to divide up the trust property successively among several beneficiaries arose as had led to the development of the doctrine of estates. That made it inevitable that the beneficial interest in the trust property should itself be treated as an estate, susceptible of division into several estates giving successive rights to possession; and since it was protected by the Chancellor in the exercise of his equitable jurisdiction, it became known as the equitable estate, in contrast to the trustee's interest, which, since it was protected by the Common Law Courts, came to be known as the legal estate. In more recent times the term equitable interest has been substituted for equitable estate. So there is not one object of ownership, a physical thing, but two separate ones, the legal estate owned by the trustee for the purpose of managing the land, and the equitable estate or interest owned by the beneficiary for the purpose of enjoying the land.

At the present day it would be easier to satisfy anyone who wanted to know who owns the land itself, for the trustee can almost always sell the land, and holds the proceeds of the sale in trust for the

[12] See p. 45 above. [13] See p. 19 above.

beneficiaries. Thus the sale will hardly ever be in breach of trust and there can seldom be any question of the purchaser's being a constructive trustee of the land.[14] Since the beneficiary can very rarely insist on the trustee's retaining the land, his equitable interest really exists not over the land but over a trust fund, of which the land is only the present manifestation. This would not be quite so true of corporeal movables, for the trustee would not be able to sell them as a matter of law, but in practice he is almost always given an express power of sale. Thus it would not now be grossly inaccurate to say that the trustee owns the individual assets comprised in the trust property, though his ownership is limited by the rights enjoyed by the beneficiary.

These various divisions of ownership are cross-divisions; no one is a subdivision of any other. Thus they may or may not coincide at the will of the donor or settlor, as the person who establishes a trust is called. For instance, A, who has a fifty-year lease of Blackacre from B, may give it to C and D (who will be joint tenants of the legal estate in the land, which they will hold as tenants of the landlord, B) in trust for E for life and thereafter to F and G as tenants in common (each of whom will have a present equitable interest analogous to an estate in the land). But almost anything in this settlement could be altered without implying any alteration in what was left. Thus, if the land placed in trust had been not leasehold but freehold (in which case the only tenure would have been the shadowy tenancy under the Crown), nothing else need have been changed. Or again the land might have been vested in only one trustee, for instance, a trust corporation such as a bank; in that case there would have been no joint tenancy, but again nothing else need have been changed. Or again the only change might have been to settle the land in trust for only one beneficiary, or, on the other hand, there might have been only one remainderman. However, some changes would necessarily have implied others. Thus, if F and G had been given an absolute interest immediately without the interposition of a trust, they could not have taken the legal estate as tenants in common, but must have become joint tenants of the legal estate; and we shall see later[15] that E could not now have a legal life estate or F and G legal estates in remainder.

[14] There is one real exception. If I convey land to X in trust for Y and Y is of full age and in his right mind, there is no settlement, and X cannot convey the land to a third party free from Y's equitable interest in it, unless, of course, the third party takes for value without notice either actual or constructive. But Y can force X to convey the legal estate to him.

[15] p. 83 below.

VI

THE RECONCILIATION OF FRAGMENTATION WITH THE NEEDS OF THE MARKET

So far our attention has been concentrated on the possible ways in which several abstract things can be made to exist in relation to one physical object; and in so doing we have been thinking of property mainly as income-producing capital. But physical objects demand attention on their own account, for the ultimate source of income must be the use made by someone, however remote, of a physical object or collection of objects. A share in a mining company may be treated as a separate abstract income-producing thing, but there would be no income without the mine which the company exists to exploit.

Now people do not want to limit their purchases to fragments of income-producing capital. They need also to buy actual physical objects, such as, for instance, machinery and land to build a factory to put machinery in. Moreover, the policy of the law may well be to have as free a market as possible for physical objects, so that they may be bought and sold without difficulty; and one difficulty which will then have to be avoided will be that of having to obtain the consents of several persons with fragmentary interests in them. For this purpose the fact that each abstract thing connected with the physical object is itself freely marketable is irrelevant, for not all the owners of such interests may be willing to sell at the same time and to the same person; moreover, some interests may not be vested in any living persons but may have been limited, as we say, to unborn persons. This difficulty occurs much more rarely with corporeal chattels because they are not permanent enough for an income arising from them to be divided among several persons in succession. But it is important for land and for such incorporeal chattels as stocks and shares or copyright.

Now, if one is impressed with the need for a free market and if at the same time one thinks almost entirely in terms of physical objects, one is forced into accepting the view that the ownership which attaches to physical things must in principle be indivisible; and if one is also forced, as seems inevitable, to allow real rights less than ownership to exist over physical objects, one must limit their number and treat them generally with suspicion. If, on the other hand, one thinks in terms of abstract things and if among those abstract things one admits the possibility of creating trust funds, one can reconcile the need for a free market for physical things with the need for flexibility in the handling of income-bearing lots of capital.

Voluntary methods of reconciliation

This can be done either voluntarily or compulsorily. It can be done voluntarily by a settlor if he deliberately vests in trustees the legal estate in physical things to its widest possible extent, conferring on the trustees full powers of management and alienation. The physical things thus constitute present investments of a trust fund and can be varied from time to time by the trustees, who may, however, be restricted by the trust deed or by the law as to the new investments they may make of the proceeds of any sale. This makes the physical objects freely alienable without the consent of any persons other than the trustees. On the other hand, great freedom can be allowed to create a most luxuriant growth of simultaneously existing abstract things, such as concurrent or future interests, within the ambit of the equitable interest, for all these will amount to limited rights to shares in the income arising from the trust fund, whatever it is invested in for the time being. Of course there is a danger that the trust fund may, by unwise or fraudulent management, be reduced in value or even disappear, but that is a necessary price to pay for freedom to buy and sell physical objects. This is the solution commonly adopted in the United States.

Compulsion by statute

It is perfectly admissible for a settlor in England also to give the full legal interest in property, together with full powers of management and sale, to trustees in trust for a number of beneficiaries in succession. But English law has taken a further step. Now by statute, whether he likes it or not, a person who settles land on several persons in succession finds that he has automatically separated the control of the land itself from the beneficial interests existing in it and has given to some person or persons, who may indeed include a beneficiary, wide powers of managing and alienating it.

The need for keeping physical objects freely alienable could be most effectually reconciled with the desire to carve up into fragments the right to receive income from them if it were enacted that the only interest that could be held in a physical object was absolute ownership, while at the same time such objects were allowed to become component parts of a trust fund and the income from the fund to be divided up with the utmost freedom.

In practice this solution cannot be accepted without qualification. Some fragmentation of the legal estate in the physical object must be allowed and some restrictions must be placed on the power to carve up the equitable right to income produced by the trust fund.[1]

Some place must be found for leases, under which the legal interest in the land itself is divided between lessor and lessee, and for mortgages or other charges, under which the mortgagee or chargee can have a legal interest in the land as well as the mortgagor or chargor. If it were not possible to have leases a farmer would always have to buy his land outright and one could not adopt the very convenient arrangement under which a landlord provides the fixed capital and the tenant farmer the working capital necessary for carrying on the farm. For if the only legal interest in the land itself were vested in the farmer, the landlord could not get adequate security for the payment of rent, the more so if at the same time it was made impossible for him to take a mortgage giving him a legal interest in the land. If only the landlord was given an interest in the land, he could sell the land over the farmer's head and force the latter, at best, to accept a money compensation, which would be not at all what the farmer intends or needs.

Similarly, if the mortgagee alone had a legal interest in the physical object, he could force the mortgagor out of it in return for compensation, whereas if only the mortgagor had a right to the physical object the mortgagee could only have a slice of the income arising from a trust fund, and a trust fund is by no means as safe as the physical object itself.

Rationale of the distinction

Thus, a certain amount of fragmentation of the ownership of the physical object itself is necessary, and the most that the law can do is to keep it down to a minimum. This it can do by allowing fragmentation only where it is necessary to give one person the physical use of an object and at the same time to give to another person a right to hold or to take the physical object as security for a right to income or even capital. Thus the tenant farmer needs the land, but the landlord cannot be satisfied with a mere right to the share in the income produced by the land which is constituted by the rent. He is not sufficiently secure if he has to accept the farmer not merely as his rent-paying tenant but also as the trustee of a fund out of which the rent is to be paid.[2] The mortgagee needs such protection even more, for without powers exercisable over the land itself he would have

[1] A discussion of these restrictions is postponed to pp. 138–46.

[2] The landlord of an efficient farmer is now very much in that position in consequence of the legislation designed to protect tenants; but this was not so at the time when the 1925 legislation was being prepared.

nothing more than a preferential right to receive his interest and eventually his capital.

The Law of Property Act

Accordingly, in 1925 Parliament provided, by Section 1 of the Law of Property Act, that the only legal estates that could be held in land were to be the fee simple absolute in possession and the term of years absolute. Those were to be the only interests in land which could guarantee the holder continued possession of the land and ensure that no one else could sell it over his head and force him to accept money compensation. Mortgages were to be made by giving the mortgagee a term of years or a legal charge, either of which in effect gave the mortgagee certain powers to enforce his security, notably by selling the land or acquiring the full interest in it for himself.[3]

The fee simple, as we have seen, approximates to absolute ownership, and this approximation is enhanced by the rules that, to be a legal estate, it must be absolute, that is to say, it must not be liable to come to an end if a condition is fulfilled or be given to last until the occurrence of a future event, and also that it shall give a right to immediate possession, that is to say, that it shall not constitute a future interest. Estates in fee simple which break these rules, for example such as exist in reversion or remainder, though they may subsist as equitable interests, that is to say, as interests in a trust fund, cannot be legal estates. However, if the owner of the fee simple demises the land to a lessee for a term of years, although he is said to give the lessee possession and to be henceforth a reversioner, that is only for one purpose; since he is entitled to the rents and profits of the land, he is for that purpose regarded as still possessing the land and so is held to retain the fee simple in possession. The fee simple in possession and the term of years in possession coexist as legal estates throughout the term.[4]

To be a legal estate, a term of years also must be absolute, but it need not be in possession. However, a term must, with one exception, be limited to take effect not more than twenty-one years after the date of the instrument creating it. Thus it must conform to the modern rule against perpetuities, which will be discussed later.[5]

There is nothing in all this to prevent a person *possessing* land by virtue of a grant for life or for an entailed interest or having a right to possession in the future as a reversioner or remainderman; but since all these interests can only exist as equitable interests, they are liable to be overreached, that is to say, converted into money or some other object, and so are in reality only interests in a trust fund of

[3] See further p. 156 below.

[4] See further pp. 118–19 below.

[5] See pp. 138–45 below.

which the present form is land. There will always be some person or persons who can sell the land itself, though, as will be seen later,[6] there are ways and means of preventing them from doing so where a sale would be improper.

Rentcharges

Since rentcharges are as subject to the doctrine of estates as land itself, the same problems arose in relation to them, and the same solution was applied. Thus they can exist as legal interests only if they are in possession and either perpetual or for a term of years absolute. But rentcharges caused a special difficulty.

When land is bought in consideration of rent secured by a rent-charge accompanied by an express right of re-entry,[7] the fee simple in the hands of the purchaser is defeasible by a condition subsequent. It was difficult to think of such a fee simple as absolute and therefore capable of subsisting as a legal estate. Hence a special provision was inserted in the schedule to the Law of Property (Amendment) Act, 1926, to the effect that 'A fee simple subject to a legal or equitable right of entry or re-entry is for the purpose of this Act a fee simple absolute'.

Tenancy in common and infants

A single subsection of the Law of Property Act, 1925,[8] brings together into what is at first sight a strange juxtaposition tenancies in common and infants, for it declares that 'A legal estate is not capable of subsisting or of being created in an undivided share in land or of being held by an infant'. There is, however, a common element in the extreme difficulties which both tenancy in common and infants may cause to conveyancers.

Any property interest which is vested in an infant is for the time being immobilized. Thus if the land itself which is comprised in a settlement is to be freely alienable, the legal estate must always be vested in some person or persons who have power to convey it. An infant cannot convey, and so steps have to be taken to vest the legal estate in persons of full capacity. On the other hand, there is no reason whatever why the infant's right to receive income from the land comprised in the settlement should be tampered with at all during his infancy, and so he is left with an equitable interest.

It has already been explained[9] that, whereas tenancy in common is appropriate to the beneficial enjoyment of land, joint tenancy is much more appropriate to the management of property by trustees. Moreover, for the conveyancer joint tenancy has another great advantage over tenancy in common. Since all the joint tenants own the whole,

[6] See p. 115 below.
[7] See pp. 75–76 above.
[8] S. 1 (6).
[9] See pp. 64–65 above.

there is only one title, whereas since tenants in common each hold a separate, though undivided share, there is a separate title to each share. Therefore, if a purchaser wants to buy land from a number of tenants in common, he would not only have to get all the tenants in common to concur in conveying the land to him, but he would also have to investigate the title to each undivided share. That could easily become a very burdensome task, for each original share might in course of time have become vested in quite a number of other persons, so that a purchaser might have to consider the validity of one transaction in respect of one share, two transactions in respect of another, three transactions in respect of the third, and so on. It has been known for as many as a hundred separate titles to exist in respect of the same piece of land, and for it to be more expensive to investigate all these titles than the land was worth. Accordingly, it is much more convenient for a purchaser to deal with joint tenants than with tenants in common, and as it is the legal estate in land that a purchaser usually wants to buy, an easy solution was found in the Law of Property Act, 1925, namely, that a legal estate in land cannot be held by tenants in common, but only by joint tenants.

On the other hand, there is not the same objection to the holding of equitable interests in common, and, since they represent rights of enjoyment, there is everything to be said for excluding the unfair operation of survivorship. Thus equitable interests can be held in common and indeed equity presumes such a holding. If, therefore, it is now desired to give land to A and B in common, the legal estate must be vested in them as joint tenants, in trust for themselves as tenants in common. The Act also provided that the number of joint tenants of a piece of land must generally be limited to four, to ensure that the assent of not too great a number should be needed for an alienation of the land.

Legal ownership in common is still possible in the case of personalty. Presumably it was thought unlikely that the shares in any movable property, or even in stocks and shares, would become very numerous, and further that no serious attempt would be made to investigate the title to each share. But in fact it is very unlikely that anyone would want to vest the legal ownership of a movable in a number of persons to hold in common. Usually the only purpose of giving several persons undivided shares in a movable, as indeed of land, would be to give them shares in the income produced by it, and it is more convenient to entrust the payment of such shares of income to trustees than to make the various tenants in common get hold of the income and divide it among themselves. Probably no harm would have been done if the same rule had been applied to personalty as to land.

Joint tenancy can be turned into tenancy in common by a process known as severance. That can be done deliberately by agreement between the joint tenants, or, perhaps more commonly, by one joint tenant alienating his interest to an outsider. In such a case the outsider will become a tenant in common with the other joint tenant or tenants; but if there are several other joint tenants, they will continue to be joint tenants among themselves. Now, although most joint tenants hold their property as trustees, there is nothing to prevent a joint tenancy from coming into existence among persons who are intended to enjoy the land, and such persons may very properly wish to sever their joint tenancy and become tenants in common. If, however, land was given to them merely as legal joint tenants, they would not be able to sever their joint tenancy, since there can be no legal tenancy in common. Therefore, in such a case they must be made legal joint tenants in trust for themselves as equitable joint tenants. They can then, if they wish, sever the equitable joint tenancy and become equitable tenants in common.

Personalty

In theory precisely the same considerations should apply all along the line to chattels as to land. It would seem that there is the same need to keep the physical object or the specific stocks and shares or other securities marketable, to allow the income derived from them to be divided among several persons, and to allow physical objects to be parted with temporarily for use. However, there has never been much tendency to keep physical chattels, other than pictures or other heirlooms, inalienable; stocks and shares, other than shares in private companies, have always been regarded as marketable commodities, and settlors have therefore usually given trustees full power to sell them and reinvest the proceeds; and whereas the unique character of each single piece of land naturally creates monopoly conditions, which must be counteracted as far as possible by making all land in principle freely alienable, such monopoly conditions rarely exist in physical chattels and, at any rate, have nothing to do with alienability or the reverse.

Whatever may have been the precise force of these considerations, the question of alienability has never been for chattels a matter of public concern as it has for land. Thus when in 1925 it was made a matter of principle that land should be freely alienable and that therefore, with very few exceptions, trustees should have wide powers of sale, no alteration was made in the law governing trusts of personalty. It was apparently thought unnecessary to abolish fixed trusts of personalty in which trustees are given no power of sale, or perhaps they were overlooked.

VII

OWNERSHIP

It is now time to see what meaning, if any, can be given to the word *ownership* in English law.

It must be said at the outset that the word is not very often used in the professional literature of English law, that is to say, in authoritative writings such as enactments and reports of decided cases; and that where the word *owner* is sporadically used in statutes it has been given many different meanings, sometimes in the definition sections of the statutes. On the other hand, no book on Analytical Jurisprudence would be complete that did not contain a full discussion of the nature of ownership.

The analytical jurists have this concern for ownership because they have for historical reasons had their eyes fixed on Roman law and the so-called civil-law systems which are in large part derived from it. Now, one of the most striking institutions of Roman law was *dominium*, upon which all the civil-law systems have modelled their treatment of ownership. *Dominium* was, in the final form it received in the *Corpus Juris* of Justinian, as near to being absolute as any private-law institution can be. The owner had an absolute title, he had an absolute right to dispose of the thing he owned, and his right to use it was limited by so few restrictions of a public-law character that it, too, could almost be called absolute. The kinds of incumbrances with which it could be burdened were kept down to the lowest possible number, and where they existed they were carefully distinguished from the *dominium* over the thing, which was regarded as retaining its character of a general undifferentiated right over the thing capable of resuming its original plenitude by the mere disappearance of the incumbrance.

Now, the concurrence of these various absolutes in a single institution was really a very remarkable peculiarity of Roman law. Doubtless it was and still is very convenient for a person to be able to say: 'This thing is mine; my title to it is absolute; I can do what I like with it subject to certain very obvious restrictions that have to be put on the use of everything of the kind; and, if I wish, I can vest all these rights in another person by transferring the thing to him.' Many persons can say those things at the present day in England. A tenant in fee simple with the legal estate in registered land is in that position, at any rate if his holding is subject to no incumbrances. If he grants a lease he parts with the use of the land for the time being, but when the lease comes to an end there is no need to revest the right of user in him; he automatically resumes it as part of the fee simple.

However, as we have already seen, absolute titles are rather rare in English law, and so it is not surprising to find that when the term *ownership* is used in relation to title, it is merely contrasted with *possession*, and means little more than *title*, or at most a title with no obviously better title outstanding. The owner is a person who has something better than mere possession. But no technical significance attaches to the term, for what he alleges in an action to recover possession is that he has a right to the immediate possession of the thing, which is almost invariably relative.[1]

As regards use of the thing, ownership rarely comes in question. It is the occupier who is normally liable in nuisance and has the full right of use within the limits set by the law of nuisance. Where the right to use a thing or to enjoy the income from it is divided among several persons nothing is gained by attributing ownership to any one of them. The situation is described much more clearly by talking of bailor and bailee, lessor and lessee, tenant for life and remainder-man, and the like.

When the question is asked whether a person can alienate a thing to a third party, for land the answer is quite clear: he can alienate his estate or interest; and the same is true of interests in a fund. For chattels the matter is not quite so clear; lawyers do often speak of the owner as having the right to alienate, and indeed the policy of the law has always been to concentrate interests in movables as far as possible so as to make them marketable. We have seen that the same policy has been extended to land.

Since it seems a pity to have to jettison excellent words like *ownership*, *owner*, and *own*, the last of which, as a verb, has no real equivalent in other languages, and since English law is not at all committed to any particular usage, there are two alternatives open to us. We can say that the owner of a thing, whether land or a chattel, is the

[1] In actual practice the Roman position cannot have been very different. If a plaintiff was protecting his possession or seeking to recover it from a defendant who had dispossessed him directly, he merely proved his possession; if the defendant had come into possession peaceably and indirectly, for example by acquiring the thing in question from one who had dispossessed the plaintiff, the latter had in principle to prove his ownership. But this meant that he must prove that he had previously acquired the thing by what an English lawyer would call a good root of title and had kept it for a certain length of time. Moreover, if the defendant had not possessed the thing before the plaintiff, the latter need only prove an earlier possession starting with a good root of title. There is little that looks 'absolute' in this, and what there is is further diminished by the rule that no one could become owner of stolen goods, however good his root of title or the length of his possession. See for a fuller discussion Buckland and McNair, *Roman Law and Common Law* (2nd edn., 1952), pp. 76–81.

person who can convey the full interest in it to another person, i.e. the person who is already often called the owner of a chattel or the person who has the fee simple of land, or on the contrary that what a person owns is an estate or an interest in a trust fund or generally his interest in a chattel. In the former case we attach ownership to the physical object at the cost of reducing the number of owners; in the latter we enlarge the number of owners but attach ownership in every case to an abstract entity. At present the usage, for what it is, is ambiguous, for whereas the Sale of Goods Act clearly speaks of the owner of goods, the Law of Property Act speaks of an *estate owner*, who is defined as the owner of a legal estate, which includes, not only the fee simple absolute in possession of land but also a term of years absolute.

VIII

THE IMPACT OF PUBLIC LAW

PROPERTY law has always been considered the heart of private law. Indeed, three and a half centuries ago every lawyer contrasted government and property. Bacon, for example, said: 'I consider that it is a true and received division of law into *ius publicum* and *ius privatum*, the one being the sinews of property, and the other of government.' In so far as a distinction can be made in England between public and private law, property belongs to the latter.

Nevertheless, it would give a totally false impression of the present status of property in this country if public law were left entirely out of the picture; and in fact property lawyers now devote much more of their attention to public law than to what would formerly have alone been considered to deserve the name of property law. A solicitor acting for his client in purchasing a house may take comparatively little trouble over the investigation of title—which belongs entirely to private law—knowing from past experience that the title is almost certainly good; he will, however, be extremely careful to find out whether public law imposes awkward restrictions on use. Similarly, whereas the old conveyancers were anxious to draw their settlements in such a way as to carry out a purely family policy and within the four corners of it to protect each person concerned against possible encroachments on the part of the rest, their successors are willing to quite a great extent to trust those persons to behave decently towards each other, if only they can protect all of them against the big bad wolf, the tax-levying state.[1] Finally, more and more property becomes vested in the Crown and other public authorities, whether local authorities such as counties and boroughs or public corporations such as the National Coal Board and the British Transport Commission.

This impact of government on property will be discussed in some slight detail later; thus town and country planning and the control of agriculture follow as a natural pendant to the private-law restrictions on the use of land, whereas taxation is best dealt with in connexion with settlements. But it is well to say a little by way of general preparation here.

[1] See further p. 130 below.

Historical development

From the Reformation to the middle of the nineteenth century the development of property law was almost entirely in the hands of the conveyancers and the merchants, who were constantly inventing and trying out new combinations of the simple elements provided by common law, equity, and the older statutes. The efficacy of their efforts was constantly being tested in the Courts, which produced an immense mass of case law; and this again was brought into systematic form by a number of very remarkable eighteenth- and nineteenth-century writers of whom the most famous were perhaps Fearne[2] and Butler.[3] During the whole of that time, Parliament intervened little to alter the law, mainly because the conveyancers and merchants were able, by manipulating the existing law, to satisfy the needs of the great landowners and men of business who between them governed the country. Moreover, the whole tendency of the time was increasingly in favour of leaving each man to manage his affairs for himself. Towards the end of the period the followers of Jeremy Bentham were able to get rid of unnecessary fictions and to bring the forms of conveyancing more into line with the substance, but without making much change in the latter.

Land and agriculture

In 1846 the landed interest was forced to renounce protection for its products, and in the 1870's the efficient transport of large quantities of cheap American grain started an agricultural depression which lasted, on and off, until guaranteed prices came in shortly before the Second World War. It had several serious effects on the law of property.

For some time past Parliament had allowed landlords to apply to a court to sanction, in the interest of persons entitled under settlements, sales of land which it had been in principle desired to render inalienable, but now it intervened in the interest of the land itself to enable impoverished landowners to raise capital for improving the land still left to them or simply to give place to persons better able to look after the land. It was this new parliamentary concern for the land itself that differentiated the Settled Land Acts,[4] which gave effect to it, from the older Settled Estates Acts.[5]

The same change of policy is seen at work in the series of Agricultural Holdings Acts,[6] which started about the same time. The agricultural depression made the position of tenant farmers much more

[2] Charles Fearne (1742–94), best known for his *Essay on Contingent Remainders and Executory Devises*.

[3] Charles Butler (1750–1832), best known for his edition of *Coke upon Littleton*.

[4] 1882–1925.

[5] 1856–77.

[6] 1875–1948.

difficult than hitherto. Many emigrated and others went into the towns; yet others began to press for greater protection against landlords whose very impoverishment made them more exacting or against new landlords who were more commercially minded and less affected by tradition. At a time when land was being turned over from arable cultivation to permanent pasture, there was little temptation to improve land and still less if a landlord could evict his tenant without paying compensation for improvements. Hence it is to the 1880's that the first of these Acts go back. They were passed partly in the interest of tenant farmers but perhaps even more in that of the land itself.

However, little was done for agriculture until the years just before the Second World War; and the present system really dates from the War itself. In return for guaranteed prices both farmers and landowners were compelled to submit to a form of control exercised by farmers and landowners themselves under the supervision of the Ministry of Agriculture and Fisheries. At the same time tenant farmers were given ample security of tenure. Thus at the present day landowners, or more properly land agents, work almost entirely in a network of statutes and regulations and one land agent has been heard to say that his landowner regains his independence only on the death of his tenant. Doubtless these new arrangements make the survival of really inefficient farmers and landowners less probable than formerly, but it is doubtful whether they ensure the height of efficiency that was formerly achieved by an enthusiastic improving landlord anxious to attract to himself the best tenant farmers. Moreover, there is less chance of the moderately inefficient farmer's being weeded out by bankruptcy.

The fact is that these reforms are to some extent a compromise between three forces, the natural desire of governments to enforce efficient production, an equally natural desire to help the underdog against monopolistic landlords, and the great voting power of the farmers, especially, but not exclusively, with Conservative governments. But the strongest immediate impulse came from war and the fear of war.

Tenancy of houses and business premises

The same mixture of motives has caused analogous protection to be given to various classes of house tenants and tenants of business premises. Wars caused shortages of house property and led to the notorious Rent Acts and the control of furnished houses and lodgings. Unfortunately, these forms of control have on the whole worked against the maintenance of dwellings in full repair. Tenants of business premises came to be protected largely because the long building leases of the Victorian period began to fall in before and after the Second World War. This and other causes helped to create great insecurity, while at the same time landlords had to be given some protection against falls in the value of money. All these factors have caused the old contractual way of handling leases and tenancies in terms of bargains between lessors and lessees to give way in great part to arrangements, made no doubt in the first instance by bargaining, though often within limits set by legislation, but afterwards continued or modified under the same or other legislation. Here again the parties look less to the law of property and contract than to legislation in order to ascertain their rights and duties.

Housing and slum clearance

Other lines of development have led to the modern law of housing and town and country planning. The ordinary law gave no assurance to tenants that their houses would be fit for human habitation or kept in repair. It was open to persons who, by reason of wealth or otherwise, were able to take care of themselves to see that appropriate terms were inserted in leases or tenancy agreements, but the vast majority of the population, especially members of the working classes, had to take what they could get. Even had the general law of the land been favourable to them, landlords might, and perhaps would, have insisted on contracting out of their obligations under it. Thus Parliament felt bound to insist that, whatever landlord and tenant might say or do, the landlord should be bound to warrant that a house was fit for human occupation. Doubtless this reform again was the product of mixed motives. It was not a coincidence that it came shortly after the greater part of the working class, in town and country alike, at last acquired the vote. But Parliament was also concerned to stop the production of slums. Gradually three different lines of development became evident.

In the first place, speculative building, which had always been extremely chancy, ceased to be generally profitable, and the creation by the Rent Acts of large numbers of privileged tenants paying what had come to be an uneconomic rent made it still more difficult to build houses at a cost acceptable to purchasers or tenants. Hence came several fluctuating policies, now in favour of subsidies to private builders, now of the direct provision of houses by local authorities, but all imposing some charge on the taxpayer or ratepayer. This is not a matter for the property lawyer's consideration.

Slum clearance was and is a very different matter. It looks indeed one way to public law, as involving invasions by public authorities of what might in general be considered the citizen's rights, and to the procedure to be adopted to give him fair protection. But it is certainly also a matter for the property lawyer. Local authorities were progressively given power to close houses in their opinion unfit for human habitation until such time as the landlord put them in repair; and in bad cases the power was extended to demolition. Where more wholesale clearance became necessary the question arose what compensation should be paid, and Parliament eventually decided that the only value to be taken into account was the value of the site cleared of buildings. In other words, the owner of slum houses could be deprived of them without compensation. It is true that this legislation could be treated as merely extending the boundaries of nuisance; an insanitary house was a nuisance and its owner could be forced to abate it by allowing a public authority to acquire it without paying compensation. None the less property rights were less secure than they had been.

Town and country planning

Town and country planning started as a way of preventing slums from coming into existence. It has now come to be a method of ensuring, as far as possible, that the best use shall be made of the land, whether in town or in country. To a great extent, as in the control of agriculture, the State and other public authorities have taken over tasks which used to be performed by enlightened landlords.

Variation of investments

The Settled Land Acts were considered a moment ago from the agricultural point of view as means of enabling capital to be spent on encumbered estates. There was another side to them which has proved more important to the property lawyer. For, far from causing the destruction of settlements, they merely substituted one form of investment for another, land frequently being turned into mortgage loans or stocks and shares. Thus the property comprised in the ordinary aristocratic settlement has ever since the 1880's been by no means exclusively land, but balanced between agricultural land, house or business property, and chattel interests such as stocks and shares; and the settlement itself became a settlement of a fund rather than of land. Often enough the mansion house, the park, and the surrounding land could be kept going only if subsidized out of other sources of wealth.

Taxation

The Settled Land Acts came just in time to facilitate the sales of property which new forms of taxation made inevitable. The first Act imposing Estate Duty was passed in 1894; and it is significant that, although it was not passed by reason of war or even in contemplation of war, it helped to pay for an important measure of naval rearmament. The previously existing legacy and succession duties had been relatively unimportant, and have ultimately been abolished, but estate duty from the start imposed a burden which was felt by men of property. It now bears down on them with crushing effect unless they can contrive to avoid its incidence in whole or in part. It is enough to say that estates of between £50,000 and £60,000 pay 35 per cent. in estate duty, estates of £100,000 to £150,000 50 per cent., and estates of over £1,000,000 80 per cent. Income-tax has risen at the same rate, until now it is impossible to keep a net income of much more than £6,000 a year.

This burden of taxation has had three marked effects. First, it has forced a great deal of property into the market that would not otherwise have been sold. It has therefore intensified the need for cheaper conveyancing, for land has changed hands just as much as personalty. Secondly, it has reduced enormously the proportionate amount of land and other property subject to settlements of one kind and another, for the very simple reason that on the whole settlements were only made by the richer classes and there has been a drastic levelling of wealth. Finally, it has changed radically the usual form of settlements. The old strict settlement formerly used by the aristocracy and landed gentry, with the primary intention of keeping land in the family, attracts taxation in the most disastrous way, whereas now the main purpose of settling property is to avoid taxation. This form of legal activity has long been known in America by the euphemistic name of 'estate planning'. We now call it, more brutally, 'tax planning'. In truth, everywhere in all Western countries no important decisions are taken in business without considering the possible incidence of taxation. It may make all the difference between prosperity and ruin.

Property of public authorities

Much property, including large areas of land, now belongs to the Crown, other public authorities and public corporations such as the National Coal Board, the British Transport Commission, the B.B.C., and the Port of London Authority. In other countries such public property is often governed by an entirely different system of law and is excluded entirely from the law of property. In England there is no such distinction of principle. Of course, property such as government buildings in Whitehall or town halls or other municipal buildings seldom come into the market; property acquired compulsorily for specific purposes, such as building a railway, cannot be used for other purposes; the Crown has certain peculiar rights and privileges by virtue of the Royal Prerogative; and such bodies as the National

Coal Board and the B.B.C., by the mere fact that they have a statutory monopoly, cannot alienate their property in such a way as to constitute competitors. But if none of these peculiar factors comes into play, public authorities and public corporations hold or own property in precisely the same way as private persons. Thus Crown Lands are governed by legislation closely modelled on the Settled Land Act.

Compulsory purchase

Public authorities and public corporations can acquire property in the same way as private persons, that is to say, normally by purchase. But sometimes the purchase is compulsory, in the sense that the private owner from whom it is sought to acquire it is forced to sell. In normal times the right of compulsory purchase applies only to land, for there is not usually the same monopoly of chattels that there always is in practice in land. Although compensation must always be paid for land taken under compulsory powers, the amount payable is often restricted to such a degree as to produce partial confiscation. This bare allusion to compulsory purchase must suffice for an elementary book on property law.

IX

THE PHYSICAL USE OF PROPERTY

1. GENERAL

WE have now to consider the use that can be made of physical objects and the explanation will be clearer if we start with persons who enjoy the fullest right over things that the law recognizes, that is to say, the full ownership of movables and the fee simple absolute in possession of land.

It is often said proverbially that a man may do what he likes with his own. Although the many restrictions placed on the exercise of powers by an owner make that statement false, it is still the best way of dealing with the content of ownership to start from the presumption that an owner can make unlimited use of a thing he owns and then to outline the restrictions placed on such use.

Such restrictions may be imposed by the general law, and if they are infringed, tortious or criminal liability will ensue. The property lawyer is not concerned with most cases of tortious liability for the use of things, and in all probability never where the thing used is a movable.

There are rational grounds for regarding liability for the use of movables in this way. In the first place, movables normally pass from hand to hand so often and so rapidly that it would be difficult to restrict their use unless they are of an obviously dangerous kind. On the other hand, one can say quite simply that a particular use of one piece of land will reduce the value of a neighbouring piece of land, so that it is appropriate to think of the two pieces of land without troubling about the persons who have them.

That is not to say that a person may do what he likes with, for instance, a motor-car or a gun; but if he damages another person, attention will be directed not to the motor-car or the gun but to his conduct in using it. He will be liable if he has used it negligently or intending to hurt the other person, and the peculiar nature of the thing used will come into consideration only in deciding whether more or less care should have been taken in using it. Sometimes, indeed, the nature of the thing is more directly relevant; thus there are statutes and regulations governing the storage of explosives. But such restrictions depending on the nature of the object almost always belong to public law.

Conversely, the value of a person's property may be increased if he is able to do something to the property of someone else. Here again, there is little to say about movables. A person is hardly ever empowered to make use of movables belonging to anyone else unless he has bargained for such use by way of contract; and his right is then strictly personal to him and affects the movables only as long as they are owned by the other contracting party. Moreover, it is impossible to create permanent relationships of this positive kind between one movable object and another.

However, such rights can be created in such a way as to give the owner of one piece of land rights over another piece of land in such a way as to enhance the value of the former.

The law itself imposes restrictions on occupiers of land in favour of their neighbours in the absence of any agreements they may have entered into. Thus they must not commit nuisances, that is to say, they must not do anything that interferes to an unreasonable degree with the comfort of their neighbours or the proper use of their land. The law of nuisance is habitually dealt with in books on criminal law and the law of torts, and all that need be said here is that it imposes liability on an occupier to pay damages for any injury caused by excessive noise or the escape of fumes, smells, or electric current or by interfering with his natural right to support for his land or the natural flow of water in a stream, and that he can be restrained directly by an injunction or indirectly by a prosecution from allowing the injury to continue.

2. SERVITUDES

But a man may feel the need to impose other duties on his neighbours if he is to obtain the full value out of his occupation of land; and, while not imposing those duties itself, the law may enable him to stipulate for them by agreement with his neighbours or to acquire some of them by exercising them peaceably for a long time.

A tenant of land may always lawfully bargain with his neighbour for any advantage whatever, so long as it does not fall within the very narrow class of what is illegal or immoral or against public policy; and such advantages may even include the right that his neighbour shall perform a positive act, such as keeping a wall in repair. But most bargains of this kind will operate only in the law of contract, that is to say, they will bind only the actual person making the promise, or his personal representatives,[1] to the person to whom it is made; though the benefit of the promise will pass to anyone acquiring the land of the promisee, provided it 'touches and concerns

[1] i.e. his executors or administrators; see pp. 165, 170–2 below.

the land'. It will not bind anyone who buys or otherwise acquires the land of the promisor. If the advantage is one strictly personal to the promisee, then the benefit of it will not pass either.

Now, this is by no means satisfactory for the promisee, who wants to secure an advantage which will exist permanently and irrespective of the identity of his neighbour. Otherwise he will have to make a new bargain every time the neighbouring land changes hands; and he is likely to be held to ransom every time. It is not sufficient for the benefit to 'run with' his own land; the burden must 'run with' the neighbouring land. In other words, what is needed is not merely a personal right against the original promisor but a real right over his land, a species of property in another person's land.

Now, the law allows such property rights to be created, but subject to definite rules, far more restrictive than those which control the formation of contracts. For a contract creates rights and duties only between the contracting parties, and they are usually temporary; although contractual rights can be transferred to other parties, yet the restriction of contractual duties to the original promisor in itself restricts the operation of contract so closely that the law can refrain from imposing any further restrictions. But real rights operate so widely and are so apt to affect all comers that the law is bound to limit the kinds of real rights that can exist. Moreover, there is a serious danger that real rights, especially if they are unrestricted, may make land subject to them of so little value as to be unmarketable.

Thus, with one unimportant exception, which will be discussed later, real rights over another person's land must be 'appurtenant' to one's own land. That means that there must always be not only a 'servient tenement', which is burdened with the duty, but also a 'dominant tenement', for the benefit of which it exists. This has two separate implications. In the first place, the burden on the servient tenement must be of permanent value to the holder of the dominant tenement, whoever he may be. It must exist to accommodate the dominant tenement and be reasonably necessary for the full enjoyment of it. Thus the diminution in value of the servient tenement caused by the existence of the duty may be expected to be roughly made up by the enhancement in the value of the dominant tenement. If, however, the advantage to be expected is personal to the then holder of the dominant tenement stipulating for the right, there is merely an uncompensated diminution in the value of the servient tenement.

Secondly, although the original person stipulating for the right can in some cases enforce it, if need be by an action for damages, against the original person granting it, no one can enforce it against any subsequent holder of the servient tenement unless he is himself holder of the dominant tenement.

All these rights are best designated by the Roman law term *servitudes*, and are of three kinds, easements, *profits-à-prendre*, and rights created by restrictive covenants.

From the point of view of the holder of the servient tenement all servitudes are negative, in the sense that they impose no duty on him to act but only not to act or to suffer the holder of the dominant tenement to do something on the servient tenement.

(*a*) *Easements and profits*

No one has yet been able to frame a satisfactory definition of an easement, but easements can be described as comprising two classes of rights, namely, first, rights to do something on the servient tenement other than taking something from it and, in the second place, exceptionally, a strictly limited number of rights to prevent the doing of certain specific acts on the servient tenement. Thus, from the point of view of the owner of the dominant tenement, easements are said to be either positive or negative.

Positive easements, which, it must be remembered, confer a right on the person entitled to them merely to do something positive on the servient tenement and not to exact a positive act from the owner of the servient tenement, are unlimited in variety and number, provided, of course, that they obey the rules which have been set out above as governing all servitudes. They can include, besides the more obvious rights of way and of diverting the course of a stream for irrigation purposes, such non-apparent rights as that of laying gas mains or electric cables, with the ancillary rights to enter the land in order to inspect and repair them, and such at first sight surprising rights as those of going upon the land of another to open sluice gates or of storing casks and trade produce on land.

On the other hand, negative easements, which give a right to restrain activity on the servient tenement, seem to be strictly limited in number, and comprise only (1) the right to light, that is to say, that the light flowing to a window shall not be unreasonably obstructed, (2) a corresponding right to the free flow of air through a defined aperture, such as a ventilator shaft, (3) the right of support to buildings, that is to say, a right to restrain any use of the servient tenement or buildings on it which will interfere with the support afforded by them to adjoining buildings on the dominant tenement, and (4) a right to restrain any interference with the continued flow of water through an artificial watercourse. There is a good reason, which will be explained shortly, for limiting such negative easements to a small number of well-defined instances. It is worth mentioning at once that although they are all in a sense negative, they all start at the earliest with some act on the part of the owner of the dominant tenement, namely, the creation of a window or ventilator or the erection of a building, or the construction of an artificial watercourse.

Profits-à-prendre, or, more shortly, profits, are rights to take part of the soil or of the produce of the soil of a servient tenement, for instance, to take game or fish, to pasture one's animals, or to cut turf. They may for practical purposes be divided into two classes. Some, which conform to the usual rule requiring the presence of a dominant tenement, are survivals of old manorial customary arrangements, whereby the tenants of a manor had the right, for instance, to pasture their animals on the waste of the manor. They were, like easements, necessary for the proper cultivation and use of their holdings. On the other hand, some profits are said to exist *in gross*, that is to say, may belong to a person as such and not as holder of a dominant tenement. Thus he can alienate them freely. If a landowner grants a lease of shooting or fishing rights for a defined term, a profit of this kind is created. Probably most existing profits in gross have this sort of origin.

(*b*) *Restrictive covenants*

Restrictive covenants always impose purely negative duties, such as not to use land for the purpose of building a factory or a shop or carrying on any trade which would be unsuitable for a residential neighbourhood. Such covenants often take the form of binding a landholder to use premises only as a private dwelling house. This, although apparently not restrictive in form, is certainly restrictive in substance.

Restrictive covenants have an entirely different history from easements and profits. In the first place, the first case in which a restrictive covenant was enforced upon the holder of a servient tenement was only a little over a hundred years ago, whereas easements and profits go back to the Middle Ages. In the second place, easements and profits have always been protected at common law, for a person who infringed an easement was liable to an action of nuisance and a person who interfered with a profit could be sued for trespass. Both easements and profits have always conferred rights *in rem*.

On the other hand, restrictive covenants started as mere contracts between vendors and purchasers of land. A person on selling part of his land would exact a promise from the purchaser not to do certain things which would reduce the value of the part of the land retained by the vendor. At first such a promise bound the actual purchaser to the actual vendor; no other person could be bound and no other person could have the benefit of the promise. However, it came to be thought that a subsequent purchaser who had notice of the restrictive covenant and had perhaps paid less for the servient tenement because of the existence of the covenant, would be acting unconscionably if he disregarded it, and in the year 1848 such a covenant was enforced against a person who had purchased land with notice of it. After a good deal of hesitation restrictive covenants were subjected to the general requirement applied to other servitudes, that they must exist for the benefit of a dominant tenement. But they differ from other servitudes, and especially from easements, in several ways.

In the first place, they started by being enforceable only against persons who had notice of them. For that requirement has now been substituted in most cases a requirement that they shall be registered; and, since registration is held to constitute notice, a registered restrictive covenant is now good against anyone who acquires the servient tenement. Easements and profits operate automatically even though the owner of the servient tenement had no notice of them when he acquired it. It is often said that easements and profits are notorious in the sense that their existence can be detected by anyone who inspects the land. That is true enough of rights of way, and perhaps even of rights connected with watercourses. It is not certainly so of profits, and it is certainly not so of easements connected with underground mains. But doubtless there is a better chance of detecting most easements by inspection than restrictive covenants.

However, the most important difference between restrictive covenants and easements is in the ways in which they can be acquired.

All these various rights over another person's land can be expressly created by an act on the part of the owner of that land. In the case of an easement or profit, it will be what is called a grant by a holder of the servient tenement or a reservation in a conveyance to a holder of a servient tenement by a holder of a dominant tenement; in the case of a restrictive covenant it will be an express promise, but one which has long since acquired most of the characteristics of a grant. Easements are almost always at the present day acquired by grant or reservation, but they can also be acquired by what is called prescription, that is to say, a person can effectually claim the right to exercise them on the ground that he has actually exercised them for a long time.

Prescription

The detailed rules of the law of prescription, which is fictitiously presumed to rest on a grant made by the holder of the servient tenement in the remote past but the evidence of which has since been lost, need not be considered here. It is enough to say that the exercise of the right on which the person seeking to prove his right relies must have been uninterrupted and as of right; and the exercise is as of right if it is not by force against the will of the owner of the servient tenement, or secretly without his knowledge, or with his permission. Thus it is always open to the latter to prevent prescription from operating by either interrupting the exercise, for instance, by locking a gate across a path, or by insisting on the payment of some sum of money, however small, as an acknowledgement that the exercise is by his leave. Both of these practices are in fact very common. Thus, if a person makes an opening for a window in a wall which will depend for its light upon the owner of the adjoining land not building in such a way as to obstruct it, that person, in order to preserve his right to build, will demand a periodical payment of a nominal sum, or may go so far as to put up a hoarding on his land to obstruct the access of light to the window.

Now a restrictive covenant cannot be prescribed for; the restriction established by it must always have a definite beginning in an actual covenant by the owner of the servient tenement. But it may be asked, why should not the restriction be imposed by way of negative easement, or rather, why should not one person claim that, having had the benefit of a restriction uninterruptedly for a considerable time, the restriction has become established permanently in his favour; for, as we have seen, the difference between the grant of an easement and the establishment of a restriction by way of covenant is illusory. The answer is surely obvious.

He has not had the benefit of a restriction but merely of a particular kind of inactivity. Now the owner of a piece of land need not use it at all if he does not want to; at least none of his neighbours can claim that he should do so, whatever the public law of agriculture, or town and country planning, may have to say. Thus it is hard to see how the mere inactivity of one person can even look like the exercise of a right by another. Or look at the matter in another way. As a famous nineteenth-century judge once said: 'You cannot acquire any rights against others by a user which they cannot interrupt.' The only way in which a person could interrupt the use of a purely negative right would be by actually doing the thing which it was going to be claimed that he could not do. Therefore he would have to do periodically every single thing that he thought his neighbour might possibly object to in the future. But the number of such things would be infinite.

Negative easements

It may be said that the so-called negative easements break this chain of reasoning. To this objection there are two answers. In the first place, as has been said above, although they are restrictive, the user has a definite beginning which is notorious to the person against whom it may operate. Accordingly, the requirement that he shall interrupt it or demand payment for it in order to prevent prescription, is not at all burdensome. Secondly, since they are definite and few in number, they escape the difficulty that arises when restrictions are sought to be derived from mere general and indefinite inactivity. In fact the need for them became obvious long before restrictive covenants were ever enforced as servitudes against owners of servient tenements. At a time when most work was done by hand in houses and shops in the narrow streets of congested towns, it was very important that occupiers should not be deprived of necessary light by the building operations of their neighbours; and in the circumstances at the time this result could be obtained only by the creation of negative easements.

Functional difference

Thus there is a valid distinction of a rational and conceptual kind between easements and restrictive covenants. But there is also a difference of function. In the first place easements appear at a much earlier historical period than restrictive covenants. There has never been a time in the history of English law when easements did not exist, whereas the first case on restrictive covenants occurred as recently as 1848. Easements confer those rights over neighbouring land or buildings which are necessary for the proper use of land or buildings but are not conferred by the law itself. The oldest of them arise out of farming needs; one farm is made to accommodate another farm so as to enable it to be used effectively. Thus easements are usually simple and affect only two pieces of property, the dominant and the servient tenement. Moreover, although they are valuable, they are valuable because they allow the performance of some physical act. They are as much part of the farmer's plant as his land, his seeds, and his stock.

On the other hand, restrictive covenants are best understood as instruments of planning. They date from a time when large landowners wanted to lay out large estates for building according to a permanent plan and arrangements which were intended to protect purchasers of property in it against each other, while at the same time they wanted to divest themselves, by sale of the land, of all further interest in it. As long as a landowner was content to let out all the portions of an estate on lease he could bind his lessees not to use their lands or houses in any way adverse to the interests of the estate as a whole. Thus he could keep the whole estate as a residential estate or could restrict shops or factories to specific sections of it. It was not so obvious that he could maintain these restrictions if he sold the land outright. It was still less obvious that any one of his purchasers could enforce them against any other of his purchasers. But if this was impossible, town and country planning would become impossible, for there was no question until the present century of either the State or local authorities starting to plan as a matter of public law. Thus restrictive covenants operating reciprocally between neighbours as part of a comprehensive plan for the development of an estate became necessary if landowners were not to do as they liked and incidentally ruin the market value of neighbouring land.

In fact large residential estates were laid out on these lines in both towns and suburbs until quite recent times, and the law had become satisfactory and complete. Where the proper steps had been taken by the vendor, each owner of a plot was able to hold every other holder within the estate to his covenants. Before 1914 there was no need to plan the countryside on similar lines, largely because it was still to a very great extent in the hands of large landowners but also because motor transport had not yet caused the towns to spread inordinately or ribbon development to make its appearance along the main roads.

3. DEVELOPMENTS IN PUBLIC LAW

Before 1914 the use of land was controlled almost entirely by arrangements made under private law. Since that date, and more especially since 1939, it has become much more a matter for the exercise of public law powers by public authorities.

Many factors have contributed to this new development.[2] In some cases the growth in voting power of the working class has made it necessary to pay peculiar attention to their interests. In almost every case it has become more and more important in the public interest to keep property in order and to plan future development. Public authorities have had to intervene largely because landholding has become steadily more commercialized, so that landowners have had less personal interest in the land and have been more exclusively concerned than previously to make money out of land or buildings. Finally, some of the most urgent problems have arisen from the simple fact that buildings were getting old and out of repair, and in some cases their owners were too poor to do the necessary repairs.

Accordingly, Parliament intervened to give powers to public authorities to deal with (*a*) housing, (*b*) town and country planning, and (*c*) agriculture.

[2] See pp. 91–94 above.

(*a*) *Housing*

It is an old and hardly defensible rule of law that 'fraud apart, there is no law against letting a tumble-down house'. However, since members of the working class were not usually in a position to exclude the rule by forcing a landlord to put a house into repair before letting it, Parliament intervened to insist that where houses are let at a low rent—not exceeding £40 a year in London and £26 elsewhere—a condition should be implied that the house is reasonably fit for human habitation at the beginning of the tenancy, and an undertaking by the landlord is implied that he will keep it in that condition throughout the tenancy. This provision cannot be excluded by any contrary agreement between landlord and tenant.

So far protection is given to the tenant against the landlord, by statutory and compulsory modifications of the tenancy agreement or lease. Local authorities were later given powers to deal with insanitary or ruinous houses as such. They have now powers to close houses until necessary repairs have been done, and, if necessary, to demolish houses which cannot be usefully repaired. They are also empowered to make schemes for slum clearance. In all these cases the owner has an appeal to the Minister of Housing and Local Government.

(*b*) *Town and country planning*

Even before 1914 it was becoming obvious to far-sighted people that slum clearance was not enough; the growth of slums should be prevented by town planning. However, nothing was done, except by the initiative of isolated local authorities, until 1919. Not until 1936 was an attempt made to solve one particular part of the general problem, namely, ribbon development, which, though profitable to builders and house-owners who were saved the expense of making up roads and laying sewers, made the suburbs of large towns sprawl in a way inconvenient to agriculture and dangerous to traffic.

It would serve no useful purpose to describe the history of the law on this topic. The present position is briefly as follows.

Local planning authorities, that is to say county and county borough councils, must prepare development plans for approval by the Minister of Housing and Local Government, and must reconsider such plans every five years. These plans specify the uses—residential, industrial, or otherwise—to which the several districts under their jurisdiction may be put; but they give only a general indication of the authority's intentions and do not bind it to give or refuse permission to develop any piece of land. However, they are very important and enter into the calculations of all landowners.

The most radical feature of the law is the requirement of planning permission, that is to say, the permission of the local planning authority, before any development of the land can be undertaken. So important is this requirement that an intending purchaser will always insist on being informed what, if any, planning permission has been granted before he even signs a contract to purchase land. For development is defined in very wide terms to include (1) the carrying out of building, engineering, mining, or other operations in, on, over, or under land, or (2) the making of any material change in the use of any building or other land; though development for the purposes of agriculture or forestry is not included in it. Moreover, if land is acquired compulsorily, as it often is for public purposes by a public authority, no account is to be taken in fixing the price of any possible future development; only the present use value is to be paid.

Any person who is refused planning permission by a local authority can appeal to the Minister of Housing and Local Government.

(c) *Agriculture*

During the Second World War it was found necessary to control agriculture in order to secure the maximum production of food, and in 1947 this public discipline was continued permanently in return for guaranteed prices. Part of the scheme, which gave security of tenure to farmers as against landlords, will be discussed later in connexion with leases, but control was imposed on landlords in the interest of good estate management and on occupiers, whether owner-occupiers or tenant farmers, in the interest of good husbandry. The plan is operated by the Minister of Agriculture, Fisheries, and Food through County Agricultural Executive Committees. Where either landowners or occupiers are not fulfilling their duties of ensuring good estate management or good husbandry respectively, they may be placed under supervision, and if satisfactory improvements have not been shown more drastic steps can be taken. If estate management is bad, the Minister may purchase the land compulsorily; if farming is bad, then (*a*) if the occupier is not the owner, the owner may be required to farm the land himself or to let it to a new tenant approved by the Minister; (*b*) if the occupier is also the owner, he may be required to give up possession of the land and let it to a tenant approved by the Minister. Against any order of any of these kinds there is an appeal to an Agricultural Land Tribunal.

4. PRICE MAINTENANCE CONDITIONS

Generally speaking, a person who sells goods has no further interest in them, but within the present century manufacturers have frequently adopted a policy of maintaining retail prices for their goods and have attempted to attach conditions to them binding any person into whose hands they may come not to sell them for less than a fixed price. This policy has had a chequered career. In the past the courts refused to enforce such conditions directly except where the goods were patented; but they also refused to treat as an actionable conspiracy an agreement among manufacturers to blacklist persons who sold at less than the listed price.

However, by the Restrictive Practices Act, 1956, Parliament, while outlawing the practice of blacklisting, now allows price-maintenance conditions to be attached to goods, provided they are reasonable.

The change is perhaps more apparent than real. At any rate there is no obvious change of policy. For it was always hard to decide how far the Courts were actuated in the past by notions of public policy and how far by mere technical reasons of private law. Probably public policy did little more than make them disinclined to overcome technical difficulties; for where such difficulties did not exist, they did not refuse their aid in maintaining prices. Thus, as has already been mentioned, they tolerated the practice of blacklisting; and where a retailer had fraudulently induced a wholesaler to sell him goods which were price-listed, the manufacturer was able to make him liable for wilfully interfering with the manufacturer's contract with the wholesaler.

X

THE COEXISTENCE OF PROPERTY INTERESTS IN SEVERAL PERSONS

1. GENERAL

WE have just been considering the physical use of things by persons who have the entire and exclusive interest in them. We have now to consider cases where the interest in property is divided among several persons. One case we have considered sufficiently already, namely that in which several persons enjoy a thing in common, sharing simultaneously either the physical use or the income derived from it or both.[1] The other cases fall under two general heads, leases and settlements.

The immediate enjoyment of a thing may be divided between two persons who have interests adverse to each other. On the other hand, one person or group of persons may enjoy the thing completely and exclusively for a time, being then succeeded by one or more other persons or groups of persons in succession. The former division is effected by leases of land and bailments of chattels by way of hire, the latter by settlements.

In lease or hire one of the parties, the lessee or bailee, has the exclusive physical use of the thing and pays a periodical rent, which, from his point of view, is the price of his enjoyment. From the point of view of the lessor or bailor, the rent is the return from an investment, and the thing is that which produces it. Thus the income is divided between the parties, for both derive something of pecuniary value from it, but only the lessee or bailee has the physical use of the thing. The two parties enjoy the thing in different ways.

On the other hand, if a piece of land or the income from a trust fund is given to A for life with remainder to B, A has the exclusive and complete enjoyment of the land or trust fund during his lifetime, including not only the whole of the income from it but also the physical use of any land or physical chattels which are included in it. When he dies, B will have the same kind of enjoyment of it that A had. From the present point of view it is irrelevant that B has already a present interest in the land or trust fund which he can sell and turn into money.

However, whether the division of interest arises from a lease or

[1] See pp. 63–65 above.

bailment or from a settlement, the person who has the physical use of the thing has it only for a period of time and after that time the possession will fall to another person, whether he be a remainderman or a lessor or bailor. Thus the former has only the income, in the broad sense of the term, and the latter the capital. Now certain problems always arise when one person is entitled to the income from property and the other to the capital. These are essentially the same whether one is dealing with leases or bailments or with settlements, though the solutions are not precisely the same.

From this point onwards we shall be dealing with complex entities rather than the simple elements that have hitherto engrossed our attention. To adopt the language of technology, we shall now be dealing not with the equivalents of hand tools but with machines. Moreover, just as machines, though compounded of various elements which could conceivably be put together in an infinite number of ways, tend to become themselves standardized, so the leases, settlements, and mortgages tend to assume a relatively small number of stereotyped forms. This is common enough in all parts of the law; it is especially marked in the law of property.

2. CAPITAL AND INCOME

Whenever property is given to a person to hold for a limited period some means must be found of protecting the person or persons who are to take it after him. In other words, he is entitled only to the income (including in that term the physical use of corporeal things comprised in the property) and must not touch the capital, which must be transmitted as far as humanly possible intact on the termination of his interest. This distinction between income and capital meets the student at many points and, although the rules governing it vary with the various kinds of limited interest, it deserves a brief introductory treatment of a general kind.

Income-tax lawyers, above all other persons, know that the question what is income is not a simple one; but this is largely because Parliament has had to check in detail devious ways of disguising income as a capital gain and so securing exemption from income-tax. Property lawyers do not have to face this mass of repulsive detail, but their task also is sometimes difficult.

Trust funds

The easiest case to understand is that of trustees holding a fund in trust for one person for life, remainder to another person absolutely. Their primary duty is to preserve the capital of the trust fund, and to pay to the tenant for life only the income as it falls due, after deducting the expenses of administering the trust. Formerly the rules governing the various possible situations were fairly clear, though not always easily stated.

If the trust fund consisted from the start of gilt-edged securities, the person entitled to the life interest had to be paid the income from the securities as it fell due. The securities would normally retain their capital value and it was to this alone that the remainderman was entitled.

Nor is the position difficult where trustees have money in their hands to invest. Unless the settlor increases their powers, they must still invest it within a narrow class of so-called trustee securities which can be expected to retain their capital value and so to produce a steady, more or less uniform income. For it is the primary duty of trustees to preserve the capital of the trust fund and to apportion income as fairly as possible among the persons successively entitled to receive it.

More difficult questions arise where the trust fund includes other kinds of securities when it comes into the hands of the trustees. Some of them may be speculative and others may be either wasting or reversionary in character. In most cases the trustees will have a discretion whether to retain or to realize them, a discretion with which the Court will not readily interfere, and they must pay the income from them to the persons immediately entitled to interest in the fund. However, where wasting or reversionary securities are settled as residuary personalty on death, the so-called rule in *Howe* v. *Lord Dartmouth*, with its corollaries, applies. A wasting security is one which is likely to lose its capital value at some future date, such as an interest in a mine which will probably be exhausted. If such a property were retained, the persons immediately entitled to the income might get a very high rate of interest on the investment, but there might be no capital to transmit to their successors. A reversionary interest is the converse of this. Until it falls in, there is no income and so the person entitled to the capital will be unduly favoured at the expense of the person immediately entitled to the income of the trust fund. Accordingly, the rule in *Howe* v. *Lord Dartmouth* says that the trustees must within a year realize wasting and reversionary securities and reinvest the proceeds in property of a permanent and income-bearing character. For it is their duty to hold the scales evenly between those successively entitled to the income. Moreover, until realization, they must not pay the whole income arising from wasting securities to the person entitled to the limited interest, but only 4 per cent. on the estimated capital value of the securities, accumulating the residue of the income as capital. Similarly, when reversionary securities fall in, part of the capital must be used to pay arrears of income to the person entitled to the prior limited interest.

Much of this law has recently become unrealistic, for so-called trustee securities are pre-eminently subject to reduction in real value through devaluation of currency and inflation. Accordingly, settlors, if they are well advised, extend the powers of trustees to allow them to invest in what economists and business men call equities, that is to say, in land or other securities of a commercial or industrial kind which, it may be hoped, will adjust themselves to changes in the value of money and maintain their real and not merely their nominal value.[2] But, whatever happens, trustees must try to preserve the capital of the trust fund in order to accord equal treatment to the tenant for life and to successive remaindermen.

Waste

The problem of holding the balance even between capital and income is more complicated where the enjoyment of a physical object is divided between several persons successively. It is hardly worth discussing apart from land.

In its relation to land the problem first arose in the form of waste. There is an ever-present temptation to the temporary holder of land to waste it by exhausting the soil or letting buildings fall into disrepair. Accordingly, the reversioner or remainderman was given an action for damages against him; but once the Chancellor was willing to grant an injunction restraining the commission of waste, that remedy was preferred to the former. Around these remedies a body of substantive law grew up, simple in its general outlines, but running to complications in detail.

A primary distinction is made between so-called permissive and voluntary waste, the former comprising mere omissions to act, such as failing to repair a farmhouse, the latter comprising positive acts diminishing the capital value or changing the nature of the land, such as pulling down a barn. Even the replacement of an old house by a new and more valuable one is voluntary waste, but such *ameliorating* waste would give rise to a claim for only nominal damages and will not be restrained by injunction.

Whether a person is to be held liable for permissive or voluntary waste depends on whether he is a life tenant or a tenant for a term of years such as a lessee. Thus, a life tenant is not liable for permissive waste and is often, perhaps usually, expressly made by the settlor unimpeachable for waste, in which case he may even commit voluntary waste with impunity, though he can be restrained by injunction from committing what is called *equitable* waste, i.e. wanton damage. The liability for waste of tenants holding under a lease or a tenancy agreement, in practice unimportant, varies with the kind of tenancy.

[2] See further pp. 151–2 below.

Improvements

The converse of waste is improvement. It might be thought that if the remainderman or reversioner can restrain the holder of a prior limited interest from waste, he should on the other hand have to pay for any improvements made by him. Yet the common law gave the latter no right to compensation and even forced him to leave any fixtures which he had annexed to the soil or buildings. Even when at a later date he acquired the right to remove most fixtures, such as trade fixtures,[3] any unexhausted improvements that increased the fertility of the soil inured to the benefit of the remainderman or reversioner. That was not likely to worry a tenant for life, who would ordinarily be the father or mother of the remainderman and would willingly improve the land for his benefit, but it could enrich a landlord unfairly at the expense of his tenant. Any tenant for an indefinite period did indeed have one privilege, that of taking *emblements*,[4] i.e. of reaping after the termination of his tenancy an industrial crop sown by him. This was to encourage him to cultivate the land properly, free from any fear that he might not reap where he had sown. A tenant for a term of years was not given that privilege, for he was held to have known all along when his term would come to an end.

However, all this learning about waste, improvements, and emblements is now hardly more than the foundation for an entirely different body of law erected by statute or act of parties. Put shortly, the tenant for life has been turned into a manager of the land for the benefit of himself and those coming after him.[5] Accordingly he has been given much wider rights and powers than at common law of making alterations and improvements in the interest of the family, though his beneficial interest remains limited to his life. On the other hand, the relations between landlord and tenant became a matter of contract between them, until various statutes intervened, first to protect the tenant against his landlord despite the terms of the contract, and, later, to ensure the proper cultivation of land in the interests of the public at large.[6]

These developments will be considered in greater detail when we treat of leases and life interests respectively.

3. LEASES AND SETTLEMENTS

Although the existence of limited interests in property always gives rise to common problems, of which the most obvious are those relating to the fair treatment of both capital and income, there are fundamental differences between limited interests arising from business arrangements and those arising under family settlements. Two call for examination here.

[3] See p. 21 above.

[4] See p. 21 above.

[5] See further pp. 148–50 below.

[6] See further pp. 122–6 below.

Popular notions of ownership

In the first place it is much easier to apply ordinary popular notions of ownership to the former. If A lends or hires out his car to B, he will naturally say that although he has lost the possession of it for the time being, it is his car; and B would neither contest that statement nor claim that the car was his. Nor would the doctrine of estates get seriously in the way if A let his house to B; he would still say it was his house and B would not say that it was his. There might indeed be doubts if B had a long lease with many years to run, for B might then say that the house was his, and A might content himself with the remark that he was entitled to a ground rent.

But when under a family settlement C has a life interest in property followed by a remainder in D, neither would say that the property was his. If indeed the property is land, the tenant for life is usually called a landowner, improperly, for not only has he at best a limited beneficial interest, but he corresponds, not to the lessor, but to the lessee, that is to say, not to the person who claims that the land is his but to the one that admits the other's claim.

Commercial and family interests

The fact is that the essential purpose of a family settlement is to give to several persons the income from property for successive periods. The income may include the physical use of the property, especially if it includes land, but it is not so much the land that is owned by anyone as the temporary income arising from the exploitation of it.

At any rate, that was the point of view that the Legislature took in 1925 when it streamlined the law relating to limited interests. It drew a distinction between cases where one person bargains with another commercially for the temporary physical use of land and cases where several persons enjoy the temporary physical use of land one after another under a family settlement. It said in effect that whereas in the former case the physical use is the paramount consideration, in the latter it is only a way of enjoying the income. Hence comes the second fundamental difference between interests arising from business arrangements and interests arising under family settlements: in the latter case, if for some good reason it is proper to insist that the temporary beneficiary shall enjoy the income in another form, the mere fact that hitherto it has consisted in the physical use of land is to be no obstacle to a sale of the land and the reinvestment of the proceeds in other securities, whereas in the former case such a solution is inadmissible.[7]

[7] See p. 82 above.

Two factors which may have contributed to this decision are perhaps not sufficiently noticed. In the first place, what may be called the commercial interest in land arises from a bargain between two persons, usually a lessor and a lessee or a mortgagor and a mortgagee. Hence any power granted to either party to force the other to submit to a variation in his investment, by selling the land over his head and compensating him with a lump sum or an alternative investment, would have been a power to vary the original bargain without the consent of the other party. The Legislature could indeed have enacted that such a power must be read into every lease or mortgage, but that would have rendered the position of lessees and mortgagees extremely insecure. In fact, as will be seen later, the whole tendency of legislation has been in precisely the opposite direction, to enhance the security of the lessee at a cost to the lessor which is sometimes quite unfair.[8] On the other hand, there is no contractual relationship between the persons successively entitled to income under a family settlement, nor does the obligation which a trustee is under to successive beneficiaries arise out of bargains made between him and them. The beneficiaries have not the same right as a lessee to insist on retaining the land in specie. The most they can do is to ask a court to say that an attempt to alienate the land is bad for the settlement as a whole, that is to say, that the proposed variation of the investment is improvident. Thus the existence or nonexistence of a bargain creates a sound distinction upon which to base the distinction made in 1925 between limited interests normally arising out of a commercial bargain, where the physical use of the land is guaranteed, and limited interests arising under a family settlement, where the beneficiaries may have to submit to a variation of investments, involving a deprivation of the physical use.

Realty and personalty

The other factor is indeed expressed in the title of the Law of Property Act, 1922, which introduced most of the innovations reenacted in consolidated form in the 1925 Acts. That title, 'An Act to Assimilate the Law of Real and Personal Estate', has been criticized on good grounds, but it does at least help to explain the particular innovation that is now being discussed.

Down to the year 1925 very much the same distinction was in fact observed in relation to personalty as is now observed as a matter of law in relation to land. One person bargained with another for the temporary physical use of a chattel, or a settlor might include chattels in his family settlement. Only choses in possession could be the object of physical use, whereas, apart from heirlooms, such as

[8] See pp. 122–6 below.

pictures or jewels, choses in action, especially stocks and shares, were the most likely chattels to be included in a settlement. Where a person bargained for the temporary possession of a chose in possession he usually desired to use it physically or to hold it as security for a loan. As a bailee he was protected against third parties, and in practice his contract gave him sufficient protection against his bailor. If choses in action were contained in a family settlement, they had to be held by trustees in trust for the successive beneficiaries, and in a well-drawn settlement the trustees were given wide powers of sale and reinvestment;[9] for choses in action were then regarded merely as sources of income.

Accordingly, when dealing with chattels, one can make a rough distinction between things which will normally be regarded as objects of physical use and things which are more naturally regarded as producing an income; and one could with no great degree of inaccuracy equate the former class with physical chattels and the latter with some varieties at least of choses in action. However, no analogous distinction could be applied to land, for two reasons. In the first place, all land is corporeal whereas all interests in land are incorporeal. In the second place, it would have been absurd to regard certain kinds of land as appropriate to leases and others as appropriate to settlements. On the other hand, such a distinction might be properly made among *interests* in land; and such a distinction was in fact made between leasehold estates and limited freehold interests.

It is true that formerly a term of years, the so-called 'portions term',[10] was an essential element in the strict settlement in its fully developed form and that it was not uncommon for a person to take a lease of land for his own life or for the lives of a number of selected persons.[11] In other words, leasehold estates appeared in settlements and freehold estates less than the fee simple were once objects of commerce. However, the primary and common use of the term of years is to create a lease, which is a matter for commercial bargaining, and freehold interests other than the fee simple came to exist only in settlements. Thus no harm was likely to occur if they were allowed only in settlements and as equitable interests behind the 'curtain' of the legal estate. Moreover, in this way the law relating to real estate was almost exactly assimilated to the practice governing personalty. Oddly enough, as has been explained,[12] the opportunity was not taken of bringing the law governing personalty into strict conformity with that governing land.

[9] See p. 81 above.

[10] This was used in order to provide for members of the family other than the eldest son.

[11] See p. 71 above.

[12] See p. 86 above.

XI

LEASES AND THE HIRE OF GOODS

1. GENERAL

WHY people hire things is easily understood. They may not want them permanently but only for a time, and it may be inconvenient for them to buy and resell. If they want them for a considerable period of time they may yet either not have the capital to buy them outright or may not want to sink a large amount of capital in them. Sometimes they may be prepared to provide what is called the working capital, whilst hiring the fixed capital from someone else. This is the key to traditional tenant-farming in England.

Why people let things out is also easily understood. They have something that may be made to yield an income and they either cannot or will not exercise the physical use that ultimately produces the income and therefore leave that to someone else who will hire the thing from them.

Where there is hire, each party enters into obligations toward the other. In other words, there is a contract between them, the terms of which are either expressly agreed between them or implied by law or partly the one and partly the other. The contractual aspect of hire is not a matter of interest to the property lawyer as far as concerns physical chattels such as animals or furniture. It is otherwise with leases of land because the benefit and burden of covenants must be made to run with both the lease and the reversion. Leases are ordinarily of longer duration than the hire of chattels and so both leases and reversions are regular articles of commerce. That being so, it is important that any two persons who are lessee and reversioner for the time being should be in the same contractual relation to each other as the original lessee and lessor, in so far as it touches and concerns the land.

In Roman law hire was nothing more than contract. In English law, however, it is much more. Here again we must distinguish between chattels and land. When a chattel is handed over by way of hire a bailment takes place, and thereby the hirer is put in possession of the thing. For land the corresponding transaction is a lease, and here too there is a transfer of possession. So far the two are very similar, though whereas the lessor always retains what is misleadingly called 'possession',[1] a bailor who bails goods for a fixed term loses

[1] See p. 119 below.

possession, and although a bailor at will, that is to say, one who is entitled to bring the bailment to an end whenever he likes, is said to retain possession, the authority for this proposition is scanty and not universally regarded as sound. The fact is that the real or proprietary, as opposed to the contractual, aspect of bailment has been so little developed that quite a number of possible questions remain unanswered. For this reason it is best to start with leases.

2. THE REAL ASPECT OF LEASES AND BAILMENTS

The property lawyer looks at leases in two different ways. In the first place a lease creates a term of years, which is a leasehold estate. Thus it divides the ownership of the land on a plane of time, between a termor, who holds the land now, and the reversioner, who will come into possession of the land at the expiration of the term.[2]

On the other hand, it divides the present income from the land between the lessor and the lessee, the former taking a fixed rent and the latter the undefined residue of the profits arising from the exploitation of the land.[3] Thus the interests of the lessor and the lessee are simultaneous in two different senses, first, in the ordinary way in which all estates are simultaneous, in that they have a present capital value although they may give successive rights to possession, but secondly, in giving them simultaneous rights to shares in the income.

This second, much more important, aspect of the lease always made it difficult to fit leaseholds into the feudal system. They were indeed, and have always been, a commercial intruder into a way of looking at property which was essentially uncommercial and which was primarily concerned with the public duties owed by holders of land. Thus the medieval lawyers were late in dealing with them and this lateness has caused the word 'possession' to be used in connexion with leases in two very different senses which are apt to cause confusion in the mind of the student.

Originally only freehold tenants[4] were given actions by which they could recover their holdings in case of dispossession. In order to establish their claim they had to prove that they were 'seised' of the land and they were therefore said to have 'seisin of the freehold'. Seisin was possession based on a title which varied with the particular

[2] For leasehold estates see pp. 69–71 above.

[3] It is assumed above that there will be enough income from the land to pay the lessor rent and leave something over for the lessee. This is, of course, not inevitable, and if there is not enough income from the land even to pay the rent, the lessor is still entitled to receive his rent in full. In practice he may find it hard to enforce his claim.

[4] See p. 69 above.

action—of which there were many—but it always served to differentiate the freeholder who had an estate in possession from one who had merely an estate in expectancy, and also the freeholder from the leaseholder, who had originally no action and no estate. When later it became necessary to protect the leaseholder by affording him an action of trespass, the medieval lawyers gave to the relation to the land which he had to establish in himself the name 'possession'.

This distinction between the seisin of the freeholder and the mere possession of the leaseholder was fundamental. Thus if a freeholder seised of the land granted a lease, although the lessee got possession, he did not get seisin, which remained in the lessor. On the other hand, if he gave a particular estate of freehold to another person, say for life, he lost the seisin, which passed to the tenant of the particular estate, and in that case his reversion was incompatible with seisin.

Unfortunately the word 'seisin' has disappeared from the working vocabulary of the real-property lawyer and has been replaced by the word 'possession'. It became the practice to distinguish freehold estates as estates in possession and estates in expectancy according as their holders were or were not seised of the land. Thus a tenant in fee simple in possession of land who grants a lease of it, though he loses possession of the land to the lessee, is still said to have a fee simple in possession in the sense that his freehold estate is not in expectancy. It is in this sense that section 1 of the Law of Property Act, 1925, includes a lessor among persons who have a fee simple absolute in possession and so a legal estate; it is at pains to distinguish that estate from a fee simple absolute which would fall into possession only on the termination of a particular estate of freehold such as a life estate.

This is the historical and technical way of explaining a curious confusion of terminology, but the Act also defines a fee simple absolute in possession in terms of economics, as including the estate held by a person who is entitled to the rents and profits of the land, and this is clearly applicable to a lessor out of possession of the land.

A bailee always has possession of the goods bailed to him, whereas the bailor, except in one doubtful case, namely where the bailment is at will, so that he can bring it to an end at any moment without notice, has not possession. There is no need to attribute an artificial possession to bailors in general since there is nothing in the law governing chattels comparable to the requirements of section 1 of the Law of Property Act that, in order to be a legal estate, a fee simple must be in possession. Hence the possession of goods always has one meaning and is free from the ambiguity attaching to the possession of land.

3. THE FORMAL REQUIREMENTS FOR A LEASE

The formalities for the creation of a lease are the subject of much intricate historical and legal learning. Nothing would be gained by explaining it in an elementary introduction to the law. Here it is enough to say that fairly indiscriminate use is made of actual leases and agreements for leases. Leases for not more than three years at a rack rent, that is to say, the best rent obtainable, may be made verbally without any formality; and this rule applies to periodic tenancies, such as tenancies from week to week, from month to month, or from year to year. However, it is advisable to have some sort of document, for otherwise there will be no permanent record of any special terms agreed upon by the parties.

All other leases must be made by deed, i.e. a sealed writing executed by the lessor. There will in fact be a counterpart to the lease executed by the lessee, which will be necessary if, as is invariably the case, the lessee enters into covenants binding him to do or not to do certain things.

An agreement for a lease is nothing more than an agreement between the parties, evidenced in writing, by which the one promises to grant and the other to accept a lease. At common law it confers on the tenant no interest in the land, but merely a right of action for damages if the landlord does not grant the lease. However, the tenant is entitled in equity to obtain specific performance of the promise and so, in pursuance of the maxim that equity regards that as done which ought to be done, the tenant has already an equitable interest in the land analogous to a lease. That equitable interest, if registered as an estate contract, is good against all the world. For practical purposes an agreement for a lease is treated as equivalent to a lease and the stamp duties payable in respect of the two are the same.

4. COVENANTS

All leases, besides creating real interests in land, also contain covenants, that is to say, reciprocal promises between the lessor and lessee. But although the real and personal rights so created must, for purposes of analysis, be kept distinct, the latter must in some way or other be made to 'run with' the former so as to bind all persons who acquire the estate of the lessee to all persons who acquire the estate of the lessor and vice versa.

This is not so easy as it sounds. All legal systems are reluctant to allow one person by contract to give another person rights against a third person. Thus in principle A should not be allowed to promise B that C will do something for him with the effect that C is bound to B. English law, though not most other modern laws, also puts serious difficulties in the way of one person bargaining with another person for a right in favour of a third person. A cannot bargain with B that B will do something for C with the effect of giving C a right against B. Thus if recourse could be had only to the general law of contract, it would be impossible for a lessor or a lessee by covenant to bind to the other party to the lease any persons to whom they might alienate the reversion or the lease respectively. Nor, at the time when the law on this subject was being worked out, could either party bargain for the benefit of the covenants to vest in subsequent holders of their interests. Thus special rules had to be evolved for leases. In the end those rules have become reasonably clear and sensible.

Privity of contract and privity of estate

It is said that the rights and duties created by a contract operate only between those who are privy to it, that is to say, the actual parties. Between the parties there is said to be privity of contract. Such privity of contract exists between the original lessor and lessee. An analogous but different institution is privity of estate, which exists between persons who have or have acquired the estates of the original lessor and lessee. Thus there is privity of estate between the landlord for the time being and the tenant for the time being, that is to say, not only between the original lessor and lessee, but also between the lessor and an acquirer of the lease, between an acquirer of the reversion and the lessee, and between any acquirer of the reversion and any acquirer of the lease. As the lessor is the landlord of the lessee, who is his tenant, the substance of the matter is that there is tenure between them and the covenant is, as it were, annexed artificially to the ordinary incidents of tenure.

Now, where there is privity of contract, any covenants which are not illegal, immoral, or against public policy have binding force. On the other hand, persons between whom there is only privity of estate are bound only by covenants which run with the land, and those covenants are, put shortly, only such as 'touch and concern' the land, or, to put it in another way, have reference to the subject-matter of the lease. In other words, they must not merely affect a person exacting them, but must affect the nature, quality, or value of the subject-matter, or the mode of using or enjoying it.

Where there is neither privity of contract nor privity of estate, covenants do not bind at all. This is especially important where subleases are concerned. If a lessee sublets land, he does not alienate his estate to the sublessee, but carves a particular estate out of his own estate, retaining for himself the reversion to the sublease. Thus there is no privity of estate between the head lessor and the sublessee, but, on the other hand, it does continue between the head lessor and the head lessee. That means in effect that the head lessee retains the benefit of any covenants entered into by the head lessor and he will have to pass it on to the sublessee, though the head lessee alone will be able to sue for an infringement. Conversely, if a covenant entered into by the head lessee is infringed by an act or omission of the sub-lessee, only the head lessee can be sued. He is in fact responsible for his sublessee to the head lessor.

It is worth mentioning that privity of contract survives all alienations of reversion and lease respectively. Thus the original lessor and lessee guarantee each other permanently against the possibility of infringements of covenants by any subsequent acquirers of the lease and the reversion respectively. But a person who acquires either lease or reversion and subsequently alienates it never had any privity of contract, and with the alienation ceases to have any privity of estate, with any lessor or lessee respectively.

5. THE STATUTORY PROTECTION OF TENANTS

Until a hundred years ago the relations between lessor and lessee were almost entirely based on contract, though the lessor had also certain rights, such as that of distraining on the lessee's goods for non-payment of rent, which depended partly on common law and partly on medieval statutes. The lessee made the best bargain he could with the lessor and had to stand by it. His bargaining power varied considerably from time to time and according to the subject-matter of the lease. In days when the business of speculative building was profitable, a house tenant might have his choice of houses and need not be victimized. In times of agricultural depression, when farmers were steadily emigrating to North America or the Antipodes, a landlord might find it difficult to obtain tenants on any but the most favourable terms. On the other hand, landlords of agricultural land, business premises, or houses might, by the force of circumstances, acquire something like a monopoly and could, within reason, impose what terms they liked. Before commenting on such terms it is well to know what forms in general they took.

Standard covenants

The primary and essential term was, and is, that the lessee shall pay an agreed rent to the lessor; and this was sanctioned by a term allowing the lessor to re-enter on the land in case of non-payment and forfeit the lease. Thus the lessor was not left to bring a personal action on the debt and to exercise his right to distrain on the lessee's goods, but could, if necessary, evict him by bringing an action of ejectment.

The second term bound the lessee to keep the premises in good repair. Here a difference was made between different subject-matters. Tenants of agricultural land, of business premises, and of substantial house property were commonly subjected to full repairing covenants, which threw the full burden of repairs on the lessee. Sometimes tenants of house property undertook merely internal repairs, leaving external repairs to the landlord. Landlords of small dwellings, normally occupied by the working class, found it impossible in practice to throw the duty of repairing them on the tenants. If the houses were not to fall into ruin, the landlord had to do the repairs himself, no doubt endeavouring, as far as possible, to recoup himself by a higher rent.

In the great days of high farming, which lasted for about a century, from about 1770 to 1870, landlords regularly exacted strict improving covenants from their farm tenants. That is to say, they insisted on their tenants improving the land and, incidentally, the farm buildings. At a later date this became much more difficult to ensure.

Very commonly leases of buildings contained a covenant not to assign the lease or create subleases without the consent of the lessor, though generally with the proviso that the consent should not be unreasonably withheld.

All these various covenants were sanctioned, like the covenant to pay rent, by a term in the lease empowering the lessor to re-enter on the land on breach of any covenant and to forfeit the lease.

The contractual aspect of the lease, so apparent and so predominant in what has just been described, has now receded so much into the background that the reader must be warned of the fact that landlords and tenants now look for their rights much less to the terms of their leases than to the statute book. Some classes of tenants, especially tenants of houses of a moderate or high rateable value and, oddly enough, tenants of council houses,[5] still have no statutory protection or have recently lost it.[6] Others can appeal to statute against the terms of their leases. How this has come about is a long story.

Agricultural holdings

Where the old agricultural system was properly worked, it was good for the land and not necessarily bad for the tenant. It required

[5] That is, houses let to them by local authorities.

[6] See p. 126 below.

the employment by the landlord of an agent who supervised continually the operations of the tenants, and it paid the landlord himself to supervise his agent. It also paid him to have happy and efficient tenants. The great agricultural depression, which started in the late seventies of the last century, did much to make relations between landlords and tenants more difficult, and brought to a head certain possibilities of abuse which had long been present. These were remedied by a long series of Agricultural Holdings Acts, which were eventually consolidated in the Act of 1948.

A tenant farmer who is unsatisfactory for some such reason as that he is in arrear with his rent or has made a composition with his creditors or is not cultivating his land in a way which the Minister of Agriculture considers consonant with the rules of good husbandry gets no protection from the Act, but can be evicted by the landlord in accordance with the terms of the lease or tenancy. But a satisfactory tenant is entitled to one full year's notice terminating at least twelve months after the end of his tenancy or lease. He can accept such notice if he chooses but is then entitled to compensation for disturbance, which will amount to at least one year's rent. On the other hand, he can, if he chooses, in effect appeal to the Minister of Agriculture and can insist on continuing his tenancy, except in certain special circumstances, of which the most important is that the land is needed for some approved purpose other than agriculture. Thus a satisfactory tenant farmer has the security of tenure which is necessary for efficient agriculture.

Business premises

A similar security is necessary for the conduct of business on leased premises. Here development of the law did not start until the Landlord and Tenant Act, 1927. The present position is rather complicated, and differs a good deal from that of agriculture. In general, if the tenant is given notice to quit he can apply to a court for a new tenancy, which must be granted. When the new tenancy ends the process can be repeated again indefinitely. But here again there are exceptions. Thus an unsatisfactory tenant may be evicted in accordance with the terms of the lease but only at six months' notice; and a landlord can successfully oppose the granting of a new lease if he intends to demolish or reconstruct the premises or, except where he has bought them within the last five years, if he intends to occupy them himself. In certain cases an evicted tenant can obtain compensation for disturbance. On any grant of a new tenancy the rent may be adjusted so as to conform to the open market rent, and other terms of the tenancy may also be revised by the court. A tenant is also entitled in certain cases to compensation for improvements.

The Rent Acts

The control of house lettings varies according as they are unfurnished or furnished. For some years before 1914 there had been a decline in speculative building, and the war produced a shortage of accommodation which threatened to put tenants at the mercy of landlords. Accordingly in 1915 the first Rent Restriction Act was passed, which had for its purpose the fixing of rent and mortgage interest at the figure prevailing immediately before the war, and also of protecting tenants against eviction. These two purposes have continued to operate until the present day, but defects in the drafting of the original Act have combined with judicial interpretation and a long series of amending Acts, the last of which is the Rent Act, 1957, to make the law of rent control one of the most complicated and obscure departments of English law. Here all that can be given is a very brief sketch of some of its most important features.

The Rent Acts apply only to the tenancy of unfurnished dwelling-houses. This excludes mere licences, but includes premises, such as self-contained or non-self-contained flats or unfurnished rooms, separately let as dwelllings. Certain landlords, such as the Crown and local authorities, and certain premises, such as public houses and agricultural holdings, are outside the Acts.

Control extends only to premises with a rateable value not exceeding £40 in London or £30 elsewhere, but the Minister of Housing and Local Government has power, by order approved by resolution of both Houses of Parliament, to modify the limits so fixed. It does not extend to any tenancy beginning after 6 July 1957, whatever the rateable value of the premises, unless it is granted to a sitting tenant of controlled premises.

The Acts protect tenants of controlled premises in two ways, by providing that the Courts may not make any order for possession in the landlord's favour except on certain specified grounds and by prohibiting the exaction from them of more than the 'recoverable rent'. Mortgagees are similarly restrained from enforcing their security or raising the rate of interest.

The Acts create in favour of a tenant, after the termination of his contractual tenancy, what is called a 'statutory tenancy'. This is not an estate but a right restricted in scope, protecting from eviction the sitting tenant, and after his death his widow or, if he does not leave a widow, any member of his family who has resided with him for at least the previous six months. Moreover, the statutory tenancy can be taken over by a member of the family on only one occasion. The tenant cannot dispose of his statutory tenancy.

The tenant can be evicted on several grounds. Some of them are based on his misconduct, such as non-payment of rent or allowing the premises to fall into disrepair. Among others may be mentioned the need to let to a new servant a house let on a service tenancy; and proof by the landlord that reasonably suitable alternative accommodation for the tenant is or will be available. But in all cases the Court must be satisfied that an order for possession is reasonable.

Landlords can charge as 'recoverable rent' not more than twice the gross annual value (which is between one and a quarter and one and a half times the rateable value) of the dwelling together with certain permitted increases for rates, services, and improvements. This power is subject to various conditions and restrictions.

The 1957 Act decontrolled premises of a rateable value between £40 and £100 in London and between £30 and £75 elsewhere, all of which were subject to different kinds of 'standard rent' plus permitted increases. The Act secured the tenants of such premises from eviction or increase of rent for a period of fifteen months.

Furnished lettings

The control of furnished houses dates only from an Act of 1946, which empowered the Minister of Health to set up Rent Tribunals on the application of local authorities. Any tenant who occupies premises under a contractual tenancy at a rent including payment for furniture or services, but not board, can apply to the local tribunal to have his rent fixed. The tribunal can, at its discretion, approve or reduce the rent and its decision is without appeal. On a change of circumstances the tribunal can either approve, reduce, or increase the rent. Once the rent is fixed it governs all lettings of the premises, whoever is the landlord and whoever the tenant; moreover, lest tenants should be victimized for referring their cases to a tribunal, any tenant who has referred a contract to a tribunal can be given successive extensions of tenure for three months at a time.

The Rent Act, 1957, excluded from the control of furnished lettings all dwellings the rateable value of which is such as to exclude the operation of the Rent Acts.

XII

SETTLEMENTS

1. GENERAL

So far we have been considering cases where the current income from property is divided between several persons as it accrues, proportionately between tenants or owners in common, or by a reservation of a rent to the owner of a rentcharge or to a lessor, leaving to the owner of the land burdened with the rentcharge or to the lessee the residue of the income. Only in one of these cases is the time element important, namely in leases, where the lessor has a right to retain the whole income on the termination of the lease, and hence has a freehold reversion during the currency of the term.

We have now to consider cases where in principle the current income is not divided, but the whole of the income and the physical use of the objects from which it is derived are enjoyed by more than one person in succession to each other. Where arrangements are made for this purpose there is said to be a settlement; indeed section 1 (1) (i) of the Settled Land Act, 1925, defines as a settlement, *inter alia*, any instrument under which any land is 'limited in trust for any persons by way of succession'. Limited interests other than terms of years can only exist as parts of settlements.

Two further observations are called for here. In the first place, the law treats many arrangements as settlements which would not ordinarily be regarded as such, to such an extent indeed as to apply the rules governing settlements to nearly all cases where some obstacle stands in the way of the alienation of land. These extensions need be no more than alluded to in an elementary account. Secondly, a settlement is by no means invariably an elaborate document governing large masses of property; a mere indication in a will that one person is to occupy a house after another will be held to create a settlement. Probably very many testators of modest means create settlements unawares.

Large masses of English property law have been built up round family settlements, and it is not too much to say that to the practice of securing the enjoyment of property to several generations the English law of property, especially the law of real property, owes its most peculiar features.

But it is the family settlement that causes most difficulty to students beginning the study of real-property law. Why should one person try to make complicated arrangements to make his property go in a particular way? Why should the law allow him to do it? On the contrary, why should the law not allow him to do what he likes with his property, even to the extent of stopping other people doing what they like with it in their turn? Finally, if the law thinks that each person should not necessarily have the full control of his property, unfettered by any arrangements that the previous generation may have tried to make, has the law made an intelligible compromise between the competing interests of successive generations?

It is difficult to avoid treating this subject historically, but the temptation must be resisted as far as possible. In fact some explanation can be sufficiently divorced from history.

Protection of widows

Let us take first the simple case of a man who has a wife some years younger than himself and children. He is about to make his will and he has to contemplate the possibility that his wife may survive him, may remarry, and may have children by her second marriage. He has considerable property but not enough to be able to make an outright gift to his wife to keep her for the rest of her life and sufficiently large outright gifts to his children. He does not want to trust his widow with the whole of his property, partly for fear lest she should favour the children of a second marriage in preference to his own children. Surely a very natural way of disposing of his property will be to give the whole or part of it to his widow for life with remainder to his children.

From a very early time widows have acquired life interests in property. Sometimes the law itself has secured them such life interests; for instance, the common law of England gave a widow a life interest in one-third of her husband's freeholds. This right was known as dower. It persists in many, perhaps most, of the States in the United States. Even where the law itself does not give such a right, it is extremely common for testators to give life interests to their widows by will. The arrangement is indeed very natural and requires little justification. What is more natural or more normal than for a man to feel that he has duties to two separate generations, his own in the person of his widow and the next one in the persons of his children?

This is a very simple and common form of settlement. Settlements are indeed infinitely various and may be established *inter vivos* or by will. But they tend to conform more or less to a fairly small number of types. It is by examining some of the more complicated of them that we can best become acquainted with the various interests which can be held in succession to one another.

The strict settlement

The most famous is the strict settlement by which the lands of the aristocracy and gentry were kept together in families for generations. Although it is extremely improbable that any new settlements of this kind are now being made, so fatally do they attract both income-tax and estate duty, many must still survive. Moreover, so many of the most characteristic institutions of English real-property law are only intelligible as elements of a strict settlement that, in spite of its lack of practical importance at the present day, it deserves some attention even in an elementary book.

Its main purpose was to ensure that the land should be kept undivided in the hands of one person in each generation, but that minor interests should be secured to other members of the family, such as wives, widows, and younger children. How those minor interests were secured is a complicated story which lies outside the compass of an elementary introduction. The primary object of the settlement was effected as follows.

The land was given on marriage to the husband for life with remainder to his sons successively in tail, that is to say, the eldest son to be born was given an entailed interest in remainder, and a similar entailed interest was given to his next younger brother in the event of his dying without issue, and so on. Since an entailed interest is smaller in duration than a fee simple, the settlor, that is to say the person providing the land, has a reversion in the land, so that if the husband's line dies out, the land reverts to the settlor. This settlement had to be renewed every generation, for reasons which will appear later,[1] with the result that all living persons of full age in the direct line of succession held only life interests, in possession or in remainder, and the entailed interest was vested in an unborn person or in one who was still under age.

The trader's settlement

A much commoner settlement is that made by persons who do not want to found a family but wish to control the property in it for more than a single generation. Since it was not primarily concerned with land but rather with the money that a person had made in business, it was formerly known as a trader's settlement. On marriage the husband and wife each bring in property which is vested in trustees in trust to sell it and to hold the proceeds of the husband's trust fund to pay the income to him for life and of the wife's trust fund to pay the income to her for life. The survivor is given the income for life from both trust funds. The husband and wife are given a special power of appointment by virtue of which they can, acting together,

[1] p. 133 below.

distribute the trust funds according to their choice among the children of the marriage. If they do not exercise the power in conjunction, it can be exercised by the survivor. If it is not exercised at all, the trust funds are distributed equally among sons of the marriage who reach the age of twenty-one and daughters of the marriage who reach the age of twenty-one or marry under that age.

Tax avoidance

Many settlements are now made with the express purpose of reducing liability to income-tax and excluding liability to death-duties altogether. Hitherto the most successful types have involved a grant of the property to trustees, who must take no beneficial interest themselves in the settlement, with an absolute discretion to make payments of income or capital at such times as they may choose to such members of a broadly defined class, such as members or servants of a family, as they choose. As such beneficiaries have no right to such payments, no interest can pass to anyone else on their death, and so there is nothing to attract estate duty. Every precaution is taken to prevent the concentration of the beneficial interest that used to be assured to the head of the family by the strict settlement. For, with an income-tax bearing on incomes, not proportionately but so progressively as to be penal in its exactions, such concentration automatically ensures impoverishment of the family property. It is far better to arrange for as much as possible of the expense of upkeep, including payments to servants, to be borne by the trustees. Of course the beneficiaries have to pay for these privileges by committing themselves to the unfettered discretion of the trustees, who may, so far as the law is concerned, stop payments at any moment and for any or no reason.

The beneficial interests which demand more special attention as elements in settlements are life interests, entailed interests, and future interests.

2. LIFE INTERESTS

There is very little to be said about beneficial life interests; indeed most of what is usually said about life interests relates to management and not to the beneficial enjoyment of property. But it is perhaps worth while to contrast the life interest with the Roman usufruct, for thereby its essential nature is brought out.

The Romans thought of the usufruct as inseparably attached to the person enjoying it, so that, although he could, as it were, sublet the enjoyment of the property, he could not alienate his usufruct. Moreover, as if this personal connexion were not enough, a usufructuary was usually made to enter into a personal undertaking by contract towards the owner of the property to hand it over intact and in good condition.

In contrast to this the English life interest is inseparably connected, not with the person for whose life it is created, but with his life. Thus he is in no way prevented from alienating it, but it cannot last longer than his life. In the hands of the alienee it is not an interest for the alienee's life, but is known as an interest *pur autre vie*, that is, for the life of the alienor.

3. ENTAILED INTERESTS

Entailed interests are usually explained historically. This is on the whole rather unfortunate, for the emphasis on their history, which is usually given in a highly technical form, tends to thrust into the background the true economic and social reasons which made entailed interests of great practical utility until very recent times.

We must start from the point that an entailed interest was used only for the purpose of ensuring that large masses of property should be kept together in perpetuity, so far as the law would allow, in one direct line of descent or, failing such line, in the next nearest line or lines of descent. Thus a person would want most of his property to go for ever to his eldest son, and then to his son's eldest son, and so on in a direct line, but, if the direct line was in danger of dying out, then, for example, to the brother or nephew of the last childless person in the line and to the issue of that brother or nephew, and so on. That is the pattern that the creator of an entailed interest would have in mind; and the next question is, how the entailed interest would help to ensure its continued existence.

Now the nature of the entailed interest is determined by two different factors, first, its essential character and, secondly, what it can be turned into.

A restricted succession

Its essential character can best be grasped if it is compared to the fee simple. It is a question of intestate succession. If a person dies intestate any lands which he holds in fee simple will go to his issue or, if he has no issue, to his ascendants or, failing ascendants, to collaterals, such as brothers or sisters or nephews or nieces. If, on the other hand, he holds an entailed interest at the time of his death, that interest can only go to his issue, and only to the eldest male in each generation or, more exceptionally, to the females equally. It can never go to either ascendants or collaterals but, on failure of issue, will revert to the donor, i.e. the person creating the entailed interest.

Thus the original mark of an entailed interest is a restricted succession; and in fact the older name, fee tail, comes from the Latin *feodum talliatum*, that is to say, a cut down or truncated fee or feudal holding.

Barring the entail

Now for what can be done to it. Put quite shortly, the tenant in tail can, if he is of full age and in his right mind, bar the entail, wholly or partially, and so improve his position at the expense of those entitled to take after his death. Three cases must be distinguished.

(1) If the person entitled to the entailed interest has actual possession of the property, if, that is, he would formerly have been called the tenant in tail in possession, he can by executing a disentailing assurance, which may be a deed or a provision in a will, turn the entailed interest into an absolute interest, and so make himself or his devisee, that is, the person to whom he has bequeathed it, tenant in fee simple of such portions of the entailed interest as consist of land. (2) If, however, his entailed interest is in remainder, if, for instance, it will take effect in possession only on the death of some other person, probably his father, who holds the land as tenant for life, there will be a person known as the protector of the settlement, who will usually be the tenant for life but may be someone else. Now, if the holder of the entailed interest executes *inter vivos* a disentailing assurance with the concurrence of the protector of the settlement, he can turn the entailed interest into an absolute interest just as though he had been in possession himself. (3) If, on the other hand, he disentails without the concurrence of the protector he can create only what is called a base fee.

A base fee is technically described as a determinable fee simple; that is to say, it is a fee simple which will come to an end on the happening of a certain event, which in this case will be the failure of B's issue. If B dies without issue or if he leaves issue which eventually fails, the land subject to the base fee will pass either by way of remainder to any person entitled to an entailed interest in default of B's entailed interest, that is to say, to one of B's brothers or the issue of that brother, or, if there are no such persons, by way of reversion to the grantor. In other words, a base fee will last only as long as the entailed interest it supplants, but the person entitled to it has during that period the same full control over its subject-matter as if it were a fee simple or an absolute interest in personalty. Thus he can, though with difficulty, raise money on the security of a base fee.

Now, a base fee must always start as a remainder, since if the person executing the disentailing assurance has an entailed interest in possession he will inevitably turn it into a fee simple; and hence its value would in any case depend on the expectation of life of those entitled to any particular estates that precede it. This factor alone might reduce it to something very small. Moreover, although there are ways of enlarging a base fee into a fee simple absolute or an absolute interest in personalty, none of them can be accomplished without the permission of the protector of the settlement until, at the earliest, the time when the base fee ceases to be a remainder and falls into possession. Hence a strong speculative element must enter into the calculations of anyone buying or lending money on a base fee. The owner of the base fee may never live to enlarge it, and in that case it would cease if his issue failed. The purchaser or mortgagee would then get nothing, any more than if he had bought a life interest in remainder, whereas if he had bought a fee simple absolute or absolute interest in personalty in remainder, he would have had something to show for the price he had paid for it, even if it proved ruinous. It follows that base fees are not readily marketable, though moneylenders have been willing to speculate in them.

From what has been said, it must be obvious that if it is desired to ensure that the property be kept in the direct line, no entailed interest must ever be allowed to fall into possession, for then the tenant in tail could disentail and alienate the property. Nor should any entailed interest be even allowed to be for any length of time at the disposal of a remainderman who, being of full age and capacity, could turn it into a base fee; for although he might get very little for it, if he was in great difficulties owing to extravagance or misfortune, he might clutch at any straw. Hence steps must be taken to keep the entailed interest always in the hands of a remainderman who is not yet born or has not attained the full age of twenty-one years.

Resettlement

Accordingly the practice was to resettle the property every generation. When the tenant in tail in remainder reached the age of twenty-one, the first occasion on which he could perform a valid act, he was induced to disentail the property and immediately make a new settlement to deal with his entailed interest, giving himself only a life interest—which would of course fall into possession after his father's life interest—and successive entailed interests to his own children, born, or to be born. The entailed interest would then be safe for another generation.

Now suppose that the young man was disinclined to play his part. There were an inducement and a sanction. The inducement was a provision in the new settlement he was invited to execute giving him a settled income during his father's life independent of his father's control; the sanction was twofold, first, that his father could keep him on very short commons, and secondly, that he could raise money only on the base fee which was all he could create without his father's concurrence.

It remains to be said that the entailed interest, which has been abolished in most other common-law jurisdictions, is hardly used today even in England. The severity with which income-tax bears down on large incomes makes any attempt to keep property together in one pair of hands ruinous, and the general tendency is to divide income among large numbers of members of a family or their servants so that each portion attracts as little taxation as possible. But the learning of entails is something that every student is expected to know, and it affords an interesting insight into the functions that the doctrine of estates was expected to perform.

4. FUTURE INTERESTS

Some interests, as we have seen,[2] exist in possession, that is to say, the person who has the interest also has possession of the land. Others exist in expectancy, that is to say, the persons entitled to them must wait until some time in the future before they can enter into possession of the land. Since the coming into force of the Law of Property Act, 1925, which restricted legal estates in land to the fee simple absolute in possession and the term of years absolute, all interests in expectancy, with the exception of certain terms of years, necessarily take effect only as equitable interests.[3] It has been well said that that Act, as it were by a side wind, simplified the law relating to future interests enormously.

Formerly future interests were of many kinds, some operating at common law, others under the Statute of Uses and the Statute of Wills,[4] and others in equity, each governed by its own appropriate rules. Now that all operate in equity, they are subject to only a few rules of universal application. It is, however, still customary for the books to deal with the older law of future estates, which governed them when they could still exist as legal estates. The reason for so doing is partly historical and partly practical, and it is practical because conveyancers may still have to look at old title deeds containing future limitations of estates in order to trace title from a date before 1925. That reason will soon have little force because a vendor is bound to trace title only from a document not less than thirty years old; and thirty-two years have already passed since the Act came into force. But there is another good reason for including in this book a short discussion of the old law relating to future interests,

[2] See p. 68 above.
[3] See p. 83 above.
[4] See p. 137 below.

namely that it will be rendered more useful to students learning their law in jurisdictions where the Law of Property Act is not in force. For it is only in England and Wales that virtually all future interests have been forced behind the curtain of a trust.

No limitation after a fee simple

The only estates in expectancy which could exist at common law were reversions and remainders, and of the latter some were vested and the others contingent. All reversions were vested. Now all these estates were governed by what may be called a very elementary rule of mathematics according to which if a person created a fee simple, he had given away all that he had, and had exhausted his estate in the land. Therefore nothing could be made to follow after a fee simple. So literally was this rule applied that even if the fee simple was made subject to a condition subsequent, no estate could be limited to take effect after it. Thus if, for instance, a grant were made to A in fee simple, but if he marry a foreigner, then to B in fee simple, the grant to B would fail and the fee simple in A would be absolute.

Seisin

Other rules rested on feudal policy. Feudal doctrine required that there should always be some person seised of the land so as to be able to perform the services due to the lord. Accordingly in any limitation of real estate the seisin must be immediately given to someone, and hence a limitation to a person to take effect at some future date, as for instance to A when B dies, was invalid unless it was 'supported' by an immediate grant of the seisin to someone else. Thus a grant to A when B dies could take effect if B were given a life estate. A's remainder was then said to be supported by B's life estate.

Further, since only persons enjoying freehold estates could be seised, termors having not seisin but only possession,[5] the estate supporting the remainder had to be a freehold estate, that is to say, a life estate or an estate tail.

Moreover, there must never be a gap in the seisin, or, in the technical language of the law, the seisin must never be in abeyance. As soon as the tenant of land ceased to be tenant, by death or otherwise, some other person must be ready to take the land. If there was a mere grant of the fee simple, then the tenant would be automatically succeeded by his heir. If he had not the fee simple, then his so-called particular estate would be followed either by a reversion or by a remainder.[6] If it were followed by a reversion, the reversioner would be ready to take at once and there would be no abeyance of seisin. The same

[5] See pp. 70, 118–19.

[6] See p. 68 above.

would be true if the remainder were vested. But what if the remainder were contingent?[7]

If the remainder was still contingent when the particular estate came to an end, that would be because some necessary contingency had not come to pass. There would therefore inevitably be an abeyance of seisin, which could not be tolerated. Hence the contingent remainder failed. Certain kinds of contingent remainders could not fail naturally for this reason. For instance, if land was limited to A for life, with remainder to his eldest surviving son, the identity of the son would automatically be ascertained the moment A died, and so the remainder would vest simultaneously in interest and in possession. The result would be the same if the limitation were to A for life with remainder to such of his children as were alive at his death. But if the limitation had been to A with remainder to the first of his children to reach twenty-one, the remainder would fail if no child of his reached the age of twenty-one before or at the moment of his death.

Destructibility

Moreover, whether the remainder was or was not liable to fail naturally through an abeyance of seisin, it could always be destroyed artificially by some event which brought the particular estate to an end prematurely. Thus if the tenant for life forfeited his life estate or surrendered it to the person who was entitled to the next vested remainder, the contingent remainder dependent on it would be destroyed. Hence destructibility was an essential characteristic of contingent remainders. However, partly by the ingenuity of the old conveyancers and partly by direct legislation, this liability to destruction was removed, and then even the liability to failure by natural means.

The old rule against perpetuities

A final rule restricting the limitation of contingent remainders was that a remainder to the unborn child of a living person could not be followed by a remainder to the unborn child of that unborn child. This rule came to be known by the name of a late nineteenth-century case in which it was upheld, long after it had originally been formulated and held to apply, namely as the Rule in *Whitby* v. *Mitchell*, or the Old Rule against Perpetuities. The Courts had come to regard liability to be barred as attaching indelibly to estates tail,[8] and they set themselves against any attempts to evade it. Of the rules they elaborated only the rule in *Whitby* v. *Mitchell* need detain us here. Its purpose is quite clear: if land could be limited by successive contingent remainders to the persons who would naturally have been

[7] See pp. 68–69 above.

[8] See pp. 132–3 above.

entitled to an estate tail had it not been barred, the effect would have been to create an unbarrable estate tail.

These and other rules relating to future interests at common law created a strict legal grammar which, although it has been progressively relaxed, has given a permanent tone to the English law of Real Property. English property lawyers naturally think and act along lines of exact and even pedantic mathematical scholarship.

Springing and shifting uses

In the later Middle Ages a practice emerged of giving lands to one person to the use of another, in a way that resembled the modern practice of settling property on trust; indeed the medieval use was the remote ancestor of the modern trust. The Common Law Courts refused to enforce the use, leaving the person for whose benefit the use was declared without a remedy and the person to whom the lands were given, the so-called feoffee to uses, answerable only to his own conscience. However, the Chancellor came to enforce uses and to attach to them many of the characteristics of legal estates. It then became possible, by employing the use, to sidetrack many of the rigid grammatical rules just described. Thus, provided the seisin was immediately given to the feoffees to uses and continuity of seisin was assured in them and their successors, limitations of the use itself were not embarrassed by rules connected with seisin. Thus the use could be made to spring into existence at a future date, and it could be allowed to lapse and spring up again in accordance with arrangements which, had there been no use, would have involved a gap in the seisin. Finally, the use could be made to shift from one person to another upon the occurrence of a prescribed event or the fulfilment of a condition or even after a term of years.

The Statute of Uses and the Statute of Wills

All these limitations by way of use operated, as we should now say, in equity and amounted to manipulations of the equitable interest. The Statute of Uses, which was passed in 1535, executed the use and so conferred legal estates, with their attendant seisin, on all the persons entitled to the use. Thus a grant to X and his heirs to the use of A and his heirs at twenty-one would now give to A a legal estate when he reached twenty-one, and a grant to Y and his heirs to the use of B and his heirs, but when C reaches twenty-one then to C and his heirs, would give to B a legal fee simple which would shift to C when he reached twenty-one. In other words, springing and shifting uses now conferred legal estates. By the Statute of Wills, passed in 1540, the same protection was extended to devises, that is to say, gifts in wills. Thus a mere devise to A and his heirs at twenty-one would give

A a legal estate at twenty-one. Such devises were called executory devises and they and springing and shifting uses were grouped together as executory interests.

Indestructibility

Thus legal estates limited by way of use became indestructible and the possibility of perpetuities reappeared. Some check was imposed by the so-called rule in *Purefoy* v. *Rogers*, which provided that where, but for the fact that it was created by way of use, a limitation would be a contingent remainder, it must be treated as such and therefore destructible. But in the end the best solution was found in the Modern Rule against Perpetuities, which ultimately came to govern all limitations of future interests. For when the trust appeared in its modern form, it provided the same freedom that uses had possessed before the Statute of Uses.

Now that in England and Wales all future freehold interests exist only as equitable interests, all the rules governing legal contingent remainders have died a natural death. Moreover, the Statute of Uses has been repealed and the rule in *Whitby* v. *Mitchell* abolished. Thus only the Modern Rule against Perpetuities remains to govern the creation of future interests.

5. PERPETUITIES

There is no limit to the kinds of interests that can be created in funds. In other words, the enjoyment of the income from a fund may be made to pass from one person to another upon the happening of any kind of event whatever or upon the fulfilment of any kind of condition which is not illegal or immoral or contrary to public policy. Moreover, there is no need for the right to income to pass immediately from one person to another; there may be a gap.

Nevertheless, although no limits are placed on the types of interests which may be created nor on the kinds of events or conditions upon which they may be made to depend, they are subject to restrictions in respect of time. Those restrictions were first formulated to deal with settlements of land as such and not with settlements of capital funds, and they were undoubtedly intended to prevent land from being kept out of the market for too long periods.

The Modern Rule against Perpetuities

Only one such rule survives at the present day, the so-called Modern Rule against Perpetuities. It is a rule designed to prevent interests from coming into existence at too remote a time. It may be stated as follows: 'Every limitation of a future interest to arise on a contingency is void, unless the contingency is such that it must happen, if it happen at all, within the period of a life or lives in being and twenty-one years after.' The rule is not self-explanatory.

Vested and contingent interests

The first point to make is that it applies only to contingent and not to vested interests. The difference between them has already been explained.[9] The reader may be reminded that for an interest to be vested it need not be *vested in possession*, that is to say, the person entitled to it need not have a right to the immediate possession of land or to draw an income immediately from a fund. All that is needed is that the nature and *quantum* of the interest and the identity of the person entitled to it should be known. It is then *vested in interest*. If, on the other hand, the identity of the person entitled or the *quantum* of his interest, or both, are not yet known, and will be known only on the happening of a contingency, the interest is contingent. Thus if the beneficial interest in a fund is given to A for life, remainder to B, B's interest is at once vested, whereas if it were given to A for life, remainder to B when he reaches the age of twenty-five, B's interest would be contingent, and would wait to be vested until he reached twenty-five.

Now the Rule against Perpetuities does not deal at all with vested interests. In other words, it does not deal at all with interests which are certain to be enjoyed, but only with the vesting of interests which are at present contingent and so, in a sense, inchoate. And the event which must, under the Rule, happen within the perpetuity period, is the event which turns the contingent into a vested interest. Thus, in the example just given, the event which is to take place within that period is B's reaching the age of twenty-five.

The 'lives in being' mentioned in the statement of the Rule must be persons who are alive at the time when the instrument takes effect, that is to say, in the case of a gift *inter vivos* at the time when the instrument is executed, and in the case of a gift by will at the death of the testator. The persons may be expressly specified, though if need be in general terms; for instance, it is quite usual to make the perpetuity period last until the death of the last survivor of all the descendants of King George V living at the death of the testator;[10] for, so long as they are specified in the instrument, they need not be

[9] See pp. 68–69 above.

[10] Such a 'royal lives clause' is regularly used so as to create an artificial perpetuity period which shall not depend on the lives of any persons included in the settlement. The royal lives are so chosen as to warrant the expectation that the period will last for about eighty years, and indeed the Law Reform Committee recently suggested that the law should be altered so as to make possible the express creation by a settlement of a perpetuity period of eighty years, in order to make it unnecessary to have recourse to a 'royal lives clause'.

given any interest by it. If, on the other hand, no lives are expressly specified, then in most cases they are taken to be either the beneficiaries or their ancestors. Thus, for example, if the gift is to the first son of A to land on the moon, A is the life in being, whereas if it is to A's son B when he lands on the moon, B is the life in being; the first gift is void because the event may take place more than twenty-one years after the dropping of the life in being, namely the death of A, whereas the second is valid because if the event takes place at all it must take place within the lifetime of B, who is the life in being.

Class gifts

The operation of the rule is beset by many complexities which make the subject of Perpetuities one of the most difficult in English law. Only one of them may be noticed here. Sometimes an interest may be given to all the persons belonging to a particular class in existence on the happening of a particular contingency. Such gifts are called class gifts. For instance, the trust property may be given to A for life, with remainder in equal shares to such of his grandchildren as reach the age of twenty-one years; or it may be given to A for life, remainder to any wife whom he may marry if she survives him, remainder in equal shares to such of his descendants as survive both A and his wife. In both cases the class of persons entitled to take will be determined only on the happening of a contingency, in the first case the attainment of majority by the last of A's grandchildren to do so, in the second the death of A, or of A's wife if she survives him. Here the uncertainty is less as to the existence or identity of the persons entitled to take than of the size of each one's share; but in as much as that size must be determined within the perpetuity period and it depends on the number of persons in the class, it must be certain from the start that the class will be complete within the perpetuity period. In both the examples given above the remainders to the grandchildren and the descendants will fail, because the only life in being is A (there being no certainty that his future wife is yet in existence) and the contingency may be fulfilled more than twenty-one years after A's death.

Not allowed to 'wait and see'

It must be emphasized that one is not allowed to 'wait and see' whether the vesting takes place within the perpetuity period. One must be able to predict when the instrument creating the interest takes effect whether the vesting will so take place. Therefore if there is the remotest possibility of its taking place outside the period, the gift will be void, and the interest will not vest even though, as events have turned out, it would have actually vested within the perpetuity period. Some of the possibilities envisaged, such as that a woman of ninety might have a child, are so absurd, and the reason for taking possibilities rather than actualities into account is so obscure and uncertain, that serious proposals have been made for introducing the contrary principle of 'wait and see', as indeed has been done in Massachusetts and some other states of the United States.

Reforms

Quite recently the Law Reform Committee has reported in favour of far-reaching reforms. Whether they will commend themselves to the Legislature remains to be seen. Meanwhile, however, one beneficial relaxation has been made by the Law of Property Act.

Quite often gifts are made to persons at some such age as twenty-five, under the impression that they are too young at twenty-one to take proper care of their property; and sometimes such gifts failed because the perpetuity period was exceeded. The Law of Property Act provided that where such gifts can be saved by substituting the age of twenty-one for any other age specified in the gift, the substitution shall be made.

Charities

The Rule is often said not to apply to charities, but this statement must be taken subject to qualifications.

The law permits certain forms of charity which it regards as beneficial to the community to be the objects of permanent endowment.

Unfortunately there is no simple way of deciding whether a purpose is charitable or not. But a starting-point can be found in the judgment of Lord Macnaghten in a case in 1891, where he lists charitable trusts under the following four heads: (1) Trusts for the relief of poverty; (2) Trusts for the advancement of religion; (3) Trusts for the advancement of education; and (4) Trusts for other purposes beneficial to the community not falling under any of the preceding heads. The Courts have had to decide in individual cases whether a purpose is charitable or not, and the natural tendency to favour good works has been counteracted by a disinclination to take property out of commerce and, above all, to confer on it the exemption from income-tax accorded to all charities. The resulting case-law is not completely intelligible.

A gift to charity is subject to the Rule against Perpetuities in the sense that it must vest in the charity within the perpetuity period. On the other hand, a gift over from one charity to another may be valid even if it may occur at a more remote time in the future. It is said that all charities are regarded as one single object and the change merely a matter of internal arrangement. But that is obviously only a way of restating the rule. Probably the true explanation is that the law regards a gift to charity as taking property permanently out of commerce, but has to admit that its particular object may become obsolete. In that case a Court may at some remote time in the future have to devote the property, as it is said, *cy-près*, to some similar object; but if that is the case, there is no good reason why the original benefactor should not specify the event which will make the object, in his eyes, obsolete and also provide for the substitution of another object. But this reasoning, for what it is worth, opens the door to abuse.[11]

The Rule against Inalienability

The treatment that the law accords to charities emphasizes the fact that the Rule against Perpetuities is not a rule against inalienability; it only strikes at remote vesting of interests. Nevertheless, the close control that is exerted over the purposes for which property can be given to charity would be absurd unless the law disapproved in general of arrangements whereby a settlor can take property out of commerce; and the disapproval is announced expressly where property is given in trust for a non-charitable purpose such as keeping a gravestone in repair. Such trusts would in any case be precarious both because they are not exempt from income-tax and because there is no one to enforce them, whereas charitable trusts can be enforced at the instance of the Attorney General and trusts for the benefit of persons at the instance of those persons. However, they are not in principle invalid. The trustees can hold the property and apply it to the trust purposes.

The danger is that they will do so and thereby keep property out of commerce for purposes which the law does not positively favour, though it does not treat them as illegal. The Rule against Perpetuities can do nothing to stop this, for if the legal interest in the property is vested in the trustees within the perpetuity period, the Rule is obeyed. Hence a rule has been devised, by analogy with the Rule against Perpetuities, that it must be possible to spend the capital or wind up the trust within the perpetuity period, or the gift is void. However, the perpetual fulfilment of a non-charitable purpose may be assured by giving property to a charity so long as the non-charitable purpose is fulfilled, with a gift over to another charity on non-fulfilment. Thus, in the leading case, a testator bequeathed a large sum of money to the London Missionary Society with a request that they should keep his family vault in repair and with a direction that if they failed to comply with the request the money should go to the Blue Coat School. But care must be taken not to impose a duty to fulfil the non-

[11] The temptation has not been resisted. See below.

charitable purpose. It is also obvious that it must be made worth the while of the charity to fulfil the condition; hence the non-charitable purpose can hardly be other than subsidiary to the charitable purpose.

Corporations

The same tendency to take property out of commerce would seem to exist whenever property is given to a corporation, for such a corporation is not subject to the natural incident of death, though it may be dissolved. In truth, the accumulation of landed property in the hands of ecclesiastical corporations has at various times in the past taken too much property out of commerce. As long ago as 1279 a Statute of Mortmain was passed to prohibit the giving of land to corporations without a licence from the Crown. The policy has been maintained, though with exceptions which show its true purpose in the modern world. Thus municipal corporations do not need a licence, for they are in any case only able to acquire land for municipal purposes authorized by statute. The acquisition of land by ordinary commercial companies incorporated under the Companies Acts does not take it out of commerce and so, being without danger to the public, does not require a licence. All corporations have always been free to acquire chattels without authorization.

Rationale of the modern rule

Let us now return to the Rule against Perpetuities in its most normal application, namely to gifts to individuals, and try to ascertain as precisely as possible its present *raison d'être*. Two points must be made by way of preparation.

First, although the Rule does not avowedly strike at inalienability but only at the remote vesting of interests, it has very much that effect. For as soon as a beneficial interest vests in an ascertained individual, which must be within the perpetuity period, it becomes alienable. Moreover, once all the beneficial interests are in the hands of living persons of full age and capacity, those beneficiaries can call on the trustees to wind up the trust and distribute the assets.[12]

Secondly, the original purpose of the Rule has disappeared. Having been devised for the purpose of preventing land from being kept too long out of the market, it was subsequently applied to all other property interests without, in all probability, very much thought being given to the changed environment in which it would work. Since the passing of the Settled Land Act, 1882, much more efficient means

[12] It is, of course, true that an infant may have to wait until he is of age before he can spend freely, but this only extends the period by twenty-one years at most. If a beneficial interest falls into the hands of a lunatic, it may remain tied up for a long time; this is an unavoidable exception which does not cast doubt on the general proposition in the text.

have existed of keeping land alienable;[13] and indeed there is no longer any question of how long land can be tied up for, since in almost every case any specific component part of a fund, whether it be land or a chattel, can at any moment be alienated by a tenant for life or by trustees or by both in conjunction with each other.

It would seem, therefore, at first sight that the Rule against Perpetuities can no longer have any relation to the market, in so far as it is concerned with specific physical objects or investments. It relates only to contingent rights to receive income from a fund. Accordingly, some writers regard the Rule as effecting a compromise between the interests of the living and of the dead. If we had no such rule, a person might on his death be able to settle for all time to come, subject to the vicissitudes of the market for securities, the interests which the persons included in his settlement are to take. If, on the other hand, he were allowed to give interests only to persons alive at the time of his death, that might appear to be too great a restriction on his power to deal with his own. There is no particular virtue in the Rule as it stands. Other countries have different rules which are not obviously worse. But from a comparison of those rules with our own there does seem to be a consensus of opinion that, in some cases at any rate, a person should be able to give his property to persons not yet in existence at the time of his death, but that that power should be strictly limited, so as to avoid anything in the nature of a Perpetuity and so as to return to the hands of the living within a reasonable time full control not merely of the specific physical objects contained in his estate but also of the rights to receive and dispose of income that is to accrue from time to time.

Other writers prefer a different but not incompatible explanation. They say that the Rule has still some application even to the specific objects or investments comprised in a settlement. Granted that nothing can now make them inalienable, yet alienation may be rendered difficult by making certain consents necessary and by allowing a court to prohibit alienations disadvantageous to persons beneficially interested in a settlement; and, in general, trustees have not, unless their powers are expressly enlarged, the same freedom to deal with trust property as if it were their own.[14] The purpose of the Rule is to curb trusts. Trust property is proverbially excluded from the class of risk capital. It is the prime duty of trustees to preserve the capital of the trust fund by cautious investment and not to speculate. But since progress in the modern world demands bold speculation, it is a matter of public concern to preserve a proper balance between trust capital and risk capital. The dangers attendant on an excessive accumulation of trust capital have often been felt, especially in relation

[13] See p. 149 below.

[14] See p. 111 above.

to charities, though when steps have been taken to restore trust capital to commerce, as at the Dissolution of the Monasteries, it has not always been with a single-minded intention to redress the balance in the public interest. Fortunately there is a tendency for the balance to redress itself through inflationary finance, and the Welfare State makes charitable trusts both less necessary and less easy to establish. Moreover, some of the most enlightened American benefactors have long provided for the progressive spending of capital so as to ensure the winding up of charitable trusts within a reasonable period. *A fortiori* individuals should not be unduly protected against themselves. They should have ample scope to take risks and, if necessary, go bankrupt. The economic progress of a nation is often measured by the number of its bankruptcies. Trusts exist to prevent bankruptcies. Hence they should be curbed.

A third explanation, again not incompatible with either of the former, is that, even if a settlor should be allowed to provide for the future devolution of his property, opportunities for stocktaking should be afforded from time to time. What seemed provident a generation or two ago may not be provident now. Hence, even if it is desired to keep property in settlement, one settlement should come to an end and another one begin. The need for resettlement every generation[15] was the salvation of the old strict settlement, for it allowed losses to be cut and improvements to be made. The Rule against Perpetuities helped to insure that such resettlements should be necessary.

However, the present Rule is not very satisfactory, whatever theory of its purpose is adopted. The perpetuity period can easily extend to a hundred years, which is too long for the modern world. On the other hand, the Rule can work so capriciously as to defeat the reasonable intentions of settlors. It does not curb the expert conveyancer enough, and it is a trap for the layman making his own will. It is not certain that we should lose anything if it were abolished.

6. ACCUMULATIONS

For the same or similar reasons the law restrains the indefinite accumulation of income from a fund. At common law there was no limit, provided the Rule against Perpetuities was not infringed, to the time within which income could be accumulated, and that is still the law in Ireland. However, in consequence of a fantastic will that directed accumulations for a period which turned out to amount to three-quarters of a century, and was designed to increase the capital

[15] See pp. 133–4 above.

of the estate to several millions of pounds, the legislature intervened to enact a so-called Rule against Accumulations.

The rule lays down four different periods, among which a settlor may choose only one and which need not be specified here, during which income may be ordered to be accumulated. However, a direction for excessive accumulation is void not absolutely but only as to the excess. Certain accumulations, for example for the payment of debts, are exempted from the Rule. On the other hand, if a person absolutely entitled to the income becomes of full age, he may insist on any direction to accumulate being disregarded.

7. THE FORM OF SETTLEMENTS

Although one must always expect to find physical objects playing a double role, as marketable objects in the hands of holders of the legal estate or legal ownership, and as component parts of a trust fund, the income of which is divided among several persons in succession, the two roles are kept strictly apart. For if they were allowed to get in each other's way, either the existence of the trust might make the task of proving title to the physical object more complicated and the sale of it more difficult, or the protection of those interested in the trust fund might be rendered less secure. For this reason steps are always taken, when it is disclosed in documents relating to the legal estate that its holders are trustees, to prevent any disclosure in them of the terms of the trust. This is called keeping trusts off the title. Any purchaser of the legal estate is, of course, entitled to see documents dealing with the legal estate, for otherwise he would be unable to investigate the title he is about to acquire. But he is not entitled to look behind the 'curtain' to see the trust instrument, as the document is called which sets out the terms of the trust. There is indeed no need for him to see it, for, provided the trustees have a power of sale, as they will always have over land,[16] he will not be bound by any of the trusts contained in the trust instrument. If, of course, he is buying, not the land, but an equitable interest conferred on a beneficiary by the trust instrument, then he will need and will be entitled to inspect the trust instrument.

Strict settlements and trusts for sale

So far we have spoken simply of trustees and beneficiaries and have conveyed the impression that all settlements, that is to say, arrangements whereby limited interests in property are created, are of one type. This is not true as a matter of theory, though in practice it is becoming very nearly true. The commonest way of settling

[16] Apart from the one exceptional case mentioned at p. 79 n. 14 above.

property is now to give the legal estate in land and the full ownership of personalty to trustees for sale, who are bound to sell the property vested in them (though they may postpone the sale at their discretion) and to hold the proceeds upon the trusts specified in the trust instrument. But there is another method, which is an adaptation of the aristocratic strict settlement of lands which was gradually developed during the seventeenth, eighteenth, and nineteenth centuries as a means of keeping together great landed estates. In a strict settlement the person in actual possession of the land, who in popular speech was known as the landowner, had only a life estate. As the powers inherent in the life estate were insufficient to allow him to manage the land properly in the interests of himself and his successors, he was in the second half of the nineteenth century given statutory powers to deal with the fee simple, by selling or mortgaging it or by granting leases to endure beyond his own lifetime. In 1925 his powers were further enlarged, but the opportunity was also taken to alter the basis of his powers. Instead of holding a legal estate only for life, he is now given the legal fee simple, which he holds in trust for himself for life and thereafter for the other persons interested in the settlement. The change has made little difference to the actual content of his powers but it made possible a new way of handling the title to the property similar to that employed in the trust for sale. Two documents are now used, the vesting deed and the trust instrument, the former of which vests the legal fee simple in the tenant for life and contains other terms which would interest a possible purchaser, and the latter sets out the terms of the trust. Thus in the vesting deed the tenant for life appears as owner of the legal fee simple *upon trust*, whereas in the trust instrument he also appears as the owner of an equitable life interest.

The two techniques, of the strict settlement and the trust for sale respectively, are kept carefully apart by the law, and the difference between them must always be borne in mind by would-be purchasers of the legal estate, since in the strict settlement it is the tenant for life who must be made to convey the legal estate, though the purchase money must be paid to the trustees, whereas in the trust for sale it is the trustees who both convey the legal estate and receive the purchase money. However, both are varieties of the same general way of keeping apart the physical object and the rights, sometimes fragmentary, to the income produced by it.

8. THE MANAGEMENT OF SETTLED PROPERTY

It is of the essence of a settlement that it should govern the property subject to it for a period of time. During that period not only may one beneficial interest succeed another, but the property has to be managed. Since the reconciliation between the management and the enjoyment of the beneficial interest is the very purpose of the trust,[17] it might have been expected that all that would need to be done would be to vest the property in trustees with extensive powers of management upon trust to allow the use of it and, where necessary, to pay the income to the successive beneficiaries. In actual fact things did not work out that way.

Until 1925 in a strict settlement the successive beneficiaries in the direct line were given legal estates in the land, trusts being used only subsidiarily for special purposes. For a long time problems of management had to be solved in the difficult and complicated environment so created.

The tenant for life

The law of estate management has been worked out mainly in relation to life interests. This is because under the strict settlement the person who was in possession of a great landed estate and was considered by the outside world as 'landowner' was, in spite of the dukedom or other title he enjoyed, merely a tenant for life. On the other hand, there was no one else with any power whatever to manage the land. All other persons with beneficial interests in the land had for the moment only rights to future income, whereas any trustees there might be were concerned only to see that subordinate members of the family were secured in their minor interests. Thus the tenant for life was the only manager, and his powers as such were strictly limited. On the other hand, if powers of management were to be enlarged, the additional powers would most naturally be given to him.

Waste caused no difficulty, for the tenant for life could be, and usually was, made unimpeachable for waste and so could be restrained only from committing equitable waste.[18] The real difficulty lay in the duration of the life estate itself. Any lease or mortgage must necessarily come to an end with the death of the tenant for life unless his successor chose to renew it, and accordingly it was difficult, sometimes impossible, for such leases or mortgages to be created. That was not necessarily objectionable as far as agricultural land was concerned, for a common tenancy was from year to year; it made the granting of mining leases and the development of urban property by long building leases almost impossible. The difficulty of raising money on mortgage put great obstacles in the way of improvements.

Things were not always, or perhaps often, as bad as that. Not all of a landowner's property was necessarily settled land. He might,

[17] See pp. 77–79 above.

[18] See p. 112 above.

like the Dukes of Bedford, be deeply interested in commerce, as a stockholder in the East India Company, or he might have considerable holdings in the funds, i.e. government stock, which had been a very sound investment ever since the great financial reforms of the Glorious Revolution, or he might, like others after him, marry a rich city heiress with ready money. Even if the personalty so brought in was settled, there would be trustees, who might easily be given extensive powers. However, such expedients might not cover the whole ground.

Express powers

In Scotland, where entails had been deliberately made unbarrable, relief could be obtained only by Act of Parliament. In England the need for legislative reform was staved off for a long time by the beneficent need to renew the settlement every generation.[19] When the tenant in tail in remainder by barring it converted it into a fee simple, the opportunity could be taken of selling or mortgaging some of the land or of granting long mining or building leases which would bind succeeding holders of the land.

A more effectual remedy was on such occasions to confer on the tenant for life for the time being powers to deal with the land for certain purposes as though he had the fee simple, but to safeguard the interests of remaindermen and others provided for in the settlement by insisting on the co-operation for certain purposes of the trustees of the settlement.

Statutory powers

These powers became the model for reforms by Act of Parliament, at first requiring for the exercise of powers the approval of a court, but eventually making such approval unnecessary and the exercise of the powers possible even despite an attempt to exclude them by the express terms of the settlement. The most striking effect of this legislation, which was to reduce the estates of all except the tenant for life to the status of interests in a trust fund, has already been described. Those concerned with management demand closer attention here.

The most important power is to lease the settled land for periods varying with the type of lease. The maximum periods are 999 years for building or forestry, 100 years for mining, and 50 years for any other purpose. Leases must comply with conditions intended to protect the persons entitled under the settlement after the tenant for life, and normally the tenant for life must give notice to the trustees before granting a lease to enable them to see that the conditions are complied with and apply to the Court for an injunction to restrain any

[19] See pp. 133–4 above.

abuse. The tenant for life is generally entitled to the whole of the rent; but since the working of minerals diminishes the value of land, rents from mining leases must be apportioned between income and capital. The tenant for life is entitled to three-quarters of the rent unless he is impeachable for waste[20] and the mine is an unopened one; in that case he is entitled to only one-quarter of the rent. In each case the residue must be invested as capital.

The most important of the other powers are those of effecting improvements and of mortgaging or charging the settled property for the purpose of paying for improvements or discharging encumbrances or providing money which is required to be raised under the provisions of the settlement.

These statutory powers of management given to the tenant for life are not confined to the old aristocratic family settlement, which is rarely encountered at the present day; for they are also conferred on tenants for life under much simpler settlements and on other persons who have limited interests in possession. Moreover, whenever the trust for sale is used instead of the strict settlement, the trustees for sale are given the powers of a tenant for life. Indeed, so far have the powers come to be adopted as a standard for management that they are given to the trustees of charities and, with slight variations, to the Crown Estate Commissioners and to the governing bodies of universities and colleges, all of whom are faced with the same problem of preserving capital by using it for improvements or for purposes not immediately remunerative but beneficial to the neighbourhood. They play the part in modern law that was formerly played by the doctrine of waste.

Trusts for sale

Since trustees for sale are directed to sell the land and hold the proceeds upon the trusts of the settlement, it might be thought that they would, if it were possible, be even less restricted than the tenant for life under a strict settlement in the exercise of their powers of selling, leasing, and mortgaging the land, the more so as they are expressly given by statute all the powers both of a tenant for life of settled land and of Settled Land Act trustees. This is, however, not the case, for not only are they given a power to postpone the sale, but the exercise of their powers can be made subject to the consent of specified persons. Where more than two persons are specified, a bona fide purchaser for value of the trust property is protected if the consent of two of them is obtained. Thus, by using a trust for sale, land may be made alienable only with the co-operation of the trustees, the tenant for life, and the persons next entitled to the beneficial interest,

[20] See p. 112 above.

whereas, if the land is made subject to a strict settlement, the tenant for life can act alone, except that he needs the consent of the trustees for a sale of the principal mansion house.

For this and other reasons, largely technical, the trust for sale is now generally preferred to the strict settlement. But the marriage of land and chattel investments is not altogether happy. Formerly the typical trustee was a member or close friend of the family, who was willing to perform a thankless and perhaps dangerous task for nothing. He was far enough away from enjoying the property to take a cool and impartial view of its problems but near enough to understand it and the family and take a personal interest in them. However, for various reasons, such trustees of the old school have largely been supplanted by trust corporations such as the Public Trustee or subsidiaries of the great banks, which charge for their services but provide financial security in the highest degree. Since they are expert in the art of financial management, they fulfil admirably the functions of trustees in so far as the trust comprises stocks and shares or similar chattel investments; for where the only questions relate to money, the quality of detachment outweighs all others.

Such investments are, however, already at least one stage removed from the physical objects which are the ultimate sources of wealth and from the human beings who have them in their care and keeping. Not only is the trust fund an abstraction, but the investments of which it is composed are abstractions also. On the other hand, the management of land and houses brings the managers into immediate contact both with soil and bricks and mortar and with flesh and blood. Moreover, to a great extent the occupier himself must be the manager.

The management of houses and flats has indeed largely fallen into the hands of large companies, which are impersonal enough; but the management of agricultural estates is still mainly personal, by owner-occupiers or by landlords with or without the assistance of professional land agents.

Thus, even where land is settled by way of trust for sale, it is advisable to leave the management of it to the tenant for life. Hence the trustees for sale may, if they think fit, delegate revocably to the tenant for life all powers of management, including that of letting it on leases or periodical tenancies, but not of selling or mortgaging the fee simple.

Changed conditions

Little attention has been paid here to the details of the tenant for life's statutory powers for two reasons. In the first place, they are inappropriate to an introductory survey, since they cannot be properly understood without some knowledge of estate management.

Secondly, they are already largely out of date. They were indeed appropriate only to an economy where the value of money was relatively stable. No wise settlor now wants to prescribe the physical form property subject to a settlement should take, nor does he want to limit a trustee's power of investment to gilt-edged securities. The only way to preserve property nowadays is to invest in equities, that is to say, securities which are likely to adjust themselves to changes in the value of money; and this inevitably means to indulge in discreet and informed speculation. The landowner has learnt this truth the hard way as effectually as the business man. Accordingly, the only way to discover what may now be considered to be the general law of settled property is to examine the best standard forms of settlements, which are more likely to be found in the most up-to-date books on Tax Planning than in the older books on conveyancing.[21]

[21] For a summary description of a typical modern settlement see p. 130 above.

XIII

SECURITY

1. GENERAL

THE point of exacting security from a debtor is to avoid having to prove as an ordinary creditor in his bankruptcy. What does that mean?

If you could be certain, when lending money or selling goods to a person, that he would be solvent when the time for payment came, you would probably not think of taking security from him, except perhaps to be able to put pressure on him if, though able, he was unwilling to pay. To a great extent people do lend money or sell goods without security because they are prepared to trust the borrower or buyer. Nevertheless, the taking of security is a normal part of business.

Personal and real security

Security falls into two broad groups, personal and real security. In the former the creditor insists on having the debt guaranteed by another person; that is to say, he insists on the debtor providing him with another person who agrees to pay if the debtor does not. There may be more than one guarantor, and in the ordinary case the creditor may sue for the whole debt the person who in his opinion is most able to pay. It is also possible for one person merely to indemnify another against the consequences of his giving credit to a third person, with the effect that he too becomes a principal debtor. All these forms of personal security belong to the law of contract and fall entirely outside the field of the law of property. Real security, on the other hand, is certainly a topic of property law.

The purpose of real security is to give a secured creditor something out of which he is entitled to have his debt paid in preference to the unsecured creditors. A segment of the debtor's property, which may be a piece of land, a particular movable chattel, or a number of investments, is set apart as something over which the secured creditor can exercise certain powers enabling him to ensure payment of his debt before any of the unsecured creditors. But lawyers have always been in the habit of saying that the secured creditor has a real interest in the property which is the subject-matter of the security.

Real security can be divided into three classes, namely, possessory security, proprietary security, and charges and non-possessory liens.

2. POSSESSORY SECURITY

Possessory security exists only in respect of tangible personal property, in other words, in respect of movables in the strict sense of the term. It has two main varieties, pledge or pawn, and possessory liens. A possessory lien is the right to retain the possession of the property of another person until a debt owned by that person is paid. In other words, a possessory lien arises only in cases where the thing is already in the possession of the creditor. It may be particular, giving the creditor the right to retain the thing until paid for his work on it, for instance when he has repaired it; or it may be general, giving the creditor the right to retain possession of the thing until the general balance of his account against his debtor is paid, the best-known instance being perhaps that of a solicitor over his client's papers. A lien does not give the person claiming it a right to sell the goods unless that right is expressly given to him by contract or statute.

A pawn or pledge is created, on the other hand, by an actual transfer of the possession by debtor to creditor. It is the only practical way of securing a debt on many kinds of movable objects. For if the whereabouts of a movable object cannot easily be traced from time to time, the only way in which a creditor can take it in security for a debt is to keep it himself under lock and key. It might theoretically be possible for him to acquire a proprietary interest in the thing while leaving the possession with the debtor, but if the latter chose to sell it it would in practice be almost impossible for the creditor to resume control. Pawn or pledge is a form of bailment, but the pawnee has a right to sell the thing if the debt itself is not paid at the proper time. Pawnbrokers, that is to say, persons who carry on the business of taking goods and chattels in pawn, are governed by a special statute, which requires them to be licensed and to observe certain rules in the conduct of their business.

3. PROPRIETARY SECURITY

Although pledge affords excellent security to the creditor, it is awkward for the debtor, for, since he loses possession of the object, he cannot use it. Accordingly, it is not a good way of raising security on anything which, like the plant of a business, should continue to be used if the debtor is to make enough money to pay off the debt. What is wanted in such a case is some arrangement whereby the debtor is left in possession and therefore free to use the object, while the creditor has the right to take possession if the debt is not paid at the proper time, and to sell the object or perhaps even to retain it as owner, free from any rights which the debtor may have in it.

It is easy for us now to think of these various powers as constituting in combination a separate institution which needs no justification for its existence except that it furnishes an excellent form of security. But it was originally difficult to see—it is perhaps still difficult for some old-fashioned lawyers to see—how one person could confer these powers on another person unless he vested in him either the full ownership of the thing in question or some more limited right in the nature of property. And so this form of security is called proprietary security.

Since the creditor has an actual title to the thing, he can safely allow the debtor to retain possession of it; though, for this kind of security to operate perfectly, both the thing must be readily traceable and the right acquired by the creditor must be good against third parties as well as against the debtor himself.

Bills of sale

Proprietary security can have for its object both movables and immovables. A person may desire to raise money upon the security of his furniture or all the contents of his house. In that case he may execute a bill of sale transferring the ownership of the goods to the lender. A bill of sale may, indeed, have for its object the out-and-out alienation of goods, and it is in fact so used in order to alienate ships; but its more usual purpose, with ordinary goods, is to afford security to a lender of money.

It is obvious that security of this kind could work serious injustice to the other creditors, who may well have trusted the debtor on the strength of his apparent ownership of the goods in his possession. Accordingly, the Bills of Sale Acts, 1878 and 1882, were passed in order to ensure the publicity of such transactions by requiring them to be recorded in a register. If they are not so registered within twenty-one days, they are void as against a trustee in bankruptcy, and indeed against any person executing judgment against the debtor.

As soon as they are registered they are noted by trade-protection agencies whose function it is to notify such things to their clients; and a registered bill of sale is likely to be the end of the debtor's chances of raising money.

Mortgages

Formerly mortgages of land were effected by a similar alienation of the whole of the interest that the debtor had in the land, subject to a proviso for reconveyance if the debt was repaid within six months; but although at common law the creditor could, after the expiry of the six months, treat the land as his absolutely, equity prolonged indefinitely the debtor's right to redeem the land. This right of redemption, both during the period when it existed at law by virtue of the proviso for reconveyance and afterwards when it rested on equity, came to be regarded as an equitable estate in the land and was known as the *equity of redemption.* It has survived intact the changes introduced by the 1925 legislation in the methods of creating mortgages. For practical purposes the debtor, or, as he is called, the mortgagor, was and is regarded as still owning the land, and the creditor, or mortgagee, as having a mere security. On the other hand, a lessee mortgaged his lease by granting a sublease. This again was treated as a mere security, and the mortgagee did not normally enter into possession of the land under his sublease. Here also the mortgagor acquired an equity of redemption in the lease.

The 1925 legislation abolished the method of mortgaging the freehold by conveying the fee simple and replaced it by two other methods. In the first place it applied to the freehold the method already used for leaseholds, and enacted that mortgages should henceforth take the form of a term of years, which in practice is usually for 3,000 years. A second device provided by the legislation is a charge by way of legal mortgage.

If the former mode is adopted, the mortgagor gives a lease of this enormously long duration to the mortgagee, who thus acquires an estate in the land which virtually swallows up the fee simple. Indeed, the mortgage term is really a legal fiction and it would have saved much confusion and difficulty of understanding if the only method allowed had been the charge by way of legal mortgage. This is in fact now far more commonly used. It was provided by the legislation that such a charge should give the mortgagee the same protection, powers, and remedies as if there had been a lease for 3,000 years. This example of legislation by reference only means, as will be seen later, that the mortgagee has the protection, powers, and remedies of a mortgagee.

Enforcement of security

Whatever the form a mortgage takes, the mortgagee is never really considered in any sense owner of the land. He has only a security over the thing, and this security consists of nothing more than the aggregate of the various rights he has to enforce the security if the debtor defaults in his interest payments or is unable to repay the principal debt after due notice has been given to him. Those rights are three in number.

Probably the one that is most commonly used is the power of sale. The mortgagee can, after giving due notice, sell the thing so as to vest the fee simple in the purchaser, that is to say, a greater interest than he himself has. Out of the purchase price he is entitled to retain his principal and interest and the costs he has incurred, but must pay the residue to any subsequent mortgagees and then to the mortgagor. It is, of course, extremely unlikely that there will be anything left for the mortgagor; for if there were, he would probably have been able to raise money elsewhere and pay off the mortgage by executing a new mortgage in favour of another creditor.

In exactly the same circumstances the mortgagee may, if he so wish, instead of selling the land, appoint a receiver, who enters on the land and exploits it, using the proceeds in order to pay the mortgagee his interest and costs, and out of the residuary income to pay interest to any subsequent mortgagees there may be. Receiverships are much more commonly found where it is required to enforce security against a company but at the same time to keep it as a going concern.

Both these remedies can be exercised by a mortgagee on his own authority without going to court. But if, as is quite frequently the case, he desires to acquire the land as his own and to keep it free from the mortgagor's equity of redemption, he must apply to a judge of the Chancery Division for a decree of foreclosure, ordering the mortgagor to pay the mortgage debt within six months on pain of losing for ever his equity of redemption. On failure to pay, the decree is made absolute and the mortgagee obtains the fee simple free from any rights of the mortgagor whether at law or in equity.

Clogs on the equity of redemption

The Court has always kept a tight hold on the foreclosure procedure, for it has always been considered necessary, if the mortgagor is not to be liable to oppressive treatment at the hands of the mortgagee, to prevent the mortgage from assuming the character of a sale. Thus any provision in the original mortgage deed to the effect that, if the debt is not paid at the proper time, the mortgagee shall become owner of the property is void; and indeed the courts treat as void any provision which *clogs* the equity of redemption, that is to say, either makes redemption unduly difficult or provides that the mortgagee shall retain some right affecting the property after the debt has been redeemed. Thus, for example, where the lease of a public house was mortgaged to a brewery company and one of the terms of the mortgage was that the mortgagor should, during the whole term of the lease, buy all the liquor sold in the public house from the mortgagee, the latter could no longer enforce this term after the debt had been repaid. Moreover, quite a number of transactions which upon their face appear to be out-and-out sales, are treated by the Courts as mortgages, with the result that the person who has obtained the money is treated not as a seller, but as a debtor entitled to redeem the property on payment of the debt. Thus a sale coupled with an option to repurchase in a year's time has been treated as a mortgage; and if property is conveyed unconditionally by a deed, the person executing it may yet prove by oral evidence that the conveyance was intended merely to secure a loan, and can recover the property on repayment of the loan with interest.

Priorities

It has already been said that one advantage attaching to proprietary security is that the debtor can retain possession and use the thing. Another advantage is that successive securities can be created over the same thing so that, for instance, land may be mortgaged to A to secure a debt of half its value, and to B for a quarter. In such a case A is entitled to be paid first and B after him. This possibility that land may be mortgaged successively to several persons may easily give rise to difficult questions of priority.

It is not the practice for persons to lend money up to the full value of land; indeed trustees are not supposed to lend up to more than two-thirds of the value and will usually lend only up to one-half. However, the value of a piece of land may decline seriously, and many mortgagees may not be able to realize their security in time. Moreover, there is always the chance that by some fraud or other a debtor may induce a person to lend money upon a security which he thinks is sufficient but which in fact is not. The total value of the land will then be insufficient to allow the mortgagees to realize their security in full.

If there is only one mortgagee, the solution is simple: he realizes as much as he can and loses the rest; though, since a mortgage deed always contains a promise by the mortgagor to repay the debt, he can sue the mortgagor in contract on this promise and may in this way recover some or all of the residue. But there may be several successive mortgagees and enough to satisfy some of them but not all. The question then arises in what order they are to be paid their mortgage debts, if indeed they are not to share and share alike.

It is the practice for the first mortgagee to take from the mortgagor the title deeds of the land. Any person who is approached with a request that he should lend money on a mortgage at once asks to see the title deeds in order to ascertain whether the borrower really has a right to the land which he is about to mortgage. If he finds the title deeds in the borrower's possession, he takes possession of them along with the mortgage deed. If he does not find them in the borrower's possession, he at once asks where they are and almost inevitably finds them in the possession of a prior mortgagee, who will inform him of the amount for which the land has been mortgaged.

He is then one step along the road to knowing how much money he can safely advance on another mortgage. For a first mortgagee who has possession of the title deeds takes priority over all other mortgagees; and it is not unreasonable that he should do so, because the others should have notice of his mortgage and of the amount it covers.

However, a person wishing to lend money on a mortgage is not thereby fully protected, for after the title deeds have passed into the hands of a first mortgagee, other persons may have taken subsequent mortgages. To protect him in such circumstances all mortgagees who have not possession of title deeds are enabled to register their mortgages, and they take priority according to the date of registration. Thus a mortgagee is postponed to any mortgagee who either has possession of the title deeds or has already registered his mortgage. These general principles are subject to refinements dictated by banking practice, which, however, cannot be considered here.

Mortgages of equitable interests

So far mortgages have been discussed only in relation to land, but there can also be mortgages of shares in trust funds. In fact, since 1925 all mortgages of limited or future interests in land subject to settlements of one kind or another are really mortgages of shares in trust funds. Such mortgages are made by agreement between the parties and entitle the mortgagee to the same remedies as if the mortgage were one of land. However, priorities are governed by a different principle, for mortgages rank according to the date of notice given to the trustees. Thus any person who proposes to lend money on the security of a life interest or a future interest should first inquire of the trustees whether there is any prior mortgage and should at once give notice of his mortgage to the trustees, if in the light of the information he has received he advances the money. Thus the trustees keep as it were a private register of mortgages on interests in the trust fund. Since the trustees are in possession of the trust instrument, which corresponds to the title deeds of a legal estate in land, there can be no parallel to the transfer of the title deeds to a first mortgagee.

Function of mortgages

There is a popular notion that a mortgage is the first step on the road to ruin and that the typical mortgagee is a rapacious moneylender who is waiting for the opportunity of evicting the mortgagor from house and home. Of course there is some truth in both these beliefs, but in general mortgages are a perfectly normal and proper means of doing business, and probably most mortgagees would be quite embarrassed if they had to resort to foreclosure in order to enforce their security. Indeed, the whole of mortgage business is based on the assumption that mortgagors will go on paying interest and will repay the principal of the debts at the proper time, and, above all, that not many mortgaged properties will be thrown upon the market at the same time.

For the lending of money on mortgage of land and houses is a highly respectable form of business, mainly in the hands of banks and building societies. The latter arrange their mortgages in such a way that the periodical payments made to them, weekly, monthly, quarterly, or annually, cover both payment of interest and repayment of principal, so that at the end of a certain number of years the mortgage debt and the mortgage are both extinguished. They have no desire whatever to own large quantities of houses. Their business is to earn money in the form of interest on loans made to purchasers of houses, and mortgages are merely security for those loans.

Thus a mortgage looks two ways. The mortgagee benefits the mortgagor by financing him, usually in the purchase of something, land, houses, or valuable chattels; the mortgagor benefits the mortgagee by offering him a sound investment. Because mortgages, at any rate of land and houses, usually provide excellent security, mortgage interest is usually low. Because the realization of mortgage security is not very quick, people invest in mortgages who wish for a fairly permanent investment. It is therefore only reasonable that the notice to redeem that a mortgagee must give to a mortgagor before enforcing his security should be balanced by a similar notice of his intention to redeem that the mortgagor must give the mortgagee. For the latter should be given reasonable time to find a new and equivalent investment.

So important has this investment aspect of mortgages become in certain types of cases, that the Courts have modified in order to suit them their prohibition of clogs on the equity of redemption,[1] so that, for instance, where two financial concerns of great size have agreed, the one to give and the other to take a mortgage for a fixed term of as much as forty years, the mortgagor has been restrained from redeeming the mortgage before the end of the term.

4. EQUITABLE CHARGES AND LIENS

A third type of real security involves no transfer of either possession or property to a creditor, namely equitable charges and liens. These give no right to take possession or to foreclose the debtor's interest, but can be enforced only by sale of the object over which they exist. That sale may have to be by order of a court, though the

[1] See pp. 157–8 above.

power of sale may be bargained for by the creditor in the agreement by which it is created.

Such charges or liens can be created by mere agreement between the parties, and in effect create a trust in favour of the creditor. Charges, as such securities are usually called, can be made for any purpose, but will only be enforced if the creditor has given valuable consideration, that is to say, they cannot be enforced against persons who have established them merely by way of gift. A very common way of creating a charge is to deposit the title deeds of property with a bank, which then has full security for the overdraft it has agreed to allow. Incidentally, if the debtor, when depositing the deeds, intends to create a mortgage, an equitable mortgage is at once created. In practice the bank may require a written document, in order to preserve evidence of the agreement between the parties, and if it wishes to acquire a power of sale without the order of a court, will insist on the execution of a deed.

Vendor's and purchaser's liens

The term *lien* is generally used to denote equitable securities which arise not from any agreement between the parties but by operation of law. The best known are the vendor's lien and the purchaser's lien, both of which are confined to sales of land.[2]

Once an agreement to purchase land has been made, the buyer is entitled, should the vendor fail to convey it to him, to a decree of specific performance, that is to say, a decree ordering the vendor to convey the land to him. But, in contrast to the rule governing the sale of goods, he is not yet the owner of the land at law. However, equity regards that as done which ought to be done and therefore, since the purchaser ought to be made owner of the land, he is already regarded as owner for the purposes of equity, or, in technical language, he has the equitable interest in the land.[3]

If the purchaser is unable or unwilling to pay the price when the vendor is ready and willing to convey, the latter may lawfully withhold conveyance, but even if he does convey, and thus loses both possession and title, he still has an equitable lien on the land for the price. For equity again applies its maxim that what ought to be done is to be regarded as having been done, and since it is only fair that the purchaser should give security for the price, holds that the vendor has an equitable interest in the land to the extent of the purchase-money owing him. He is entitled to be placed in the same situation (so far as a court of equity can place him) as if it had been paid.

[2] The seller's lien over goods operates at common law.
[3] See p. 47 above.

Similarly, if a purchaser has paid the whole or part of the price, but for some reason or other the sale goes off, he has a lien over the land to recover what he has paid.

What is the point of these various equitable charges and liens? How and how far do they put persons entitled to them in a better position than unsecured creditors? They really give the creditor a privilege, that is to say, a prior right to be paid his debt out of the proceeds if the thing over which they exist is sold, and if necessary the power to insist on such a sale. Thus if the debtor is insolvent, the creditor can insist on having his debt paid by the trustee in bankruptcy up to the value that the thing on which it is secured has fetched or would fetch on a sale; and he is entitled to be paid this in preference to the ordinary creditors.

This is perhaps not unreasonable; but what if the debtor sells the thing in question to a third party? Does the latter take subject to the charge or lien? Formerly equity applied to the equitable interest created by the charge or lien the regular principle that an equitable interest binds anyone who takes the thing subject to it otherwise than as a bona fide purchaser for value without notice of the interest. Now, since the Land Charges Act, 1925, an equitable charge or lien over land must be registered if it is to bind any purchaser, but if so registered it binds him even if he has no notice.

Floating charges

One special variety of charges should be noted, the *floating charge*. It is a common practice for companies, if they are short of money, to borrow in the market in return for debentures secured by a floating charge. This is a charge on all the assets of the company, but it does not prevent the company from disposing of its assets in the ordinary course of business. It must indeed continually dispose of its products and stock-in-trade if it is to earn money and so pay the interest on the debentures. However, the floating charge may at any time become a fixed charge in accordance with the terms contained in the debentures, the commonest term being that the debenture-holders may produce that result by giving notice if the interest ceases to be paid or the company becomes insolvent. The charge is then said to become crystallized and settles on the specific articles of property belonging at that moment to the company instead of affecting the changing assets considered as a fund. From that moment the company can no longer dispose of anything, even in the ordinary course of business, without the leave of the debenture-holders. In practice they appoint a receiver to manage the business on their account. The charge gives the debenture-holders preference over the unsecured creditors.

5. HIRE PURCHASE

One of the commonest of all transactions at the present day is hire purchase. It is a complex contract, the present form of which in this country is determined by the desire which actuates the supplier of goods to enjoy the security which comes from retaining the ownership of them until the price is fully paid. Moreover, he is deeply concerned to protect himself against claims which a bona fide purchaser for value from the person who has possession of the goods may acquire even against the owner of them.

A seller can reserve the right of disposal when delivering goods to the buyer, and this secures to him the continuance of his ownership until, as is usually agreed between the parties, the price is fully paid. At one time, therefore, all that a person who sold goods by instalments needed to do was to sell them and reserve the right of disposal until the last instalment was paid. As between a seller and a buyer this was, and is, satisfactory enough; and until the year 1889 it was completely satisfactory, because the general common law rule applied that a person could not give a better title to goods than he himself had. Thus, if the possessor of the goods sold them, in breach of his undertaking not to do so, to a person who paid for them and took possession in good faith, the seller could recover them from the latter. However, in 1889 section 9 of the Factors Act provided that a buyer who obtains possession of goods with the consent of the seller can give a good title to a person who buys from him in good faith and acquires possession of the goods; and this section was re-enacted in section 25 (2) of the Sale of Goods Act. He is deemed to have sold and delivered them with the authority of the original seller. It was very soon held that this covered the ordinary case of an instalment buyer selling to a bona fide purchaser goods over which the original seller had reserved the right of disposal and therefore the ownership.

The way out of this difficulty was for the supplier of the goods to make the acquirer hire them in return for the payment of periodical fixed sums of money, and for this contract of hire to be turned into a sale of the goods when the final instalment was paid. So long as the contract was one of hire, there was nothing for the Sale of Goods Act or the Factors Act to operate on. Even so care had to be taken not to impose a binding obligation on the acquirer to buy the goods by continuing to pay his instalments until the hire turned into a sale, for in such a case the Courts said that the real substance of the contract was a sale; indeed, if the two parties bound themselves respectively to sell and buy goods, even though the sale might not be complete for a matter of months or years, there would be a sale, and both the Sale of Goods Act and the Factors Act would apply in such a way as to protect a bona fide purchaser for value from the acquirer.

Accordingly, the form that a hire-purchase contract now takes is that of a hire of goods coupled with an option to the hirer to purchase the goods by paying the final instalment. The supplier is bound to sell eventually if called upon to do so, but since the buyer can back out at any time, there is no sale until he exercises his option, which he cannot do until he pays the final instalment. Until that time there is nothing that even resembles a sale, and the acquirer is a mere bailee and cannot give a title to anyone who buys the goods in good faith from him.

XIV

SUCCESSION

1. GENERAL

A QUESTION which can never be avoided in any system of law is, what is to happen to a person's property when he dies? The question is complicated by a number of factors of which the most important are the facts that, along with corporeal things such as land or goods, the estate of a deceased person may include debts due to him from other persons and, on the other hand, he may have died owing money to yet other persons; moreover, almost all modern governments insist on taking part of the estate by way of death-duties. It is, therefore, very practical, if not absolutely necessary, for the estate to be administered before it is distributed among the various persons, if there are more than one, who are ultimately to benefit from the estate. In other words, debts must be got in and other debts paid, and death-duties also must be paid, before the ultimate distribution takes place. It would be possible to choose one or more of the ultimate beneficiaries and impose upon them the duty of administration; and this is done in many countries. It is not the plan which is pursued in England. Here administration is carried out by so-called *personal representatives*, whose duty it is to administer the estate, pay death-duties, and then distribute what is left according to the provisions of a will left by the deceased, or, in default of a will, in accordance with rules laid down by the law. To the extent that the estate is not disposed of by will, there is said to be an intestacy.

Accordingly, the law of succession falls naturally into three parts, the administration of estates, wills, and intestate succession. However, the law is most easily understood if one deals first with wills.

2. WILLS

It has long been the custom for most English people of substance to make wills. No doubt the initial impulse came from the medieval church, which desired legacies, but will-making remained a popular and even necessary practice because the old law of intestate succession was felt to be unsatisfactory. Starting with the great reforms enacted in the Administration of Estates Act, 1925, the law has been progressively improved, so that the average person may safely die without making a will and leave the law to take its course; and will-making may possibly become less common than hitherto.

To make a valid will, a person must be in his or her right mind. This is all that is required of a member of the forces or the merchant navy on active service. Any other person must also be of full age, that is to say, be twenty-one years old, and must state his wishes in writing, signed by himself, and attested by two witnesses, who sign their names at the foot or end of the document in his presence and in the presence of each other. The witnesses, too, must be of full age and in their right mind. The fact that a benefit is given to a witness in the will does not make him an incompetent witness, but he cannot take the benefit which the will purports to give him. Thus, in an indirect way, the impartiality of the witnesses is as far as possible ensured.

A will can be subsequently altered. This is usually done by adding a codicil, which must itself be executed in the same way as a will. A will may be revoked either by the making of a subsequent will which expressly revokes it or is totally incompatible with it, or indeed by merely destroying the document. The interpretation of wills has given rise to untold litigation, and the rules and principles that have been developed in the resultant case law fill many volumes of abstruse and intricate doctrine. All of this would be entirely out of place in an elementary book of this kind.

The next question is, what can a testator do in his will? We may leave on one side such topics as the appointment of guardians to look after his infant children; our concern is only with property. We may also leave on one side, as too complicated, the questions whether this or that kind of person can be benefited by a will. It is enough to say that certain restrictions are placed on the capacity of corporations and charities to benefit by will. On the other hand, persons who, for want of age or complete sanity, are incapable of making wills, may take under a will, though not in precisely the same way as persons of full age and in their right mind. Thus an infant cannot take under a will a legal estate in land, which must be vested in some other person or persons in trust for him during his minority.[1]

Until 1939 a testator could leave his property as he pleased without considering the moral claims of his widow, his children, or other members of his family. It was said that a man could endow a college or a cats' home, and leave his wife and children to starve. That state of affairs was altered by the Inheritance (Family Provision) Act, 1938. It is well here to consider some of the various ways in which members of a family may be protected against being disinherited by will; for in this way the peculiar technique of the English Act can be best understood.

[1] See p. 84 above.

One technique may be exemplified by the law of Scotland. In Scotland, if a man dies leaving a widow and children, he can dispose by will of only one-third of his movable property. Whatever he may say in his will, his widow will get one-third of his movables, and his children the other third between them. Similar arrangements are in force in many other countries, according to which the will can operate on only a fixed portion of the whole or part of the estate.

A second arrangement is that of German law, in accordance with which certain relatives, if passed over in a will, can claim from the heirs a sum of money amounting to one-half of what they would have been entitled to receive if there had been no will.

Now, the English Act adopts a plan which is quite unlike either the Scottish or the German plan.[2] On the one hand, it leaves the testator free to make his will, without marking off any part of the inheritance which he must not touch. Moreover, it does not guarantee to any of the relatives any share in the inheritance. In the ordinary case the testator makes his will and his estate is distributed in accordance with his instructions. He can deal with the whole of his estate and none of his relatives has any right to insist on sharing in it against the terms of the will. But certain near relatives may, if they think they are insufficiently provided for, apply to a judge of the Chancery Division to make an order giving them something out of the estate. They have no right to be awarded a definite predetermined portion or, indeed, anything at all. Parliament deliberately left it to the discretion of the judge to decide whether to make an order in favour of the applicant, and, if so, for what amount. Since the Act was passed various judges have gradually built up a body of precedent which they normally follow in applying the Act, but not so as to bind themselves absolutely in the exercise of their discretion. Perhaps the most important general principle is that the needs of the applicant must always be taken into account. Thus a widow who is otherwise well provided for, or a son who is perfectly well able to earn his own living, will be unsuccessful in his application. In fact, the evident intention of Parliament was to maintain as far as possible complete freedom of testation, while guarding against gross abuse.

A testator need not deal with the whole of his estate. He may, for instance, distribute only some of the lands in his possession, he may mention his books but not his motor-car, he may give away specified sums of money leaving a balance unaccounted for. As to all these things which are not dealt with in the will, there is an intestacy. He may, if he wishes, say that he leaves the residue of his estate to one or more named persons; and if he follows the general practice in so doing, then the whole of his estate will be provided for. But if there

[2] The technique was first employed in New Zealand in 1900.

is anything left unprovided for, it will devolve according to the rules of intestate succession. In other words, unlike a Roman citizen in the ancient world, an Englishman may die partly testate and partly intestate.

3. INTESTACY

Although will-making has long been prevalent among persons of substance, the law of intestate succession is very important, not only because persons who have little property do not usually go to the trouble of making a will, but also because there are always a certain number of persons who die possessed of property but, from want of age or sanity, have been unable to make a will.

There are two different ways of looking at the question what is to happen to a person's property when he dies. According to one school of thought, certain near relatives are entitled, by the mere fact of their near relationship, to shares in the estate, though some compromise may have to be made with the deceased by allowing him to dispose of some portion of it. If, however, he has not chosen to dispose of such portion, they are entitled to succeed. This way of thinking starts from the assumption that the family is more important than the individual, that some at least of the deceased's estate has probably come to him from his family, and should go back to his family on his death. The next question is to decide which persons for this purpose are to be looked upon as the family; and very different solutions are to be found in different countries. But everywhere the rules of intestate succession are derived from the prevailing conception of the family and are, as it were, an appendix to family law.

Now the English point of view is very different. Individualism is strong and the family weak. It seems to be assumed that a person—a man, at any rate—has made his money for himself and should be allowed to dispose of his estate as he wishes. If he derives much property from his family it is for the family to protect itself by means of a settlement, in such a way that no one shall succeed to the settled property whether by will or on an intestacy. It follows as a natural and logical consequence that in laying down rules of intestate succession the legislature should try to find out what the average man of property would naturally have done with his property if he had made a will, and then to lay down rules of intestate succession which will give the result which he would probably have ensured if he had made a will. Obviously the best way to ascertain what the average man of property would have done is to find out what in actual fact a large number of men of property have done. This was what was done before the Administration of Estates Act was passed in 1925.

In fact the task of making an average substitute for a will was made easier by the existence of standard forms of wills in the books of precedents used by solicitors and conveyancing counsel. These forms had tended to canalize wills so that their main outlines were fairly uniform; and all that was needed was for the legislature to choose the arrangements which conformed to its ideas of fairness and therefore could be assumed to represent what would have been the wishes of a fair-minded testator. Changes in the value of money, among other factors, have made certain minor changes necessary, but the general structure of the law is the same as in the Act of 1925.

The first point to be made is that there is complete equality between the sexes and that no preference is given to anyone on account of age. Primogeniture, which was once a salient feature of English law, has been abolished apart from the succession to entailed interests.

Secondly, the only persons who can conceivably succeed on intestacy are the surviving spouse, the issue, and the four grandparents of the deceased and their issue *ad infinitum*. Thus, failing issue of the deceased, parents can take, and also brothers and sisters and their issue, grandparents, and uncles and aunts and their issue, the less remote excluding the more remote. If the deceased leaves no relatives within the family group, the estate goes to the Crown as ownerless property (*bona vacantia*), but compassionate allowances may be made to dependants, whether kindred or not.

Thirdly, all other relatives take subject to the rights of a surviving spouse. In contrast to earlier times, that person is now greatly favoured. He or she now always takes all the so-called personal chattels, which correspond to what would usually be called personal belongings, for instance, household furniture and effects, including motor-cars and domestic animals, but not money or chattels used for business purposes. In addition the surviving spouse is entitled to sums of money which ensure that he or she shall take the whole of small estates not greatly exceeding £5,000, and that his or her share of the estate shall be greater if there are no issue than if there are. If there are no near relatives, the surviving spouse gets the whole estate, however great.

One other point remains to be mentioned. All these classes, issue and more remote relatives, with the exception of parents and grandparents, may possibly include persons who are under age. Now, it would be awkward to allow a share of the estate to vest in such a person because he or she might then die unmarried under age and there would be a second intestacy, which would thus undo the effect of the vesting; accordingly it is the regular practice in settlements to provide that interests shall vest in persons only upon their reaching the age of twenty-one or on their marriage under that age. The

Administration of Estates Act, 1925, copied that practice by providing that the shares of estates devolving on all classes of persons other than the surviving spouse, parents, or grandparents should be held upon statutory trusts for those persons who are alive at the death of the intestate and who either attain twenty-one or marry, with the powers of maintenance, advancement, &c., which are usually contained in such trusts.

This law of intestate succession on the whole works substantial justice, but when the last changes were made in 1952 it was felt that certain near relatives might turn out to be just as much in need of protection against the law of intestacy as against the unfair will of a testator; and so the discretionary powers of the Chancery Division under the Inheritance (Family Provision) Act, 1938, were extended to cover cases where a person dies without making a will.

4. ADMINISTRATION OF ESTATES

So far we have discussed the ultimate distribution of an estate. If we had followed the chronological order, we should have started by discussing the administration of the estate, for, as was said at the outset, distribution takes place only after administration is complete. However, we have followed the more practical course, because administration varies to some extent in accordance with whether there is a testacy or an intestacy.

In the first place, the manner of appointing the personal representatives will be different. A testator will normally appoint an executor to administer his estate as his personal representative. If there is no will there can be no executor and some other means must be found of appointing a personal representative, who will, in that case, be called an administrator; though an administrator may also have to be appointed in three other cases, namely, if a will contains no appointment of an executor, or if the appointed executor declines to act, or if after an executor has ceased to act some property belonging to the estate still remains to be dealt with. In the two former cases the administrator is said to obtain letters of administration with the will annexed, in the third, letters of administration *de bonis non administratis* or, for short, *de bonis non*. The words *letters of administration* require further explanation.

The executor derives his office and powers from the testator and may at once take various steps which will bind the estate; but to regularize his position he must obtain a grant of probate. This he does by depositing at a Probate Registry the original will together with the executor's oath, i.e. an affidavit verifying the will and the testator's death and undertaking to administer the estate, and an

Inland Revenue affidavit giving detailed particulars of the property contained in the estate, to enable the authorities to calculate the death-duties payable. He then receives a grant of probate with a copy of the will and is fully authorized to act as the personal representative of the deceased. This, the normal procedure, is called probate in common form; but if there is a dispute about the validity or genuineness of the will, for instance on the ground that the testator was actuated by undue influence when he made it, probate must be sought in solemn form, which is equivalent to an action. A grant of probate may be revoked if, for instance, a later valid will is found.

If there is no executor, some person interested in having the estate administered applies for letters of administration. He may be a person entitled to succeed on intestacy or even a creditor, if the estate is thought to be insolvent. The applicant must take steps similar to those taken by an executor seeking probate except that he must, if there is no will, swear an affidavit to that effect and, since he has not been entrusted by the deceased with the administration of his estate, he must also enter into a bond for the due performance of his duties. One or more sureties will usually have to be provided. If the administrator misconducts himself he becomes liable under the bond to be sued for twice the value of the estate. Once letters of administration have been granted, the administrator becomes, like the executor, the personal representative of the deceased. But since there is always some little time between the death and the grant, and in the interval it is not known who will be the administrator, the estate is for the time being automatically vested in the President of the Probate, Divorce and Admiralty Division of the High Court.

The personal representative succeeds automatically to all the rights of the deceased, in so far as they do not die with him, as is the case, for instance, with a claim for damages for libel. Thus he can claim property which belonged to the deceased and bring actions on debts due to him. He can in the same way be sued to recover property belonging to someone else which the deceased possessed at his death and he can be sued on debts due from the deceased to third persons. In all these cases he acts not in his personal capacity but as a representative. Thus anything he acquires he acquires for the estate and anything he relinquishes or pays he relinquishes or pays in his representative capacity, that is to say, he does not make himself personally liable but only the estate. If, therefore, the estate is insolvent, he must pay all he can out of the estate but cannot be made personally liable for the residue. However, he must pay the debts before distributing the estate to the beneficiaries, or must keep enough in hand to pay them. If he does not, he may find that he has to pay them out of his own pocket.

The administration of an estate may be a complicated business. For a testator may leave his property to different persons in different ways, and he may leave debts of different kinds. He may make specific or general bequests and then leave the residue to another person; a specific bequest will be of some specific thing such as his car, whereas a general bequest will be, for instance, of a stated sum of money. Now, the debts are to be paid in the first instance out of residue, but if the residue does not suffice, then the other bequests must be drawn on according to rules which are too detailed to be set down here. Again, it may be that the estate is insolvent. If all the debts are of one class, then the creditors divide proportionately what is left after funeral expenses and the costs of administration have been defrayed. But if there are several classes of debts, some, for example, being secured and others unsecured, they will rank in order of priority, one class of creditors being allowed to satisfy themselves before the others lower down the list. Again a detailed description of the rules would be inappropriate here.

XV

REGISTRATION

REGISTRATION is a familiar device for preserving evidence and guaranteeing its truth, most familiar to the ordinary man in the form of registration of births, marriages, and deaths. Even in that form it is not very old in England so far as the State itself is concerned; before 1837 there was little besides various ecclesiastical registers, the most important of which were the parish registers maintained by incumbents of the Church of England. For property of various kinds it is much younger, younger than in most civilized countries.

Registration has been accepted wholeheartedly for ships, for bills of sale, and for various kinds of companies and other associations such as trade unions; and there has been no difficulty in insisting on companies keeping registers of shares and shareholders. Moreover, the practice of proving wills has always carried with it registration.

With land the story has been very different. The obvious advantages attaching to registration have had to fight against many adverse forces, of which the most important have been the desire of landowners and their lawyers to keep transactions secret and the difficulty of placing all the immensely complicated mass of interests that may coexist in land on a single register. During the latter half of the nineteenth century there were among reformers of real property law two opposing schools of thought, the one insisting that registration should be pushed forward as rapidly as possible, the other insisting on its difficulty without a preliminary simplification of the law and on the probability that it would be found unnecessary once the law was simplified. The dispute between the two schools helped to prevent anything being done on either side, but eventually the simplifiers won. Registration has been extended greatly in many ways, but perhaps not so much as if the movement in favour of it had alone held the field.

Registration of incumbrances

There are three forms of registration as regards land, one of which indeed goes back to the beginning of the eighteenth century. The most limited form goes back for many purposes only as far as the 1925 legislation, and concerns charges and other collateral transactions relating to land, such as mortgages, judgments, restrictive covenants, and estate contracts, but not the central line of documents, other than wills, which go to make a title to land. So far as this form of registration goes, a purchaser's solicitor must search in public registers for all incumbrances on the title, but he must look for evidence of the devolution of the fee simple to the title deeds disclosed to him by the vendor's solicitor.

These registers of incumbrances are so-called 'names registers', that is to say, the incumbrances are entered against the names of the persons creating them. They are therefore not always as easy to search with any guarantee of success as if the incumbrances were entered against the plots of land described in a cadastral survey. This is particularly the case with restrictive covenants, of which the original covenantor's name may no longer be known. Yet the register is conclusive: no registrable incumbrance binds a purchaser unless it is registered, but a registered incumbrance binds him whether he has succeeded in tracing it in the register or not. This form of registration is probably only a half-way house to registration of title.

Registration of deeds

An intermediate form of registration is that in force in Yorkshire (except the City of York). It was probably imitated from Scotland. Under it all deeds and other documents relating to land must be registered or they are void against all purchasers. Thus all title deeds are registrable and are always made the object of search in every transaction relating to land. But the title itself is not registered. However, although the register is a 'names register', there is no apparent inclination to change the system.

Registration of title

Registration of title is the natural culmination of land registration. Before land is put on the register it has to be identified by reference to a map, and if necessary its boundaries have to be surveyed. The holder's title has then to be proved to the satisfaction of the Land Registrar.

The land may be registered with an absolute, a qualified, a possessory, or a good leasehold title. Only the last three require explanation here.

A qualified title is one which is granted when an absolute title is applied for but some particular defect appears in the title which prevents the Registrar from registering it as absolute. It is then registered subject to the specified defect. The Registrar may in certain circumstances later convert a qualified into an absolute title.

A possessory title is subject to any defects which may turn out to have existed at the time of registration, but is guaranteed as regards anything that may happen afterwards. In other words, the title prior to first registration must still be investigated as if it had not been registered. The Registrar may in certain circumstances convert a possessory into an absolute title and must do so after a certain number of years have elapsed.

A good leasehold title is the same as an absolute title except that it does not guarantee the lessor's title to lease the land. This again the Registrar may convert in certain circumstances into an absolute title.

Except for a few reasons, the most important of which is that the registered owner knew of a defect in his title, an owner whose title is registered as absolute has an absolute title against all the world and cannot be disturbed. If some other person should prove a better title than the registered holder, he can only claim a money compensation out of an insurance fund in the hands of the Registrar which has been built up out of compulsory contributions made by holders when their titles were first registered. The existence of this fund makes it possible for the Registrar not to spend unnecessary time or trouble in investigating titles which appear sufficiently sound on their face.

Not only the title itself appears on the register, but also anything that prevents or restricts the registered owner from dealing with the land. In addition to incumbrances, there are so-called cautions and inhibitions designed to protect persons interested in settlements other than the registered owner. The most important of them warn purchasers of the existence of a trust and of the need to pay someone other than the vendor; but the interests to which those other persons are entitled under settlements are not registrable, for they will in any case be overreached by a conveyance of the legal estate, will not affect the purchaser, and will be transferred to the purchase money.

There are, however, certain so-called 'overriding interests', by which, although they do not appear on the register, a registered holder is bound. Such are, for example, easements and profits.

Once a title is on the register a certificate of title is issued to the holder, in lieu of his title deeds, and if he wants to sell the land, he need no longer prove his title in the old way but will point to his certificate and the entry in the Land Register. This ensures a great saving in time and expense. But, of course, it costs money to put the land on the register in the first instance.

Voluntary and compulsory registration

Land may be voluntarily registered wherever it may be; and much land has been registered in that way. Registration is very commonly applied for where there is some doubt as to the validity of the title which may be cleared more rapidly if the land is allowed to remain on the register for a sufficient length of time. It is especially sought where solicitors' offices have been bombed and in consequence title deeds have been lost. Registration then usually follows pretty easily upon good prima facie evidence of title.

However, the Crown has power to issue orders in council making registration of title compulsory within the area under the jurisdiction of any county or county borough, registration to be compulsory only upon the first transfer of title for value after the order in council comes into force. At the present time the following areas are subject to compulsory registration: the Counties of London, Middlesex, and Surrey and the County Boroughs of Eastbourne, Hastings, Croydon, Oxford, Oldham, Canterbury, and Leicester. The County of Kent is being brought under compulsory registration by stages. It is understood that the extension of the area subject to compulsory registration of title will be made to follow closely the progress of the new edition of the Ordnance Survey, new counties or county boroughs being brought under registration as the survey is completed for them.

The total area is small, but the task of putting land on the register is great, not only in cost but also in the number of skilled experts who are needed for the purpose. At the present rate it will take a long time to complete the process. It is a pity it was not taken in hand systematically in the days of huge landed estates, when the number of separate holdings to be registered would have been much smaller.

XVI

CONCLUSION

IN spite of the streamlining the law of property underwent in the 1925 legislation, it remains very complicated and not entirely free from confusion. Too many kinds of people have had a hand in producing it to admit of a simple orderly system consistent in all its parts. The merchants have built up the law governing the sale of goods, the financiers have moulded the law of stocks and shares, the landed aristocracy and gentry stimulated the activity of the conveyancers. Some parts of the law of property, especially those concerned with possession and title, have grown up around the common-law actions, while elsewhere the judges have thought sometimes like merchants and sometimes like the old conveyancers who presented them with the problems they encountered in creating and manipulating the doctrine of estates; and where trusts occur the trail of the Chancery is everywhere evident.

Where many people start from different points, they do not always meet. So there is a lack of co-ordination in property law. Moreover, so vast is the field covered by it that no mind has hitherto been capacious enough to master it all and at the same time familiar enough with the details to make his opinions acceptable outside a relatively small part of what is a most technical branch of the law.

If property law had been codified after the Continental fashion, the codifiers would have introduced more order into it, and in particular would have asked whether certain generalizations accepted for one kind of property were acceptable for others. A case-law system like ours naturally deals with problems as and not before they occur in practice; and some problems occur for some kinds of property and have not yet occurred for others. Occasionally lawyers are then found to say in effect that they will not occur and adopt for that part of the law a structure which in the end may prove too simple.

It has been suggested above[1] that the law of physical chattels has been over-hasty in rejecting the doctrine of estates and adopting a theory of ownership that is less practical than it might be. To ensure complete harmony in the law legislation would probably be needed; but writers on the principles of property law might profitably inquire whether the solutions found for leases could not be applied to bailments and a uniform doctrine be enunciated to cover all limited

[1] See pp. 60, 72–73 above.

interests in physical objects. They might find that the doctrines common to all kinds of property are more numerous than is at present apparent; and where there is doubt, the courts might be persuaded to apply to one kind of property by analogy doctrines which have been developed for the purpose of governing other kinds of property.

The universalizing tendency of the trust has produced much more uniformity in the treatment of beneficial interests, whatever the physical object or other investment on which their value depends. Here beneficial interests in land, goods, and intangible movables such as stocks and shares are treated alike and nothing remains to be done, in order to make the law truly uniform, but to extend the overreaching effect of a conveyance to goods.[2]

Some distinctions will remain. The land agent will always be concerned with the course of husbandry, with repairs to buildings and with servitudes. Mortgages of the fee simple will always provide a preferable security in the eyes of some people to assignments of shares; the security provided by the assignment of a bill of lading will always be a matter for specialist bankers and merchants; and not everybody wants to be a pawnbroker lending money on watches or jewels. More care will be taken in investigating title and fewer risks assumed in buying land than goods. But these will usually be differences of fact and business practice; they need not be strongly reflected as doctrinal discrepancies in the law. In other words, differences between land and movables and between corporeal and incorporeal movables should occupy only a subordinate position and not interfere with the formulation of a large body of general principle.

It is, however, clear that one distinction now outweighs all others, namely that between physical objects regarded as things to be used and enjoyed physically as specifically identified individuals and what may be in the broadest sense called investments, of which the money value alone is relevant. It may be expressed summarily as one between money and what money will buy.

It is not in essence a distinction between different kinds of things but between different ways of dealing with things; though some things are more likely to be thought of primarily, or even exclusively, in terms of their money value and others to be kept and used in their present state. If funds, such as trust funds, can be regarded as composite things, they of course constitute an exception; as funds, they are clearly money and nothing else.

Again, it is not in essence a distinction between the kinds of persons who deal with things. The trader, it is true, while he is trading thinks of all the objects he deals in, whether corporeal or incorporeal, as things to be turned into money, and of money itself as something to

[2] See p. 86 above.

be turned into things which are themselves destined to be turned into money in their turn. But he thinks of his house, his car, and his wireless set as things to be used and enjoyed in themselves. On the other hand, although the landowner values his mansion house and family portraits for themselves, he has at the back of his mind the thought that they may be turned into money in case of need. That money value will be what concerns the Government when death-duties are to be paid, but the Government also may on occasion prefer to take some objects in kind, whether because turning them into money may be awkward and even ruinous, or because it is in the public interest to keep a collection together. Stocks and shares may seem at first sight to have only a money value, but some holders may value them even more for the control they afford of an undertaking. Indeed, although one is tempted to say that the ultimate objects of the law of property are always physical, in the sense that everything is derived in the last resort from physical objects and that in the end all satisfaction comes from the enjoyment of physical objects, money being merely the instrument by which the raw materials are turned into the immediate objects of enjoyment, that is not strictly true of our complex world. Many persons obtain intense satisfaction from the process of dealing with money, if by that term we designate all the abstract intellectual creations that intervene between the use of physical objects in the way of production and their eventual enjoyment.

The law is bound to be influenced, and the balance of its parts in large measure determined, by the ways in which the various groups constituting a nation think of property and by the balance existing between them from time to time. If the groups which think of things mainly in terms of their money value predominate, the law will tend to disregard the desire of a person to keep and enjoy a thing in specie and will see no great harm in forcing him to give it up in return for a money compensation. Still less regard will it pay to one person's expectation of succeeding to specific objects under the present but temporary control of another. It will in principle give no effect to attempts to tie up land or anything else in specie. If, on the other hand, the groups predominate which attach peculiar value to the possession of physical objects themselves, the law will be much less inclined to force an acceptance of money compensation or to allow limited interests to be overreached.

Put very crudely, it is a question of how the commercial and the landed interests are balanced in a community; for, with few exceptions such as heirlooms, movables are not permanent enough for the distinction between them and their money value to be very important. A French or Irish peasant will cling to his land at all costs; a business man engaged in land speculation will sell out at what seems to him the most propitious moment and will regard as absurdly old-fashioned any restrictions which prevent the present holder of land from selling to him.

The law does not indeed always conform to what is desired by one group or another, or even express the balance of power between groups. The law may exhaust itself against the strong passive resistance of a stubborn peasantry, or a class may feel no need to translate its economic power into legal terms. It is easy to expect too much of the law; it will seldom break down deeply rooted social habits, nor do they need it for their preservation. But where the commercial and landed interests have battled for centuries with fluctuating fortunes but on fairly even terms, as in England, both have perforce had recourse to the law and the law has reflected pretty faithfully the changing social scene.

Much of the contents of the foregoing chapters is a commentary on what has just been said. It need not be repeated here. It is, however, perhaps worth emphasizing that the student must be prepared at every turn to ask himself what it is that the law of property is really talking about. Is it talking about physical objects as such, as things to be acquired, possessed, and enjoyed in specie, or is it merely talking about money? Sometimes it is only by putting this question that any sense at all can be made of the law. For instance, the continued operation of the Modern Rule against Perpetuities can be reconciled with the policy enshrined in the Settled Land Acts and section 1 of the Law of Property Act only if it is realized that it now deals with money, whereas that policy governs the alienation of the land itself.

Generally speaking, the distinction between money and the things that money will buy introduces order and system into the law. On the whole judges and legislators have had fairly clear in their minds which they were dealing with at a particular moment. Moreover, in the last quarter of the nineteenth century and the first years of the twentieth century it was pretty clear that the law generally took a commercial view of property, in that it favoured the circulation of land as well as corporeal and incorporeal movables. It was bound to secure tenants in their holdings and mortgagees in their security, but only to the extent that they had bargained for their rights. Such interests had from the very beginning been looked on as essentially commercial in character and so the protection of them formed no exception to the general policy of the law.

However, the Rent Acts[3] marked a decided swing away from pure commercialism, albeit it was expected to be temporary. Tenants had their possession protected on grounds of public policy irrespective of their bargains with their landlords. The legislature was forced to pay

[3] See pp. 125–6.

special attention to the holding of specific physical objects and to refuse to allow landlords to fob tenants off with money as the price of eviction. The essential thing was to secure to a person a roof over his head, and rent restriction was enacted less for its own sake than in order to prevent eviction by forcing tenants to pay a higher rent than they could afford. Here was a direct denial of the general commercial thesis that every physical object can be adequately replaced by its value in money.

Even more far-reaching has been the change which has secured not obviously inefficient agricultural tenants in the possession of their holdings;[4] for here the public interest has been held to demand a permanent policy of protecting farmers in the physical enjoyment and use of the actual means of production. If a tenant farmer could alienate his holding so as to force his alienee on his landlord irrespective of the terms of his lease or tenancy agreement, and if the landlord did nothing but receive rent, it would be easy to say that the tenant had in reality become owner of the land subject to a perpetual rent. But that is not usually the case; the landlord retains a real interest in the land, he takes responsibility legally for certain repairs and morally for seeing that the rules of good husbandry are observed, and on the death of the tenant he regains his freedom to take the land into his own keeping or let it to another tenant. Moreover, the tenant cannot, so long as the present policy continues, insist on buying out his landlord. Thus both have interests in the land itself which cannot be overreached.

So far we know where we stand, and the only warning to be given the student is not to exaggerate the effect of the general commercial bias displayed by the law. In spite of its general tendency to favour the free alienation of physical objects, it allows itself to be deflected by considerations of public policy in the direction of maintaining tenants in their holdings. But sometimes there is real doubt which line of thought should prevail. There are gaps in the powers of sale granted to trustees by the 1925 legislation, which can be filled in only by the benevolent action of the courts. The courts may, however, not be willing to act in such cases where the effect would be to disturb the occupier, and they have in any case power to grant an injunction to prevent trustees from selling where that would be unjust.[5]

It is clearly the occupier whose protection makes the greatest breach in the policy of the Settled Land Acts. Where there is no question of protecting him, English law has progressively leant more and more in favour of the money point of view. It might well have adopted as its motto the famous saying of Louis Philippe, *Enrichissez-vous*, 'Get rich'. This is in full accord with the old policy of Free

[4] See pp. 123–4 above. [5] See p. 5 above.

Trade, which was justified precisely on the ground that in the long run it made the country richer, in the money sense, than any other policy could have done, though it may possibly have made the country weaker in time of war and may have had social consequences that were not entirely admirable. Taken by and large, the law has encouraged people to get rich at the cost of sentimental or aesthetic attachments.

The merits of this general policy are, however, very questionable, though its defects are rendered more conspicuous, and perhaps in some degree are even called into being by the operation of other factors which have removed the social and moral brakes which formerly kept it in check.

The old state of balance, between a landed aristocracy interested in the land as such and a legal policy aimed not merely at economic improvement but also at the replacement of impoverished landlords by self-made men more capable of looking after the land, undoubtedly produced a very beautiful country and one that in the long run did not suffer even from the point of view of wealth. The old landlords often planned with an eye to beauty as well as money. When land came to be treated much more openly as a source of wealth, there inevitably arose a tendency to exploit it by cutting down trees without replacement, by the practice of ribbon development, and in general by treating it as something to be mined rather than cultivated.

In other words, the Settled Land Acts were originally thought of as a medicine rather than a regular food. They were a necessary safety valve in a society where the landed interest in general wished to keep the land and could be trusted to look after it. With the gradual disappearance of large-scale landholding by the aristocracy and gentry, the balance was lost. It is in process of being readjusted by planning controls exercised by public authorities.[6] How the results will compare with those produced by the old landlordism it is of course too early to say. That the burdens dropped by the old landlords should be shouldered by someone else was inevitable. It is also necessary for the student of property law to cast his eyes into what may at first sight appear to be the alien ground of public law if he is to acquire a sense of the way in which equilibrium is, somewhat painfully, being restored.

There is no need to repeat here the remarks made elsewhere[7] about the difference of intellectual atmosphere when one passes from the law relating to physical objects to that relating to what has, in a popular sort of way, been described as money. But in summing up, one question deserves attention.

[6] See pp. 106–7 above.

[7] See pp. 60–62 above.

For almost a century attacks have been made here and in other countries on what is called *conceptualism*. It may be described roughly as a tendency not to give a direct answer on the merits to a practical question but to interpose between the question and the answer one or more abstract concepts, to work out a number of legal rules and principles defining those concepts and then to see whether the concepts may be made to apply to the situation in respect of which the question arises. Those who attack conceptualism say that to interpose concepts in this way is to interpose wholly unnecessary middle terms and that it does not help in finding the right answer; whereas at worst it may distort the question, by forcing it into a procrustean bed, and so make the finding of the correct answer even more difficult and hazardous than it would be otherwise.

On the whole these attacks have found targets other than property law; they have been peculiarly prevalent and vicious in the law of torts. But property law is open to attack, though mainly where it touches on contract and tort.

It is at least doubtful whether it helps, in deciding whether a finder becomes the owner of goods, to ask whether another person was in possession.[8] There is always the possibility that a judge will decide first of all whether the finder should really become owner and will then decide whether or not to attribute possession to some other person in order to give the right result. If that is the case, the attribution of possession plays no real part in the process of deciding the main question.

In the sale of goods the attribution of what is called *property* may even commit courts to decisions which have no necessary connexion with property. For instance, whether the creditors of a seller can satisfy themselves at the expense of the buyer out of goods sold to him, and force him to prove as an ordinary creditor in a bankruptcy, is made to depend on whether the *property* has passed from the seller to the buyer.[9] Since the moment at which the property passes is in principle determined by the seller and buyer between themselves without any reference to the possible creditors of either, it is not self-evident that the rights of the creditors should be made to depend on whether the property has passed or not. It might be thought better to think out the answer to the question directly as one affecting the seller's creditors and the buyer. At any rate, in dealing with Scandinavian lawyers where a foreign element enters into a sale, it does not help in any way to say that the property has or has not passed from the seller to the buyer. They say that in doing so one is merely inserting an unnecessary middle term which, if taken seriously, may prevent one from finding the right solution to a practical question.

[8] See p. 57 above.

[9] See pp. 52, 55 above.

Indeed, our merchants also were not prepared to accept the inferences which lawyers drew from the passing of property where goods were left in the hands of the seller and then resold and delivered by him to an innocent buyer, and they insisted on the passing of the Factors Acts.[10] In an earlier chapter an attempt has been made to explain the resulting law on lines suggested by the sub-titles introduced by the draftsman into the Sale of Goods Act and to apply it to all other objects of property rights. The author would not be in the least degree surprised if his formulation were considered unsatisfactory and out of accord with practical needs.

The whole conceptual structure of mortgages has also become little more than a nuisance. All that the mortgagee needs, and all that he really gets, is a bundle of powers over the mortgaged property, namely, to apply with every prospect of success to a court for a foreclosure decree, to appoint a receiver, and to sell, all of them governed immediately by practical rules suggested by experience.[11] The mortgagor in effect remains owner of the property subject to those powers, and has a right to redeem, governed in its turn by other practical rules. Yet other practical rules decide to what extent his right to redeem can be restricted and how far the mortgagee can bargain for collateral advantages by making the loan. Nothing would be lost if the notion that the mortgagee has an interest in the mortgage property were entirely given up and the existence of the equity of redemption entirely disregarded. The essence of the mortgage is that it allows the mortgagee to satisfy himself out of certain property in preference to unsecured creditors.

It is also very doubtful whether anything is gained in many of the cases where a trust for sale is implied by the law. Indeed, there is something ridiculous in saying that trustees are under a trust to sell property and hold the proceeds of sale upon certain trusts with a power to postpone the sale, when what is really intended is that they should keep the property unsold as long as possible, should hold the property as such in trust for the beneficiaries, but should have a power to sell it if at any time they think fit. At one time it may have been necessary to frame trusts in this way. It is surely time now to bring them more in accord with reality.

However, this artificiality is a blemish mainly in the part of property law which deals with physical objects. When we are adjusting the claims of the seller's creditors and the buyer, we are really dealing with the goods themselves; when asking whether land can be sold in such a way as to overreach the claims of those entitled to limited interests, we are dealing with the land itself. When we pass into the field dominated by the conveyancer, especially that of settlements, it

[10] See pp. 52, 163 above.

[11] See pp. 156–7 above.

is clear that the law cannot help dealing in artificial concepts. Only artificiality can give the certainty of prediction that is required.[12] The doctrine of estates is certainly artificial but it serves practical purposes and has been extremely useful. Moreover, the trust fund made up of ever-changing investments is an artificial creation if ever there was one.[13] But it is not merely the invention of the lawyers. Modern finance in England and America could not now dispense with it. Incidentally it is in its application to the trust fund that the doctrine of estates now performs its most useful function. Similarly, the various commercial documents, such as negotiable instruments and documents of title, which have reached a high degree of standardization, are as artificial as they could well be.[14] If they were not artificial they could not be used, as they are used, by bankers as units in a form of commercial mathematics.

It would seem, therefore, that, speaking generally and somewhat crudely, artificiality and conceptualism, though on the whole out of place in the part of property law which deals with physical objects, are essential to that part which deals with money. In any case, what is more artificial than money itself?

Property law now needs the attention of jurists who, while seeing the need to give it the orderly and systematic treatment which it receives in books on Continental law, would still refuse to force it into the closed system of Continental categories. Whether they choose or not to adopt ownership as their starting-point is not very important, so long as they are prepared to subject it to a more profound analysis and to admit that it has no prescriptive claim to be considered indivisible. If the English law of property has anything to teach the analytical jurist it is certainly that some place must be found for a discussion first of the *quantum* of interest measured in terms of duration as exemplified by the doctrine of estates, and, secondly, of the separation of management from enjoyment. To consider the doctrine of estates and the trust as English eccentricities is surely misguided. But English property law would be much better arranged, and some of its substance would probably be improved, if jurists could be found who would look at it comprehensively after the manner of Continental lawyers. Hitherto our property lawyers themselves have been too close to it to see it as a whole.

No attempt has been made in this book to deal with the effects on property of what has been called 'The Managerial Revolution'. This is not to suggest that they are unimportant. Much property of all kinds is now owned by corporations such as limited companies, the control of which is often in the hands of small groups of individuals

[12] See pp. 16–17 above.
[13] See pp. 30–31 above.
[14] See pp. 23–25 above.

who between them own perhaps less than a quarter of the shares. If we see as the essential part of ownership the power to dispose of property, then such small groups really own enormous masses of property to which they have no direct legal title. However, what is peculiar to this form of 'ownership' belongs to company law; the rest has already been described.

SELECT BIBLIOGRAPHY

THE only recent book which deals with the Law of Property as a whole is the first volume of *Stephen's Commentaries on the Laws of England* (21st edition, 1950, with annual supplements). This is by Professor A. D. Hargreaves, who is also the author of an admirable *Introduction to the Principles of Land Law* (3rd edition, 1952), conceived on more historical lines than the present book.

Of the next order of size are G. C. CHESHIRE, *The Modern Law of Real Property* (7th edition, 1954) and R. E. MEGARRY, *Manual of the Law of Real Property* (2nd edition, 1955). The former is fuller in its explanations but less complete than the latter. Both cover the ground in considerable detail.

The most complete work on land law as a whole is R. E. MEGARRY and H. W. R. WADE, *The Law of Real Property* (1st edition, 1957). Beyond lie practitioners' treatises on special topics, many of them out of date, and also various titles in *Halsbury's Laws of England* (3rd edition, in progress), an immense encyclopedia covering the whole of English law.

Halsbury also includes several titles on personal property, a subject which has attracted few authors of general books. The only ones that are reasonably up to date are L. A. GOODEVE, *The Modern Law of Personal Property* (9th edition by R. H. Kersley, 1949) and J. CROSSLEY VAINES, *Personal Property* (2nd edition, 1957), the former of which is dry, informative, and reasonably complete, the latter lively and explanatory but selective. Very often a student is most likely to find what he wants in an elementary book on Commercial law, of which a good example is *Stevens's Elements of Mercantile Law* (12th edition, by J. Montgomerie, 1955).

Standard elementary books on Equity are G. W. KEETON, *An Introduction to Equity* (3rd edition, 1952), SNELL'S *Principles of Equity* (24th edition, by R. E. Megarry and P. V. Baker, 1954), and H. G. HANBURY, *Modern Equity* (7th edition, 1957). The two last named devote much space to the law of trusts, which may be followed into G. W. KEETON, *The Law of Trusts* (6th edition, 1954) and the practitioners' work, SIR A. UNDERHILL, *The Law Relating to Trusts and Trustees* (10th edition, by C. M. White and M. M. Wells, 1950).

On the public-law aspects of property there are, beyond the relevant chapters in MEGARRY and MEGARRY and WADE, only practitioners' books.

The following short books on special topics can be recommended to students:

J. F. R. BURNETT, *Elements of Conveyancing* (8th edition, 1952).

Chalmers' Sale of Goods Act (13th edition, by P. Sieghart, with the assistance of E. J. Prince, 1957).

J. H. C. MORRIS and W. BARTON LEACH, *The Rule Against Perpetuities* (1956).

L. M. Simes, *Public Policy and the Dead Hand* (1955), an American course of lectures which discuss the limits to freedom of testation, perpetuities, accumulations, and charities.

Sir D. Hughes Parry, *The Law of Succession, Testate and Intestate* (3rd edition, 1953).

C. H. M. Waldock, *The Law of Mortgages* (2nd edition, 1950).

Certain topics included in this book are more usually dealt with in books on other portions of English law. Thus the contents of Chapter III (The Protection of Property Interests), down to the end of the section on Title, should be followed up into the standard books on the law of torts, such as *Salmond on the Law of Torts* (12th edition, by R. F. V. Heuston, 1958), H. Street, *The Law of Torts* (1955), and Sir P. H. Winfield, *A Text-book on the Law of Tort* (6th edition, by T. Ellis Lewis, 1954). The theory of Possession is also discussed in books on Jurisprudence such as G. W. Paton, *A Textbook of Jurisprudence* (2nd edition, 1951), and Sir J. W. Salmond, *Jurisprudence* (11th edition, by Glanville L. Williams, 1958).

The assignment of choses in action and the theory of negotiability are regularly treated in books on the law of contract such as G. C. Cheshire and C. H. S. Fifoot, *Law of Contract* (4th edition, 1956). Much that is of interest to the property lawyer may be found in P. M. Bromley, *Family Law* (1957). The close interrelations between property law, family law, and certain portions of public law are admirably displayed by O. Kahn-Freund in his chapter on England in W. Friedmann, *Matrimonial Property Law* (1955).

An interesting book by an American economist is C. R. Noyes, *The Institution of Property; a Study of the Development, Substance and Arrangement of the System of Property in Modern Anglo-American Law* (1936); and the student's outlook will be greatly widened by a reading of the translated portions of the work by the great Danish authority, L. F. Vinding Kruse, *The Right of Property* (Vol. I, translated by P. T. Federspiel, 1939; Vol. II, translated by D. Philip, 1953).

INDEX